Chicken Soup
for the Soul.

The
Blessings of
Christmas

Chicken Soup for the Soul: The Blessings of Christmas
101 Tales of Holiday Joy, Kindness and Gratitude
Amy Newmark

Published by Chicken Soup for the Soul, LLC www.chickensoup.com

Front cover photo of window courtesy of iStockphoto.com/Kesu01 (©Kesu01), photo
of candle courtesy of iStockphoto.com/RomoloTavani (©RomoloTavani), photo of
gingerbread cookie and mug courtesy of iStockphoto.com/fcafotodigital (©fcafotodigital),
photo of Christmas garland courtesy of iStockphoto.com/Liliboas (©Liliboas)
Back cover and interior photo of Christmas tree courtesy of iStockphoto.com/
adogslifephoto (©adogslifephoto)
Photo of Amy Newmark courtesy of Susan Morrow at SwickPix

Cover and Interior by Daniel Zaccari

Distributed to the booktrade by Simon & Schuster. SAN: 200-2442

Publisher's Cataloging-In-Publication Data
(Prepared by The Donohue Group, Inc.)

Names: Newmark, Amy, compiler.
Title: Chicken soup for the soul : the blessings of Christmas : 101 tales
    of holiday joy, kindness and gratitude / [compiled by] Amy Newmark.
Other Titles: Blessings of Christmas : 101 tales of holiday joy, kindness
    and gratitude
Description: [Cos Cob, Connecticut] : Chicken Soup for the Soul, LLC,
    [2021]
Identifiers: ISBN 9781611590777 (print) | ISBN 9781611593174 (ebook)
Subjects: LCSH: Christmas--Literary collections. | Christmas--Anecdotes. |
    Joy--Literary collections. | Joy--Anecdotes. | Kindness--Literary
    collections. | Kindness--Anecdotes. | LCGFT: Anecdotes.
Classification: LCC GT4985 .C457 2021 (print) | LCC GT4985 (ebook) | DDC
    394.2663/02--dc23er 2018951878

Library of Congress Control Number: 2021942964

PRINTED IN THE UNITED STATES OF AMERICA
on acid∞free paper

25 24 23 22 21   01 02 03 04 05 06 07 08 09 10 11

The Blessings of Christmas

101 Tales of Holiday Joy, Kindness and Gratitude

Amy Newmark

Chicken Soup for the Soul, LLC
Cos Cob, CT

Changing lives one story at a time®
www.chickensoup.com

Table of Contents

❶

~The True Meaning~

❷

~Kindness and Gratitude~

❸

~Santa's Helpers~

❹

~Treasured Traditions~

5

~The Joy of Giving~

6

~Tales of the Tree~

7

~Around the Table~

8

~Getting Creative~

❾

~The Perfect Gift~

The True Meaning

Carols for Christmas

Let us have music for Christmas. Sound the trumpet
of joy and rebirth; let each of us try, with a song in our
hearts, to bring peace to men on earth.
~Mildred L. Jarrell

I t was four weeks until Christmas, and our youth group wanted to do something together as a Christmas project. The concept was great, but none of us seventeen-year-olds had any idea what to do.

"Maybe we could have a food drive," John suggested at our Sunday night meeting.

"That's boring," answered Gail with a frown. "Nobody wants to do a food drive."

"Why don't we raise money for one of the downtown missions that serve Christmas dinners to the homeless?" Brian said.

We could hear a couple of groans from around the table.

I sat back listening to the discussion for another ten minutes and then decided to speak. "Why don't we think about our project for a few days and then come back with three or four suggestions we can vote on?"

Everyone agreed to wait a week before deciding. I knew time was running out to get something going before Christmas, but I had no clue what we should do.

During the following week, one idea after another ran through my mind, but I was still indecisive. Thursday after school, I wandered into the kitchen as my mom stirred stew for dinner.

Without looking up, she asked, "What's wrong with you?"

"Oh, nothing," I sighed.

"Yes, there is. I can tell by the way you walked in here."

"Well, there is something."

"And what's that?"

"Well… it's…" I let out a long breath. "Our youth group wants to do something for Christmas, but we…"

"You don't know what to do."

I nodded.

"Hmm." My mom thought out loud. "There's a seniors' home I've worked with close to St. Joseph's Hospital. The residents don't get out much around Christmas with the snow and ice. It might be an idea to take a few of them out to see the Christmas lights around here. Since they don't have a lot of money, they'd appreciate seeing the lights and all the Christmas displays. After they pay for food and rent every month, they don't have much left over."

I stood still for a few moments thinking of all the houses in our neighbourhood with spectacular Christmas light displays.

"What do you think?" my mom persisted.

"I never thought about it, but it might just work."

My mom turned to me and smiled, but she didn't say a word.

Next Sunday evening, our youth group met and discussed various Christmas projects. When we voted, the Christmas lights tour won unanimous support. December twentieth would be the date for the tour, which gave us very little time to prepare.

The next week was a whirlwind of busyness as we lined up everything for the tour. First, we needed to visit the seniors' home to see if they were interested. Assuming they were, we figured we would need at least nine cars to drive them. We also decided to bring them back to our church for refreshments and a carol sing.

"Do you think we can get it all done in time?" Mark asked me on Wednesday that first week. "And what if they don't like the tour?"

"I'm sure they'll enjoy the outing even if they don't enjoy the actual tour itself. Besides, it's too late now to change our minds," I responded.

As we expected, the seniors at the home were thrilled about a Christmas tour of lights and wanted to do whatever they could to make it happen. Muriel was the leader of the seniors' social club, and she loved to organize. Tall with perfectly coiffed white hair, bright blue eyes, and a generous amount of rouge on her cheeks, she was full of energy and never still a minute. Muriel knew everyone in the home and kept a very active social calendar. One of the seniors described her as a "spark plug."

With one week to go before the tour, we lined up all the essentials, including refreshments and the cars to drive thirty-eight seniors along the route we'd take. The weather was an unknown factor, so we would just have to wait and see.

On December nineteenth, the city was hit with a major snowstorm that left over a foot of snow. Fortunately, it was cleared just hours before the tour, and the snow added a magical white blanket to our whole neighborhood. By 6:30 P.M., our cars were lined up in front of the seniors' home. All thirty-eight residents slowly found seats in our cars. Muriel supervised it all.

The residents loved the tour of lights. When we arrived back at the church, they couldn't stop talking about all they'd seen.

"This whole place is like a Christmas fairy tale," one lady announced.

"I've never seen anything like this my whole life," another joined in. "It's a wonderland."

Muriel led the carol singing, even though she was never on key. Her version of "Silent Night" had a melody that sounded strangely like "Santa Claus Is Coming to Town." But every senior joined in on the fun.

As everyone was leaving the church, Muriel put her hand on my arm. "You know, none of us down at the home have very much." She lowered her voice to a whisper. "I've lived alone for many years, and I've got very little." Muriel then took a deep breath and looked straight into my eyes. "But you've made this Christmas so special for me. Tonight is my only Christmas present this year. I'll remember this the rest of my life. God bless you." She squeezed my arm and smiled. I could see her eyes were filling up, and then she turned and walked out the door into a swirl of snow.

I never saw Muriel again because she passed away a month later. I realized we'd given her the last Christmas present she ever had by taking her on a tour of lights.

But she gave me a Christmas present I still remember — her words of thanks and the look in her eyes.

— Rob Harshman —

Christmas Far from Home

The Christmas spirit whispers softly
in my ear to be of good cheer.
~Richelle E. Goodrich, *Being Bold*

I was twenty-two and living my dream. I was working on the seventh floor of a skyscraper in Sydney as a journalist for one of the world's biggest media companies. For a while, everything was a glamorous whirlwind of cocktail parties, yacht rides, and celebrities. None of my colleagues knew I was taking a one-hour train ride each night to a dingy apartment in an outer suburb. It was so full of mold that mushrooms once sprouted in a corner of the carpet, but it was all I could afford.

Who cares! I thought. *I'm young, passionate, and always busy in the city anyway!*

Everything was non-stop and exciting… until Christmas arrived.

My colleagues packed up their desks for the holidays, talking excitedly about spending time with their children. They had decorations to hang, family to visit, and holiday dinners to attend. I had only a bare, dank, grey apartment.

I walked through the city streets hoping to absorb some Yuletide cheer from the department-store windows. But it was humid and tropical in Sydney, and all I found were gaudily decorated utility poles. Shoppers rushed frantically everywhere, and the energy felt soulless, commercial, and impersonal. There was no cozy Christmas village charm to be had.

That first Christmas, I think I ate Korean food from the only restaurant I found open. The following year, I volunteered to work in the office on Christmas Day. I had nothing else to do and nowhere else to be. By the third Christmas, I'd had enough. I took the train to an enormous discount shopping warehouse to try and find some traditional garlands. I bought a foot-high artificial tree mounted in a raffia base and spent a delightful afternoon crafting "ornaments" from red, white, green, and gold ribbons. I wrote and mailed Christmas cards to astonished friends. "You're so good," they said. "Who has time to write cards?"

At my office desk one morning in late December, I opened a package sent by a PR contact who was hoping to get magazine coverage for her brand. She'd filled it with six beautifully decorated gingerbread people, wrapped in packets with gold ribbons like party favors. It gave me an idea.

Riding the train home that night, I gazed out the window and reminisced. I thought back to my happiest childhood memories—when Christmas Eve had been shared with Polish friends at their magical farm. The Polish mother, who insisted I call her Ciotka (Auntie) even though we weren't related, always brought out her heirloom European decorations and best antique silver. Her husband used to chop down a real fir and place it in a corner of the dining room where it glittered with hand-painted wooden ornaments and strings of beads. We would begin the evening by receiving traditional *oplatki* holy Eucharist wafers, which are very thin, white, and flavorless, stamped with religious Christmas images.

Ciotka's mother, Babcia (Grandmother), had brought these special gifts from Poland, where they had been blessed by a priest. Being the eldest, tradition stated that she must break her wafer first. She passed a piece to the next oldest person and so on until everyone's *oplatki* was divided into little pieces. We went around the room exchanging our pieces for another person's piece. As we did this, we kissed and wished each other "Merry Christmas!" and health and joy for the coming year. Afterward, for the entrée, Ciotka and Babcia always served two traditional Polish recipes: bright red beetroot soup (*barszcz*) and delicious mushroom pie (*paszteciki z kapust i grzybami*).

Thinking back to those wonderful years — loved ones gathered by candlelight, exchanging gifts and *oplatki* — made my throat ache with nostalgia. No wonder Sydney felt so hollow and empty, I realised. If you want to experience magic, you must make your own!

In a surge of enthusiasm, I picked up the phone and called Ciotka, who was still living on her old farm, happily surrounded by her vegetables and flowers. "How do you make that sour red soup?" I asked her. "And what is the recipe for Polish mushroom pie?" She told me the secret was to use Maggie Beer's famous sour-cream pastry, and I found myself rolling out a pie base for the first time in my life. My idea, which had begun as a spark the day I received the gingerbread men, was growing.

I had met a few people in Sydney who, like me, were far away from their family homes. Perhaps it was time to host a Christmas celebration for us "leftovers" — the ex-pats, out-of-towners, and university students who couldn't afford to fly home. I bought the most enormous frozen turkey I could find and lugged it home on the train. I spent all afternoon preparing Ciotka's traditional soup and mushroom pie to accompany it. I decorated the table with more red-and-green crafts I'd made myself and hung one of the festive gingerbread men I'd received at work on the back of each dining chair — six place settings, five friends.

On Christmas Day, everybody arrived on time. They brought chocolate panettone and Turkish delight, marzipan, and rye bread — different offerings from each of their own countries, traditions, and memories. Although my crummy apartment practically sat on a railway line, and the windows and walls rattled every twenty minutes when a train rushed past, we barely noticed. The six of us were busy toasting each other and creating magic in a city far from home.

Together, we enjoyed the most wonderful, meaningful afternoon I can remember. As my friends hugged and kissed their goodbyes, I heard a television through the thin apartment walls and remembered that an old man lived alone next door. I looked at the beribboned, decorated gingerbread man still hanging on the back of my chair and knew what I had to do.

I knocked on his door, and he opened it. Sure enough, he'd been alone all day inside his equally grey and depressing apartment. When I offered him the gingerbread man, his old, lined face broke into a smile. He was so touched that he found it difficult to say, "Thank you." I noticed he had a thick accent and asked him where he was from. "Poland," he told me, "although I've lived here for over forty years." I was stunned.

"Wait here!" I cried. I dashed back into my apartment, placed the leftover mushroom pie on a plate, and spooned *barszcz* into a takeaway container. When he saw what I was offering him, he cleared his throat several times, and his eyes looked very wet.

"Are you Polish?" he asked me.

"No," I admitted. "I'm just a young woman learning how important it is for adults to pass on traditions and magic!"

— Rebecca Wyldewood —

My Most Memorable Christmas Gift

I will honor Christmas in my heart
and try to keep it all the year.
~Charles Dickens

My family wasn't poor as I was growing up, but we certainly weren't rich. Dad worked two jobs, if needed, to provide for us. The year I started first grade was different, though. Mom was able to take a job at a store, so we had two incomes. Christmas was always good, but that year promised to be the best yet, with way more presents than usual under the tree. My brother and I couldn't wait for Christmas morning to arrive.

Just prior to the holiday, a co-worker of Mom's passed away, leaving behind a partially disabled husband, an infant, and several other children. Everyone at the store wanted to make sure the family had a Christmas, so they banded together to provide something for each member of the family. I enjoyed helping pick out a few items for the younger children, and I found myself beginning to look at Christmas a bit differently. I began to grasp the joy of giving.

Although it seemed to take forever, Christmas morning did arrive, and my brother and I awoke to find more presents than we had ever imagined. They filled the space under the tree and even part of the next room. They seemed to go on forever.

The morning's noisy bedlam had settled down a bit when Earl, a good friend and neighbor, stopped by. He had discovered that a single mother who lived in the area had been unable to give her children a Christmas, so Earl was asking friends and family if they had anything they could donate or share to brighten the family's holiday.

Mom and Dad sat my brother and me down to tell us about the family that didn't have a Christmas. They asked if we were willing to give the children some of the many gifts that Santa had given us. We didn't hesitate. In fact, we treated it like a game and went shopping among our gifts to pick out presents for the children. It didn't take us long to box up quite a few items for Earl to take to the family.

When I look back on that Christmas, I can vividly recall so many things, but the presents I most remember aren't the ones I received but the ones I gave away. To this day, one of my favorite parts of the Christmas holidays is doing something for others. Toys for children, meals for families, hats for the homeless, or volunteering around the city — there are so many ways to lend a hand, and even the smallest act can have a tremendous impact.

My parents asked a six-year-old girl to give away a few toys, and that one small act shaped my life. They could not have given me a better gift.

— Donna L. Marsh —

A Laundromat Christmas

> *Appreciation is a wonderful thing. It makes what*
> *is excellent in others belong to us as well.*
> ~Voltaire

I t would be our first Christmas in Florida with our younger daughter, Joanne, in her new home. She and her fiancé, Mike, had moved there three months earlier and were still adjusting while also planning their wedding.

"I'm not buying a traditional Christmas tree, Mom," Joanne told me during a phone call. "I'm getting a palm tree I can plant in the back yard in January, so I'll remember this Christmas as long as I live in this house."

The forecast was for cool, damp weather, but I wasn't prepared for so much rain while we visited. We had torrential rain like I had never experienced on Christmas Eve. I wondered how we would get to church if streets were flooded.

On Christmas Day, however, the sun shone brightly upon dry streets and sidewalks. We walked to church and admired the flowers blooming along the way.

When we returned, Joanne and Mike noticed the laundromat across the street was open. "I wonder why it's open today of all days. It was supposed to be closed for Christmas," Mike said. "I'll go and see what happened."

When he returned, he told us, "Johnny, the guy who runs the laundromat, realized homeless people would need to dry their belongings after last night's rain, so he opened up and said quite a few homeless people have come in to use the machines."

"How nice of him to think of the homeless instead of enjoying his only day off and celebrating Christmas. He works seven days a week ordinarily," Joanne said.

"Would you and Dad mind if we invite Johnny to have dinner with us?" she asked. Of course, we didn't.

"Johnny is such a nice person. He's from Georgia, and his family is there," she said. Both she and Mike had used the laundromat in the past three months. I had also been there during our stay. Johnny had helped me find machines to use in the busy place. He even helped me load my wet clothes into the dryer.

When Johnny arrived at our house, he was dressed in a sport coat and immaculate shirt, but he looked uncertain. He was a young Black man about to eat with white people he hardly knew.

After he sat down, I tried making small talk with him, but he was still reserved. He might have found the blinking lights on the small palm tree strange. Perhaps, he wondered why there were so few Christmas decorations, although after seeing Joanne's frisky cats, the decoration question should have been answered.

When dinner was ready, we sat around the table. "Johnny, maybe you would like to do us the honor of saying grace," I suggested. We all bowed our heads and listened as Johnny thanked God for all the blessings he had received and was about to receive.

Joanne brought in the appetizer, and we began our feast. Soon, she cleared away those dishes and brought in the entree: shrimp and chicken grilled with a honey-maple marinade, whipped potatoes, and stir-fried vegetables — broccoli with red and yellow peppers. The table looked festive.

My husband told Johnny how his family had been migrant farm workers, picking strawberries in the late spring and beans and tomatoes in summer. Johnny visibly relaxed. As we ate a dessert of ice cream and cookies, Johnny said, "I never experienced a meal where all these different dishes got taken away so more could come."

"Oh, Johnny, we don't eat a meal with lots of courses all the time. It's just that Christmas is special. Your being here made it more special," I said. He smiled and told us he came from a family of eleven but two of his brothers had died in an auto accident.

"I am so impressed that you thought of the homeless today, Johnny. That was beautiful. You became a gift to people in need. Sharing our dinner was a small gift to you. The kindness you showed others really touched me," I said.

He smiled and said, "I've been in St. Petersburg for three years now, and this is the best Christmas I have ever had."

After he left, we all agreed it was a special Christmas for us, too. It was so meaningful to spend it with a man who was such a gift to others, who put their needs above his own in the true spirit of Christmas.

Joanne didn't need to plant that palm tree to remember how beautiful that Christmas was. She had only to look across the street to the laundromat.

— Sandy McPherson Carrubba Geary —

An International Chanukah to Remember

Strangers are just friends waiting to happen.
~Rod McKuen

The six of us stood wrapped in towels and dripping wet in the elevator. Grandma and Papu cooed over the twins, Huck and Helen, adorable at five years old but nevertheless over-sunned and overtired. However, their fussing could not dampen the jolly mood. It was winter break, and we were on a sun- and sea-filled visit to Mazatlán, Mexico. Best of all, tonight was the first night of Chanukah, and I was looking forward to our celebration.

The elevator doors opened, and two young men squeezed in. The pair spoke rapidly in another language and laughed at a joke. Amidst the banter, I picked out a couple of words. They were speaking Hebrew. "Are you Israeli?" I asked them in Hebrew.

They were so startled to hear someone address them in Hebrew in Mexico that they laughed again and answered me in English. "Yes! We are on vacation." Then one turned to the other and said something in Hebrew again that ended in the words "celebrate Chanukah."

I decided it was appropriate not only to eavesdrop on their conversation but to consider myself a participant. "Oh," I said. "Did you say Chanukah?" I had switched to English. My Hebrew was limited to

"Where are you from?" and "More chocolate *babka*, please."

My husband Steve rolled his eyes at my nosiness, and my mother-in-law beamed. She loved this kind of thing — a sort of improvisational entertainment for the captive audience one can only find in an elevator.

"Yes. Yes. Chanukah!" The elevator dinged at floor five. They gestured for us to step out and then followed behind. Five was their floor, too.

"Hey! We're both on floor five," Huck mentioned. At age five, this kind of coincidence was nothing short of amazing.

"I'm Avi, and this is Dov." The Israelis shook hands all around. "Do you celebrate Chanukah?"

"Chanukah!" Helen said as if hearing the word for the first time at this moment in the conversation. She did a dance that looked more like running in place. "Chanukah. Chanukah. Chanukah!"

Avi looked on indulgently while Steve tried to get her to avoid stepping on the adults' feet. Dov interjected, "We wanted to celebrate, but we don't have a *hanukiah* or any candles."

"Ilana, you brought a menorah, didn't you?" Grandma said, using the English word for the Chanukah candelabra. Of course, I did. I had two five-year-olds. How could I possibly forget Chanukah? I had also brought the dreidels, the spinning tops to play the traditional holiday game. Not only that, but I'd wrapped and packed little gifts for two wee children for each of the eight nights, causing an overcharge on my suitcase, which Steve had kidded "must be loaded with bowling balls."

We still stood in the hallway, smiling at one another. Clearly, there was only one thing to do.

"Why don't you come celebrate with us tonight?" I asked.

Dov and Avi erupted in smiles. "Are you sure? You have space?"

Papu said, "They insisted we get a double. It's a palace in there. There's plenty of room. Come at seven."

I pulled out the silver and blue tinsel from the depths of my suitcase and decorated the kitchenette table. I placed the menorah in the center of the table, and the kids "helped" me heat the wax on the bottom of the candles so that the unlit candles would stand up straight in their holders. We would light two candles: the center, raised *shamash* or guardian candle, and a candle to represent the first-night celebration. By the end of the holiday, we would have lit all eight candles to remember the miracle of a tiny amount of the ancient temple's oil supplies lasting eight nights.

There was a knock on the door, and Avi and Dov entered with a paper shopping bag filled with who-knows-what. "Oh, you look nice." Avi smiled at Huck, who wore a real dress shirt complete with buttons that he had buttoned himself. Huck's chin retreated and his cheeks reddened, but I could tell he was pleased.

As the sun descended, we lit the candles and sang the blessings together in Hebrew. Even Huck and Helen had learned them in religious school. "Good Hebrew!" Avi said and received shy smiles in return.

"Okay. Make room in the kitchen," Dov said. "Is it okay if I make a mess?" He began to unpack the bag: a bottle of vegetable oil, a container of salt, a peeler, and a gigantic sack of potatoes. A container of sour cream and a jar of applesauce would be the garnish. We stared in amazement.

"Are you really going to make potato latkes? From scratch?" I asked, disbelieving. Sure, I had "made" the fried potato pancakes before as a holiday treat. But I started with frozen hash-brown patties, threw them in the microwave, and covered them quickly with applesauce, hoping nobody would notice. These were going to be the real deal.

Dov cooked the latkes, two or three at a time, and we devoured them as fast as he could make them. Meanwhile, the kids tore the wrapping off the gifts from us and the grandparents. Even Dov and Avi had something for the kids — *gelt*, a traditional Chanukah gift of coins. And these were special Israeli coins. Very cool.

At last, we all sat on the floor while Grandma and Papu watched. Spinning the dreidel, we competed to see who could make theirs spin the longest. By now, the kids had warmed to Avi and Dov, and Huck especially looked to the big boys with shining eyes, spinning the dreidel and reveling in their attention and praise.

After lighting the candles, we shared a customary blessing, the *Shehecheyanu*. The Hebrew translates to: "Blessed are you who has sustained us in life and brought us together at this time." I smiled at this happy circumstance of American and Israeli strangers celebrating together in Mexico because it brought home the true point of Chanukah: An unexpected friendship is a little miracle in itself.

— Ilana M. Long —

Delivering Christmas

*May the spirit of Christmas bring you peace,
the gladness of Christmas give you hope,
and the warmth of Christmas grant you love.*
~Author Unknown

I had to run to the post office, but I told my son I'd be right back. It was a gym day for him, and it had snowed overnight. With his multiple sclerosis and use of a walker, he'd need extra time to get out of the car and into the building. I really did have to be right back.

Somehow, Christmas had snuck up on me. I needed to mail some cards and a package, and it took forever to find a parking space. Hurrying toward the post office, I noticed two older women helping each other up the steps. The snow from the night before had been shoveled away, but I could see a few places that might cause them a problem. I was about to ask if they'd like me to hold the door when one of them pushed the handicap lever. The door opened, and they noticed I was waiting behind them.

They told me to go ahead.

One explained, "We're just two old friends coming to mail our Christmas cards. We've been doing this for years."

They told me not to wait for them.

"You'd be here all day," one joked. They both laughed.

I thanked them and went inside, only to take my place in a long line. I thought about leaving but decided there'd be no good time to mail something with Christmas around the corner.

While standing there, I could hear those two older women chatting. The building was so massive that their voices echoed against the towering walls. I turned around to see where they were and what they were doing. They both saw me. They smiled and waved. That's when I noticed what they were wearing.

The two were all dressed up with clip-on earrings, long wool coats, and hats—not winter hats but dress hats with veils. One hat even had a feather in it. The two looked as if they were making a day of going to the post office. They reminded me of my father. He loved going to the post office. He always wore a tie no matter what time of the year it happened to be. If it was cold outside, he'd wear his dress hat with a red feather on the side. If it was Christmastime, he'd wear his long, wool coat. He'd always run into people he knew and spend time talking to all of them.

Now, so many people were using their cell phones while they waited. Socializing at the post office was a tradition that was dying out.

I turned my attention back to the line. The post office was extremely busy, and people were getting restless. A few had tired children. A few muttered to themselves and to others in line. A few left, which made the rest of us happy. The line got shorter.

When one particular person reached the counter with many big boxes to mail, a subdued moan went around the lobby.

That's when I noticed one of those two older women reading greeting cards for sale on a circular display. The cards that had her attention were all Christmas-themed.

One special Christmas card caught her fancy. Laughing, she brought it over to her friend. They both started chuckling, giggling, and then laughing—a from-the-belly laugh that sent tears down their cheeks. They tried stopping. They'd take a breath, but then they'd read the card again and start laughing and chuckling. Their laughter became contagious.

Others in line started laughing, and they hadn't even read the card. Strangers smiled and talked with one another. Cell phones were put away and replaced by conversations.

It felt like Christmas had arrived early in the historic post office. I could imagine my father standing in line waiting to mail the Christmas cards my mother had addressed. That day the post office delivered Christmas to me, right on time. And then I went back outside and got my son to the gym on time, too! No problem.

— Barbara Briggs Ward —

Chicken Soup for the Soul

Family First

*The bond that links your true family is not one of blood
but of respect and joy in each other's life.*
~Richard Bach

"You are going to have the best Christmas ever." We heard this ad nauseam during that cold December in 2010. After a year of adoption preparation, we were finally (and nervously) picking up our six-year-old daughter Courtney at her foster home and bringing her to her forever home.

It took about an hour to get home. The energy in our car was palpable. We talked about all the wonderful things we would be doing, the great school she would be attending, the new friends she would be meeting in ballet class, and, of course, the best Christmas ever she would be experiencing.

Our friends and family rejoiced at having a new niece, cousin, granddaughter, and goddaughter. We were starring in our own cozy Hallmark movie: Girl moves in, has new life with lots of love, clothes and toys, forgets about her past life and lives happily ever after.

Our imaginary movie started off well. We worked hard at setting the scene by visiting Santa at the mall, attending the Christmas parade, baking cookies, shopping for a new Christmas dress, writing to Santa, attending holiday-themed plays, going to parties, making festive decorations, dancing to Christmas music, decorating five (yes, five!) trees, watching cartoon classics and, the cherry on top, taking

The True Meaning |

in a live performance of *The Nutcracker*.

Expecting nothing but sprinkles, glee and giggles, you can imagine our surprise as Courtney's sadness and agitation grew with each passing activity.

Christmas morning was no exception. As Courtney opened each gift on her Christmas list, she managed to force a smile, put the gift aside, and then start on the next. It was like watching someone labour at a factory job, repeating the same task over and over. Days later, most of the toys still sat in their pristine, unopened boxes. A couple of gifts were taken out of their boxes but were set aside.

Nothing made our girl sparkle. We were sad and disappointed that we weren't getting the best Christmas ever as we had been promised.

It didn't take long to recognize that our daughter didn't see much cause for celebration. Behind all the tinsel, lights and trees was a little girl who was spending her first Christmas without her biological mother. And out there, in another city, was a mother who was spending her first Christmas without her biological daughter. Our gain was a mother's loss. We felt awful as guilt and sadness started leaking through the cracks of what we thought was a fairly solid adoption foundation.

We decided to have a family meeting where we encouraged Courtney to talk about what was making her sad. We prompted her a bit because we knew she would feel awkward talking about her mom. We encouraged her to talk about her as much as she wanted. We suggested she draw pictures and write down whatever she wanted — good or bad — about her past life. We assured her we wouldn't judge. And we also assured her that we would never disrespect or speak poorly of her biological mother.

We started sending her mother detailed letters, photos, videos, and gifts that our daughter had picked out for her. Shortly thereafter, Courtney decided that it was time to see her mom. She really wanted this to happen. Coincidentally, she had just been cast as a dancing polar bear in *The Nutcracker* with a professional ballet company. Proud of her accomplishment, she wanted her mom to attend the premiere.

Without hesitation, we contacted the Children's Aid Society and worked with them to make this dream happen. As the next December drew near, all our daughter could talk about was getting to see her biological mom again. Her excitement peaked on opening night. Courtney lit up the stage as a dancing white bear. She was beaming from ear to ear, and she really stood out. After the show, she put on her new Christmas dress and ran out to the lobby to give her mother a huge hug.

After much research, we have been able to reunite Courtney with most of her eight siblings. Her life is being glued back together bit by bit, and she is very appreciative. We have learned that in building a new life, we must include her past life. Children are not like Christmas toys that can turn on and off with a switch. If we allow them to embrace their past, they will come to realize that they are who they are because they lived through it.

A couple of summers ago, we were honoured when Courtney's mom asked all three of us to be in her wedding party. And last year, Courtney was asked to be a bridesmaid at her biological sister's wedding. Our daughter's life — and ours — continue to grow. And each Christmas gets better and better.

— Réjean Mayer —

8

The Spirit of Peace

While we may be of different faiths, we have
a strong sense of faith, family, community.
~Bob Menendez

Three days before the start of Christmas break, I stood in a fifth-grade classroom and passed out sheets of Christmas-themed writing paper. The writing prompt at the top of the paper was meant to be easy and engaging for students whose minds were on everything but school. They were instructed to write a five-paragraph essay about how their families celebrated Christmas. I smiled, finally relaxing as the students got to work. My day as a substitute teacher was going surprisingly well. There had not been a single problem all day, and this class was the last one of the day.

A raised hand drew me to the desk of a girl who had been class helper that period. She stared at her paper with obvious frustration.

"What's wrong?" I asked gently. "Do you understand the assignment?"

She looked up at me. "Yes, but I can't do the assignment. I don't celebrate Christmas. I'm Muslim."

Oh, dear. This was the kind of situation that the substitute workshops never prepared me for. Apparently, it had not occurred to the regular teacher that some students didn't celebrate Christmas. She had simply been looking for a light, easy activity to leave for the substitute (me) that would keep the kids busy and quiet.

I thought for a moment about what I knew about Islam and its holidays and what special festivals the girl would take part in.

I smiled as I crouched by her desk. "Well, Christmas is a special time for celebrating peace and love with our family and friends. There's usually a big meal when everybody brings food, and we get to see our extended families, even the people we don't get to see a lot. It's such a special time that everyone feels like getting together with their loved ones to celebrate."

"That's Christmas?" she asked.

I nodded. "That's Christmas. In fact, it's a lot like your celebration of Eid al-Fitr at the end of Ramadan. Isn't there a big meal and a special time to gather with your loved ones to celebrate the end of the month of fasting?"

A grin spread across her face. "Yes! That's just what Eid is like."

"So, here is what we will do," I said. "You write your essay about your family's Eid traditions. I'll leave a note for your teacher to let her know why you're doing that. That will make it okay."

She smiled at me again and immediately got to work. For the next fifty minutes, I sat at the teacher's desk and watched over the class while I wrote the note to the teacher. When I called for the girl to collect the papers, she made sure to put hers on top.

"Thank you so much," she said as she handed them to me before gathering her books.

I stopped her for just a minute while the other students filed out. Recalling what little Arabic I knew, I spoke to her in the language that I knew she would understand.

"*As-salamu alaykum*," I said.

Her face lit up as she recognized the words. "Peace be with you," she repeated in English.

And it was.

— Anna Cleveland —

A Florida Christmas

Christmas is a piece of one's home
that one carries in one's heart.
~Freya Stark

"I wonder what it's like around here at Christmas," I said to my husband one sultry summer afternoon in our new hometown of Lakeland, Florida. We were sitting on a wooden bench in a small downtown park. Along with the heat, I was soaking in the quaintness of the small-town life around me: charming brick walkways around the main square, mom-and-pop gift shops, streetlights resembling old gas lamps. I loved it all. Christmas, I hoped, would be just as picturesque. In my mind, I already had the Hallmark movie written.

Florida was quite a change from Chicago, where we had lived for ten years prior to our move. Now retirement beckoned, and we were ready to live life at a slower — and warmer — pace. Having lived all my life in the Midwest, I was looking forward to a winter with sun instead of snow, short sleeves instead of parkas, and sandals instead of boots.

"What have we gotten into?" I remember thinking when we first arrived in Lakeland, and temperatures reached 100 degrees. Initially leery, I hadn't been quite ready to move away from the Midwest. But my job in Chicago was unexpectedly eliminated after thirty years, so I retired early, and we moved south. "Don't worry," our new neighbors told us as I wiped the sweat from my face. "The weather at Christmas will make up for this heat."

When the holiday season arrived, I was relieved to learn they were right. The days were glorious: mid-70s and breezy, better suited for a day at the beach than for Christmas shopping. Even so, Christmas was just a few weeks away, and I hadn't found my holiday spirit yet. I was anxious to go downtown and walk through the park to see the city's decorations.

They certainly lived up to my expectations. Each path in the park was lined with lighted candy canes. They all met at the city's fourteen-foot Christmas tree. Santa had set up a small house beside the tree for his visits with the children—and the line was already getting long. Some of the children had taken off their shoes and were running around barefoot while they waited. In December! *Norman Rockwell would love all this,* I told myself.

Then I walked a little closer to the tree and noticed a ring of about a dozen newly planted rosebushes encircling the trunk. Delicate roses were in full bloom—pink, yellow and white. I was jolted. Pastel roses next to a dark green pine tree with red and gold trimming? That didn't go together at all. Even their scents clashed. Rich, hearty pine that, to me, smelled like the essence of Christmas, was paired with the soft, subtle scent of roses. That was all wrong. Norman Rockwell never would have put such roses in a Christmas painting.

In the days that followed, I noticed other holiday peculiarities around town. Festive outdoor lights were everywhere, but they decorated swaying palm trees or stately scrub oaks dripping in Spanish moss instead of hedges and pines. Beautiful? Yes. But Christmas-y? Hardly. A billboard showed a big picture of Santa's sleigh in action, but his familiar reindeer had been replaced by a team of neon-pink flamingos. Salvation Army bell ringers wore flip-flops and shorts. On Christmas Eve, I saw a family in bathing suits washing their car in their driveway and goofing around like it was an annual Christmas tradition.

Of course, the wonderful weather had lured me to Florida in the first place, but I wasn't expecting it to feel so unsettling. I hadn't realized how many of my fondest Christmas memories involved being bundled up in coats and scarves and still feeling cold. Growing up in Detroit, my siblings and I bundled up to go shopping downtown and to the

Christmas Eve midnight service each year. We bundled up to go to my grandmother's house. We bundled up to go tobogganing with the neighbor kids. Even as an adult during my Chicago years, one of my favorite holiday activities was to stuff myself in my long, down-filled coat and head downtown to Christkindlmarket, an authentic outdoor German-style holiday market.

Aside from browsing all the beautiful tree ornaments displayed by the many vendors, the best part of the experience for me was eating a platter-sized *schnitzel* and sipping warm, mulled wine from a small, ceramic Christmas "boot" al fresco. I saw my breath with every bite I took, but I didn't care.

To my surprise, I realized I missed being cold, if only for a day or two. I missed the crunch of snow beneath my feet and the soft glow of the outdoor lights against newly fallen snow. I missed the rosy cheeks on everyone's face, with color provided by the cold and not the sun. I didn't even mind the runny nose and cold ears that always came with it. THAT was Christmas as I knew it.

Looking back, I can't help but wonder if those layers of clothes I wore every winter back home served as a security blanket of sorts, a way to hold in all the good I felt around the holidays growing up because those memories were rare ones. My mother succumbed to breast cancer after a five-year illness when I was twelve, and five years after that my father suffered a fatal heart attack. My childhood memories are clouded with hospital visits, canceled family plans when Mom wasn't feeling well, and — worst of all — funeral homes and condolences from everyone I saw. The happy memories of my Christmases before all the sickness are some of the scarce "normal" ones I remember. I suddenly felt a strong need to protect them.

It was an adjustment to be sure, but in time my nostalgia peeled away like the layers of clothing I used to wear. Instead of comparing everything to the past, I began to focus on the beauty of my present. Instead of finding things that were different, I looked for things that showcased the essence of the small-town life I found so engaging. A city-wide Christmas parade with marching high-school bands and floats heralded the beginning of Lakeland's Christmas season. Each of the five lakes near our downtown had a decorated Christmas tree "floating" in the middle of the water. Magical. I realized that, while I cherished my holiday memories, I didn't want my Christmases past to take away from the very different — but equally memorable — Christmases present and future.

One morning, shortly after we rang in the New Year that first Florida winter, I took my coffee out to our lanai, which overlooks a big retention pond. I sat down and lazily watched the egrets and sandhill cranes wade along the water's edge. Our two resident swans, "The Swansons," also swam up to say hello. *This* was the life I had longed for during those blustery Midwest winters years ago, I told myself. Enjoy it! So, I got up, took off my shoes, and blissfully walked outside in my bare feet to feed the birds.

— Diane Hurles —

10

A Miracle on 27th Street

The joy of brightening other lives becomes
for us the magic of the holidays.
~W.C. Jones

I handed my Subaru keys to the Les Schwab attendant and joined the other customers waiting to have their summer tires swapped out for snow treads. My tradition every year is to procrastinate until the last minute and then wake at 5:00 A.M. to get in line the day before I drive over the mountain to my parents' place for Christmas. This year was no different. After spending an hour shivering outside along with a dozen other procrastinators, I wasn't feeling particularly social, so I gripped my coffee mug and hunkered down to read my book while I waited.

An elderly man in his late seventies took the uncomfortable plastic seat next to mine. In polished loafers, a well-pressed dress shirt, and wool coat, he stood out among the crowd bundled in Patagonia and Carhartt. It looked like he'd taken a wrong turn on his way to Saks Fifth Avenue.

I tried to use my book as an excuse to ignore him. He struck up a conversation anyway, so I grudgingly set my book aside out of courtesy. I soon discovered that he was a former justice of the peace in a small rural town one county over from where I grew up. He even knew several people my mom had worked with back in her Circuit

Court days. Engaged and surprised, I asked what brought him to town.

The man, whose name was Dewey, sat very still for a moment and gazed at the popcorn machine across the lobby. "My wife is in hospice," he said. He had driven his wife a hundred miles to Bend for a doctor's appointment, expecting to get a prescription refill. Instead, the doctor had delivered bad news and shunted his wife directly to a hospice facility, anticipating she would pass away over the Christmas holiday. His children lived across the state, and with the dicey roads and families of their own, they couldn't drive over to say goodbye to their mom.

Dewey had been by her side constantly since then but had decided that morning to buy snow tires. His car didn't handle well on slick roads, and he "just needed some fresh air." His voice was matter of fact as he told me that he was alone in a strange town for Christmas, waiting for his wife to die.

For a while, we both stared at the popcorn machine. "Life is full of surprises," he said. I had to agree.

Later that day, as I packed my suitcase and prepared to drive home, I couldn't stop thinking about Dewey and his wife. There couldn't be that many hospice facilities in Bend, so I did a Google search and figured they must be at the 27th Street hospice based on his description. I decided that on my way out of town I'd drop by with candy and flowers to brighten their day. If I'd picked the wrong hospice, I'd give the candy and flowers to my mom.

I tiptoed across the icy parking lot to the hospice entrance with a bouquet of white lilies in one hand and some chocolate in the other. My fear grew with each step. I had no idea what I would find inside. I felt inadequate in the face of grief and loss; all I had to offer was a bouquet of Safeway flowers and a box of candy from aisle 4. Surely, I would offend this couple by intruding on a deeply private moment.

I pulled open the glass door and resolved to turn tail at the first opportunity. Unfortunately, a woman in nursing togs promptly pointed me down the hall to Dewey's wife's room.

"Are you family?" she asked.

"No," I replied, proffering the lilies. "Flower delivery."

Dewey's wife was propped up in bed. Tubes pumped oxygen into her nostrils, and an IV protruded from her bruised arm. Dewey sat by her side holding her hand. His eyes widened when he saw me. Then his face turned red as he scrambled to explain to his wife who this forty-something redhead was, as if he'd been caught doing something naughty. His wife, whom he introduced as Nancy, seemed amused. She reached out a hand to me. "It's good to meet you," she said, and coughed. "Dewey always meets interesting people."

I arranged the lilies in a vase the nurse provided and listened to Dewey and Nancy chat with each other as if spending the holiday at a hospice in Bend, Oregon, was a grand adventure. They were especially looking forward to the hospice Christmas meal, wondering how it would compare to various other holiday meals they had eaten over the years. Would there be ham or turkey? Would the stuffing be moist or dry? Dewey had a complex plan to smuggle in a bottle of champagne. I was lulled by their chatter, imagining decades of such simple yet personable interactions knitting together the fabric of their marriage. For a moment, I was wrapped up in the softness of their love.

I felt strangely light as I drove to my own parents' home, and I savored every moment of a very normal holiday with my family — even more for witnessing Dewey and Nancy facing their last. Still, my mind looped back to the couple again and again: Did their children decide to visit after all? Did they smuggle in the champagne?

When I returned home, I decided I would visit one more time. I had an appointment nearby anyway. Once again, I walked across the ice and pulled open the heavy glass door of the hospice. Then I hesitated, realizing this could be a very different scene than my last visit. The door to Nancy's room stood ajar. I could see that her bed was empty, and the rumpled sheets were thrown back. Nancy wasn't there.

I pressed my hand to my lips and absorbed what this meant. Tears welled in my eyes.

Then a nurse's voice called from behind me. "They're just about to leave."

"Excuse me?" I said.

"Nancy and Dewey. They're packed up and about to head home.

She's in the car out front. I think Dewey is in the restroom."

I stood blinking in the hall for a moment, and then Dewey appeared. He didn't seem surprised to see me.

"They're sending us home," he said, his eyes dancing. "Nancy's decided not to leave me just yet." After a little more chitchat and a handshake, I watched him fold his lean, elegantly dressed body into the driver's seat and pull out of the hospice parking lot with Nancy in the passenger seat. His car didn't slip on the icy roads thanks to a new set of studded tires.

When I reflect on this episode, which spanned all of five days, I am amazed at my naivety. I thought I was giving a gift to this couple. Instead, I was the one who was blessed. I got to witness a miracle at the 27th Street hospice and was reminded that it is by giving that we receive.

— Vernita Lea Ediger —

11

A Christmas of the Heart

One of the most important things you can do on this
earth is to let people know they are not alone.
~Shannon L. Alder

It was 4:00 P.M. on Christmas Eve. A light snow had fallen, and it was windy and cold. Winter was here for the long haul. The months ahead would be cruel.

I had not been to see the old man in months. I felt a little guilty about this, knowing that he lived alone. He was ninety-three and had outlived both his son and wife. His grandson lived some miles away but checked on him frequently, or so he told me.

After the old man's wife died, I stopped by often, shoveling his sidewalk and checking on him. He seemed to be adjusting well, although every visit brought a tearful reminder of his loss. I wanted to help him more, but I feared that I was intruding, so I stayed away for longer and longer periods once I satisfied myself that he was going to be alright.

I watched from a distance then, driving by his house, passing by when I walked during the summer, and asking around to see if his grandson was still checking on him. As time passed, I began to forget about him — until Christmastime came, that is.

Christmas had always been a sad, lonely time for me. I'd always disliked the large family gatherings, the office party, the hype and fuss of it all. I had this idealistic notion of the perfect Christmas as a time to quietly show those we love how much we care for them in our own way. I never had much money for gift buying, and it seemed that I never had enough for everyone. I was always happy to see the season end.

Now, as I was getting older, there were fewer people to buy for. There were no more family gatherings, my parents were gone, and my sisters and I led separate lives. I was finally free to spend Christmas quietly at home.

So, I kept it simple. I shopped for those on my list. I put out a few decorations. I bought food only for a small family dinner. It was low-key, not like my parents' holidays at all. It made me realize acutely how small my circle of family had become.

I thought about Christmas gatherings of the past and traditions that I had let go. My mother and grandmother had always decorated their houses inside and out. Christmas lights and music filled our home when I was young. Trimming the tree was a major event, selecting from a collection of ornaments and debating over the star or the angel at the top.

There were Christmas tablecloths, the good china, and a table set with special treats. We had Christmas towels and soaps for the guests in the bathroom. The elf took his place on the mantel, and the stockings were hung there, too.

Mom always baked cookies. There were meats and cheeses, wine, and eggnog. Presents were hidden, and lots of secret wrapping took place behind closed doors. We visited relatives, went to midnight mass, and spent the holiday in a perpetual frenzy of celebration.

It was during this time of remembering that I suddenly thought of the old man. I wondered if he would be at home. Had anyone taken him to their house for the holiday? Would it be okay for me to get him a small gift? I had not seen him in so long.

Then I got a lovely Christmas card from him in the mail. He still wanted contact! It was not too late.

I bought him some snacks, a little meat and cheese, candy, and some cookies. It was just enough to enjoy but not enough to serve as a reminder that he was alone.

The general Christmas busyness kept me occupied until Christmas

Eve. It would be a quiet Christmas Eve this year. I decided to take a chance and go to see the old man.

I wondered if he was off to some family gathering, or perhaps the family was at his house. I decided I would just make a quick stop, say hello, and give him his gift. I packed the items in a colorful bag and drove up the street to his house, nervously wondering what to say.

He opened the door with a bright smile. "Nobody home!" he said with that laugh that I remembered, the laugh I had missed. But he opened the door wide, obviously glad to see me. I was excited to see him, too.

We sat at the kitchen table and chatted. He seemed more peaceful this year, although every mention of his wife brought a tear. After sixty-five years together, it was a lonely life without her. Her absence was visible in the house, with no decorations or tree. He kept things sparkling clean, though, just the way she would have liked.

He told me of his time overseas in the Navy, the fever he caught, and how he almost died. He told me how he drank whiskey once when he was young and got terribly sick. He never drank again.

He told me how he and his wife would fight sometimes, as married couples do. He always let her have the last word. He learned early on that it was the best way to stop the fight. Once, when they drove to the next state to go shopping, they got into a fight over some silly thing. The fight continued for miles on the way home. Finally, he pulled the car over about ten miles from home and told her to drive it to the house; he would walk. She tried to convince him to get back in the car, but he told her to go on alone, so she did. He walked all the way home. We laughed at the crazy things we do sometimes out of anger. I told him he sure had proven his point. He nodded but said, "I paid the price the next day. Boy, was I sore!"

We talked for over an hour until it was near time for supper. I gave him my small gift, and we parted with a warm hug. I made him promise to call me if he needed anything at all. I decided then that I would not stay away for so long this time. He was far too precious to be forgotten.

I went on my way, feeling lighter, smiling, and listening to carols on the radio. I was happy and filled with the Christmas spirit. It was what I had wanted all along—to show the people I care about how I feel, in my own way. It was the best Christmas gift I could have asked for: a Christmas of the heart, without pretense or preparations. Just two people enjoying each other's company, sharing and caring quietly. After fifty-two years, I finally got my wish.

—Carol Gaido-Schmidt—

12

Truly Blessed

*All religions are true. God can be reached by different
religions. Many rivers flow by many ways,
but they fall into the sea. They all are one.*
~Ramakrishna

My first Christmas mass was coming, and I was nervous — mostly because I'm a Jewish teacher who works at a Catholic school. It's not as strange as it seems. At my interview, the school's principal asked, "Why do you want to teach at a Catholic school?" I hesitated, considering my response while she looked over my résumé — filled with years of teaching experience at Jewish schools. "Wait a sec. You do know this is a Catholic school, right?" she asked, grinning. Of course, I did. The word Catholic was in the school's name!

"Yep. I know. But faith is faith," I answered. "To me, a school practices faith, teaches kids about respect for themselves and their community, and gives them the support to do right by the world." The fact is that Judaism has always been the cornerstone of my culture and faith. My grandpa was a rabbi. I speak some Hebrew, celebrate the holidays, and force my kids to go to religious school — religiously.

Once I was hired, I learned that every class period opened with a prayer. Each day, I appointed a different student prayer leader. I stood respectfully but silently for the call-and-response prayer. We were a few days into the first week of seventh grade when Jennifer raised her hand shyly. "Mrs. Long? I can teach you the words to the prayer after class if you'd like."

"Oh! Thank you." It was time for an explanation. "I appreciate your offer, but I ask students to lead the prayers because I'm Jewish. So, although I'm not reciting along with you, I'm saying my own prayers in my heart." They looked at me and at one another in quiet surprise, and several kids nodded in understanding.

Fall turned to winter, and the Christmas mass grew nearer. An e-mail suggested that teachers and students alike follow liturgy dress code. First, I Googled "liturgy": "A form according to which public religious worship, especially Christian worship, is conducted." Then, at home, I wrestled with the dresses in my closet, wondering what would be appropriate. I settled on a simple blue number with a modest collar, the same one I've worn to synagogue. If it worked for the Jewish holidays, it was probably mass-worthy.

I led my students into the gymnasium, and we filed onto the bleachers. Silently, respectfully, five hundred students settled into their seats. I'd never seen such a large group of kids sit so quietly. Then, the student liturgy leaders processed into the gym, bowing to the altar before taking their places near the podium. Dressed in white robes, the religious faculty followed, forming a solemn parade as they took their seats. Finally, Father Merrill entered the room, clothed in a deep red robe, his tall crimson hat adding formality to the ceremony.

On our holiest Jewish holidays, like Rosh Hashanah and Yom Kippur, my grandfather also used to wear a special white robe as he led the services, which signified a plea for forgiveness. So, both the ritual and the clothing felt remarkably familiar.

During the service, the youth choir sang "Silent Night," and I was reminded of my father who used to sing me this song in German as a lullaby. The students and faculty joined in, following the lyrics on the screens. I stood pensively, my own thoughts and prayers in my head while students read passages from the scripture and prayed for peace, health, holiness, and an open heart.

Father Merrill lifted his arms skyward and said, "Now it is time for each of you to come and receive a blessing. All are welcome," he said, "even if you are not Catholic. You may cross your arms over your chest, and we will offer an alternate blessing." I felt that his words were meant for me.

Every student and teacher began to make his or her way down toward the gym floor. Members of the religious faculty were posted around the space. They offered the Eucharist to the Catholics. To bless the non-Catholic students who had their arms folded, they made the sign of the cross and offered a prayer. Father Merrill was blessing students and staff directly below my section of the bleachers. Did he know I was Jewish? I wasn't sure.

I stood uncomfortably. The row in front of me had filed down to the gym floor, and now our row had begun to move into the aisle to receive a blessing, too. But I was frozen in place. One of my students discreetly gestured for me to step ahead of him, but I gave him the tiniest shake of my head until he moved past me.

I really did want to receive a blessing. To me, blessings are little presents—messages of comfort, peace and even belonging. Many a time, my grandpa the rabbi had held his hands together over my head and recited the Jewish priestly benediction, "Y'varechecha." The blessing ends with the Hebrew words, "Viyāsēm lekhā shalom." May you be granted peace.

As the students returned to the bleachers, I stared straight ahead, frustrated with myself for having skipped the opportunity and feeling awkward at my imagined conspicuousness. By the time the service ended, I was ready to get back to my classroom and hide—in front of my room full of kids.

But as I walked out the door of the gym, I noticed Father Merrill greeting students and wishing them a happy holiday. As I passed, I shook his hand and thanked him for the service. I nearly went on my way, but something about his warm, open expression made me pause. "Father, I'm Jewish. I didn't come down for a blessing, but I'd like to have your blessing now, if I can."

He placed his hands on my shoulders and said, "May you be blessed with *shalom*." I smiled, pleased and comforted that he had used the Hebrew word for peace. Then, with kindness and sincerity, he looked me in the eye and added, "You are very welcome here."

His words made their way into my heart, and I knew it was true. Wherever you are, faith is faith, and a welcoming gesture is always welcome.

—Ilana M. Long—

Chapter 2

Kindness and Gratitude

Everyday Miracles

*When it comes to life, the critical thing is whether you
take things for granted or take them with gratitude.*
~Gilbert K. Chesterton

"An everyday miracle," the radio commentator began, "is a wonderful or amazing event that occurs." That captured my attention. Although I was anxious to hear more, I had to snap off the radio as I was next in line at the fast-food pick-up.

Because I stopped there every morning on my way to work, I knew the elderly clerk, so it wasn't a surprise when she leaned through the window while handing me my Diet Coke and began talking.

"We're not having Thanksgiving this year," she confided. "We canceled for the first time ever. It's so sad." Her voice was flat and expressionless. "I can't afford it anymore."

I tried thinking of something comforting to say, but my mind was blank. Embarrassed, I mumbled a feeble goodbye and began my forty-five-minute commute to work.

Maybe it was the way the tree limbs stood naked against a dull sky. Maybe it was the cold November mist hitting the windshield. Or perhaps it was the carcass of a deer lying along the road. But I felt sad, too. And I couldn't get her beaten down look out of my mind. That's when I recalled the Garden Club's annual White Elephant Auction that we had held the week before.

"Please remember, ladies," the club president said before the auction started, "with so many in our community out of work, Thanksgiving three weeks away, and Christmas around the corner, the food pantry can sure use our generosity this year. They're struggling, too."

For over a decade, our Garden Club's November meeting has been a White Elephant Auction where members bring their various discards to be auctioned off. All the proceeds go to our local food pantry for holiday food baskets.

This year, however, things were different. The event was canceled due to the COVID pandemic.

So, it came as a real surprise when I received another e-mail shortly afterward: "Grab your stuff. The annual White Elephant Auction is back on!" Due to unseasonably warm weather, we were going to have the auction outdoors in the church parking lot.

Two days later, I arrived at the event with my chair and my "treasures." Just seeing each other was thrilling. The sun was out, and a light breeze was coming in from Lake Michigan. Everyone was laughing and talking at once, and it felt like old times. Even the church bells chimed just before we began, as if they too were participating.

But when I looked around, I counted only twenty-two people. "We won't make any money today," I quietly mumbled to my longtime friend, Sandy.

Always optimistic, she quickly reminded me, "Every little bit will help this year."

The auction began and so did the fun as the usual bidding and overbidding for various special items gave us all an extra dose of laughter and a pre-holiday boost. By the end of the event, our treasurer proudly reported that this impromptu White Elephant Auction had raised more than $800 for the food pantry.

Over the next couple weeks, I saw the elderly woman at the drive-through almost daily on my way to work. But we never again mentioned her Thanksgiving dinner being canceled. I felt uncomfortable talking about it.

Eventually, Thanksgiving Day came and went. The next day, I had to go into work for a few hours. Stopping once again at the same fast-food place, I placed my usual order, waited a few minutes for the cars ahead, and then pulled up to the elderly clerk's drive-through window.

Upon seeing me, she nearly jumped out the window. "You won't believe it. You just won't believe it!" She was squealing by now. "I had a Thanksgiving! It was a miracle. It was a miracle. The food pantry gave me a nineteen-pound turkey and all the fixings. I had my sister and our friends over, and we watched the Macy's parade and ate. It was wonderful." By now, she was crying. For a few moments, we both ignored the long line of cars behind me. "It was a miracle. It was just a miracle," she kept saying.

Choking back my tears, I turned onto the main road and headed for work. No music or phone calls. Just silence. In the quiet, I reflected upon the words I'd heard on the radio a few weeks earlier: "An everyday miracle is a wonderful or amazing event that occurs."

"That's it," I said to myself. That Thanksgiving dinner was an everyday miracle! Suddenly, I began to think about other "everyday miracles" being performed all around us, not just at Thanksgiving. Generally, they're done quietly, behind the scenes, and seldom recognized as miracles except to the receiver. They're ordinary things, for ordinary people, done by ordinary people. They're never important enough to make the evening news, but they're important enough to have an impact on someone's life. The neighbor who plowed the driveway and refused to take money for it. The mentor who came into someone's life at that special time. The teacher who made a difference. The friend who called and said the right thing just when it was needed. The Garden Club White Elephant Auction. Or a Thanksgiving dinner given to a worker at the fast-food drive-through when she needed it most.

Yes, indeed. God bless those "everyday miracles."

— Linda L. LaRocque —

14

A Circle of Love

Small acts of kindness can make a difference in other
people's lives more than we can imagine.
~Catherine Pulsifer

Teaching middle-school kids during the day and college freshmen in the evening had begun to wear on me. But finally, I could see the light at the end of the tunnel. "Only two more classes after tonight," I reminded myself as I pulled into the college parking lot.

Christmas Break was right around the corner.

I got a call as I entered the building. My mother informed me that my father had been taken from the nursing home to the hospital. She had little information. I told her that I would cancel my class and come join her and my siblings, but she insisted that I stay. "I'll call you when I have more information," she said.

I pulled myself together and headed in. I learned early in my teaching career how to act. The show must go on.

I told my students what was going on. They already knew about Dad's dementia and how that hideous disease had been affecting those around him.

"If I get a call," I announced, "I'm going to have to get out of here right away. We'll just stop wherever we are in the lesson, and I will send you the rest electronically. I am so sorry."

"Don't worry, Mr. Ramsey," one young lady replied. "Just concentrate on your dad."

A lump formed in my throat.

I directed the class to the online copy of the evening's story and turned on the audio version for them to follow. Almost on cue, as the story ended, my cell phone rang.

"It would be a good idea to come to the hospital now," Mom said. "They say that your father had a heart attack sometime during the day. It went unnoticed by the staff at the home. They just thought he wasn't feeling well. Come now. His heart is only functioning at twenty-five percent."

I looked up and saw every student sitting quietly, watching me respectfully. Another lump formed in my throat.

"I have to go," I announced. "I am so sorry." I packed up my things and headed for the door. "I'll keep in touch. Check your e-mail."

The students filed out quickly and quietly. Some shook my hand. Others patted my shoulder, offering me kindness in their comments.

"Good luck, Mr. Ramsey."

"I'll pray for your dad, Mr. Ramsey."

"Drive safely, Mr. Ramsey."

The rest of the week was a blur. I arranged for a substitute teacher for my middle-schoolers and for my next two college classes. I sat with my mother and six siblings in the waiting room of the hospital for days.

Finally, we all agreed that it was time to grant my father's longtime wish. It was time to disconnect him from the machines.

Dad was transferred to a hospice room and our humongous family crammed into it. Most of us sat on the floor surrounding his bed. We laughed. We cried. We reminisced. We thanked him for all he had done for us.

At one point, a nurse poked her head into the room to see what all the ruckus was about. She did not evict us, though. I'm sure that Dad enjoyed all the happy noise. It must have reminded him of so many other times when we filled his home with commotion and joy.

He died early the next morning.

One of my sisters and I proceeded with final arrangements, which we had never done before. We chose a casket, planned the viewing and the military funeral, and ordered the gravestone.

The next few days were an emotional roller coaster. The support of so many friends helped ease the pain immensely.

Even though I was physically and emotionally drained, I decided that I needed to be in class for the last day of the college semester. I had sent the final exam to my students the week before, in the midst all the funeral planning.

I informed my department chair that I would show up for the last day. I e-mailed my students and thanked them for all the positive messages they had sent during the week. "All you need to do for our last day," I typed, "is to bring in a paper copy of your final, and then you are free to start your winter break."

The next day, students streamed into the classroom with their final exams, all offering their condolences. I stood and shook each student's hand. I thanked them for a great semester, and for their support. I apologized for not being fully there for them.

More students arrived. I reminded everyone that there would be no real class. All they needed to do was drop off their exams.

But no one left. Slowly, the group formed a circle around me.

I felt a lump forming in my throat and tears leaking from the corners of my eyes.

My students reminisced about the semester. They laughed. They cried. They thanked me for all I had done for them during the semester.

They enveloped me in a magnificent Christmas circle of love.

— Tim Ramsey —

15

Seeds of Memory

Carry out a random act of kindness, with no
expectation of reward, safe in the knowledge
that one day someone might do the same for you.
~Princess Diana

"Be sure to get inexpensive, useful items. Remember, there isn't much of an activity budget, so things like tissues, lotion, maybe lip balm — those are the things that the residents will use and which we can afford." The administrator's words followed me as I headed out the door to shop for Christmas gifts for the residents at the skilled nursing facility for Alzheimer's patients where I was working as an activity director. She was a sensible, compassionate woman who possessed a good business mind, so she wanted the small budget to stretch as far as it could go, be well-appreciated... and useful.

My face burned red at the stern look I received when I returned with not only tissues, lotions, and lip balms but also packets of seeds.

"Seeds?" she said. "It isn't exactly the best time of year to plant anything, and you look like you know less than zilch about getting anything to grow. I know that fern on your desk is a rubber one that you substituted after you killed the one I gave you." Knowing that I looked redder than a Santa suit, I stammered that I thought the residents could plant the seeds in little cups and place them by the windows. The facility was certainly warm enough inside for growing things. And I was hoping that the residents, from all their years of experience tending to plants and gardens, might make up for my lack of expertise.

She reluctantly gave me the green light. "Well, I guess it will be okay. Even if they eat the seeds, they can't really be harmed. If all that results is a bunch of dirt in cups with dead seeds at the bottom, though, you have to clean it all up, Jack." So, I hoped for a Christmas miracle… and that the New Year wouldn't be heralded by cups of dirt filling the wastebaskets.

On Christmas morning, each resident received a card from me containing a packet of seeds. It seemed like my idea was a big flop. The seed packets, despite their cheerful photos of blooming flowers, were ignored. The residents paid more attention to the tissues and lip balm. They opened their small bottles of lotion with interest, and they were delighted by the gift bags from the Salvation Army containing slippers, handkerchiefs, socks, and chocolates.

My seed packets lay forgotten. Except by Frieda. She was new to the facility and in the early stages of Alzheimer's disease. She often felt restless and wanted something to occupy her time. She studied the seed packets intently. Seeing her concentration, I pulled up a chair beside her. "Frieda," I said, "I am relieved to see someone notice the seeds. I think they are a big bomb with everyone else."

Frieda looked up with a conspiratorial smile on her face and said, "Jack, these really need to be planted outside, but the weather is a bit cold. I'm not sure if they have a chance of making it this early." And then she said words that were a true Christmas gift to my ears: "But I sure as hell want to give it a try."

We both looked out at the Southern California "winter" weather, with its gray sky and temperature hovering around sixty degrees. Turning back to face each other, we both smiled. "Frieda, I like your attitude. Let's give it a try!" I said. Looking over all the packets of seeds that had been cast aside, I couldn't help but think that, by planting them outside on the facility grounds, there wouldn't be a mess to clean up if-and-when they died. I was sure that Mindy, the administrator, wouldn't deny Frieda her chance to "sure as hell give it a try."

So, the day after Christmas found Frieda and me with our hands in the dirt planting seeds, oblivious to the light mist falling upon us.

"These are Donner Party seeds," Frieda said as she wiped dirt from her hands.

"What do you mean?"

She didn't look up as she clapped her hands together to shake off dirt, but I could still see her eyes twinkle as she replied, "They are an adventure founded in a forlorn hope and most likely already doomed." Her husky laughter reminded me again why I loved my work with these residents so much: I received daily lessons in grace and dignity from the best of teachers.

That Christmas, more was planted than just seeds of forlorn hope. That Christmas, the memory of Frieda, her hands covered in dirt, was planted in my heart. It was a great comfort to me when, unexpectedly, Frieda passed away in February, not from Alzheimer's but a swift heart attack. By then, the seeds had fulfilled Frieda's prediction: They had either not sprouted at all, or they had started to grow and then died in the unusually rainy weather that winter. Frieda had managed to keep a few sickly marigolds going, but they had succumbed the day after she passed.

I showed Frieda's daughter the soggy brown marigolds when she came to pick up her mother's belongings. I shared with her Frieda's prediction about the sad destiny of the seeds but mentioned that I was so glad that we had had the time together to do something she loved.

At that, her daughter broke into a wide grin before she disclosed, "Oh, Jack… Mom hated gardening. She never was good at it. She told me that she felt so bad for you on Christmas morning that she pretended to be into gardening just to make you feel better." The husky laughter that followed made me feel that Frieda was close. Her daughter sounded just like her. "That's how Mom was," she concluded. "Mom was always a sucker for a lost cause."

These seeds of memory have seen me through some very rough times. The fact that someone facing great challenges in her own life could reach out to comfort me remains one of the greatest lessons in dignity and grace I have ever received. It goes without saying that I learned it at the hands of one of the greatest of teachers. Never have I been so honored… and so humbled… to be a lost cause. To this day, I have a handmade ornament on my tree made of an empty seed packet and a paper clip. I explain its meaning if anyone asks about it. As I hang it each year, I say out loud: "This one's for you, Frieda. We sure as hell gave it a try."

—Jack Byron—

16

The Joy of People

*The greatness of a community is most accurately
measured by the compassionate actions of its members.*
~Coretta Scott King

I t was two days before Christmas, and I was on holiday break
from my freshman year in high school. Over the summer, my
parents had remodeled the basement to be my bedroom. I even
had my own Christmas tree in front of the windows, a few feet
behind my bed.

I had gone to bed and was sleeping soundly. I woke up to a wall
of flame right behind me. I began screaming for my mother, who came
down the stairs to see what was wrong. We ran up the stairs to wake
my father. Mom called the fire department while my father assessed
the situation. He told me to run upstairs to get my aunt who lived
on the second floor and told my mother to grab my seven-year-old
sister and get out of the house. By this time, the smoke was so thick
that we could not see into the next room, but we all managed to get
out of the house.

I remember standing across the street watching the firefighters
and hearing the windows break. One fireman came out of the house
carrying our dog. He had inhaled a lot of smoke but recovered just
fine. Unfortunately, our cat did not survive.

Our neighbors across the street, with whom we had recently had
a minor dispute, forgot our differences and welcomed us into their
home for the night. Some of the other neighbors brought us clean

clothes. As my sister and I were getting ready to go to sleep later that night, I realized we did not have anything — not even a toothbrush.

As we were now homeless, it was agreed that we would stay temporarily with my aunt, uncle and two cousins. It would be crowded, but their generosity in our time of need demonstrated the true meaning of love and family.

On Christmas Day, we attended the last service of the day at our church. At one point, the priest asked for prayers and aid for our family. I was so embarrassed.

At the end of mass, the priest asked to meet with our family. He told us that one of the parishioners had a vacant apartment that we could move into until our home was rebuilt. He then handed my father an envelope containing over one thousand dollars that had been donated. Over the following days, weeks and months, the entire community donated clothes, furniture, toiletries, and other items that got us through that time.

I don't remember our Christmas celebration that year. I don't remember what we ate for Christmas dinner or what presents replaced the ones consumed by the fire. I don't remember shopping for new things or all the trouble we endured. What I do remember, what I will never forget, are my father's words at the back of the church on that Christmas Day. With tears in his voice, he kept repeating: "The joy of people, the joy of people."

— Lisa Long —

Faith in Humanity

*Christmas is the season for kindling the fire of
hospitality in the hall, the genial flame
of charity in the heart.*
~Washington Irving

O
n a Saturday afternoon three weeks before Christmas I got a call from my mom. "I made two hundred dollars selling my towels!"

"That's so awesome," I said, delighted that people bought the decorative kitchen towels she'd worked so hard to make.

For months, Mom had sat at a sewing table in the living room of her small, subsidized apartment, cutting, stitching, gathering, and appliqueing decorative towels to sell at the annual holiday craft fair in the lobby of her apartment building.

"They bought every single one," she said. "Now I have money to buy Christmas presents and some new puzzles for the girls on the fifth floor, so we don't have to put together the old ones again."

The heavy snow that had been forecasted for the weekend had already begun to fall that evening when Mom decided to pick up a ham at the grocery store. After brushing the snow off her car in the apartment parking lot and again in the grocery-store lot, Mom arrived safely back home and filled a simmering pot with the ham, potatoes, and rutabaga.

At 9:30 that night, I received a second call from her. She was sobbing.

Kindness and Gratitude | 55

"I lost my wallet and all the money I earned at the craft fair. My Christmas is ruined."

"It's okay, Mom," I said, completely unaware that she had gone out in the snow.

At eighty-seven years old, Mom often lost things, such as her reading glasses and cell phone. Sometimes, she even lost her teeth. So, at first, I wasn't overly concerned about it.

"I'll drive up in the morning," I said. "I'm sure we'll find it."

"No. It's gone. It was in my jacket pocket when I went to the store. But when I checked my jacket tonight it wasn't there."

She started to cry. "I searched the car and retraced my steps to the front door. And I drove back to the store to see if I left it. But it wasn't there either. I tried to remember where I parked, and I walked through the parking lot looking for it because it must have fallen out of my pocket. But it wasn't anywhere."

My heart broke at the thought of her out in the snowy, windy night.

"It'll be okay, Mom," I assured her. "We'll cancel the credit card, and we can replace all the rest of the things in your wallet." However, the thought of getting her a new license, along with bank, medical, and insurance cards, was daunting, even for me.

It took me several hours to drive to Mom's house the following morning, but I was overdue for a visit. Before I got there, she had already gone back to the store. With tears in her eyes, she shared her story about the money she'd earned from the sale of her towels with the store manager and asked if he could check any other places for her wallet — hoping against hope that someone might have found it and turned it in.

That, of course, did not happen, but what did happen was something that restored Mom's faith in humanity.

The store manager, who didn't even know Mom, kindly took her into his office where he searched through videotapes from the previous night. The tapes only showed Mom making her purchase and leaving the store. Wiping tears from her face, Mom thanked him for trying to help. But as she got up to leave the store, he reached for her elbow.

"Hold on a minute," he said.

Taking his wallet out of his pocket, he pulled out two one-hundred-dollar bills and pressed them into Mom's hand. "I would like you to have a Merry Christmas."

Mom shook her head, barely able to speak as she tried to push the money back. "No… I can't."

With a warm smile, the store manager squeezed Mom's hands around the bills. "It would make my Christmas if you would take this," he said.

Mom left the store in tears, and more tears fell when I met her back at her apartment. We called the police station to see if the wallet had been turned in, but no luck. I spent the night with Mom, and the police department called the following day. They had her wallet. Most of her money and all her cards were still in it.

Mom immediately drove back to the grocery store. With tears of joy this time, she gave back the store manager's money, thanking him wholeheartedly for a Christmas gift that was so much more valuable than money.

Since the manager already considered the money no longer his, he said he would donate it to a local charity that delivered baskets of food and Christmas gifts to families in need. Mom's holiday experience went from heartbreaking to heartwarming. And remarkably, thanks to a stranger's big heart and special gift, another family would have a similar holiday experience.

— Linda L. Koch —

18

The Cookie Fairy

Cookies are happy because that is their job.
Making those you know and don't know happy.
They tell people you care.
~Brent M. Jones

My mom and dad enjoyed their lovely apartment in a graduated-care retirement community. Declining with vascular dementia, Dad had recently moved into the memory-care unit, and Mom was dreading the upcoming Christmas season, knowing how hard it would be. But instead of focusing on herself and her losses, she came up with a way to bless others. "I want to give Christmas cookies to my neighbors," Mom told me.

"How many neighbors are you talking about?" I asked, thinking she meant those who lived in the other apartments on her floor.

"A lot. Maybe thirty or thirty-five, but some are couples," she assured me. I nodded. I had a funny feeling about where this was headed.

"Could we bake them at your house? Your kitchen is bigger than mine." She paused. "And I don't want people to smell the cookies baking. I can bring my mixer and ingredients."

Mom and I have been baking Christmas cookies for as long as I can remember. Christmas Cookie Baking Day is an annual holiday at our house, celebrated on what others know as Black Friday. With a refrigerator loaded with Thanksgiving leftovers and no need to cook, we let the hungry fend for themselves. We recruit help from all corners and jump headlong into this task, the official first step in our annual Christmas preparations.

Batches of snickerdoodles, peanut blossoms, gingerbread hearts, raspberry thumbprints, mint-surprise cookies, sugar cookies, and orange cookie bars reappear annually, just like the familiar ornaments we love and the Christmas music playing in the background. Whether the house is filled with children and grandchildren, or it's just the two of us with my husband washing dishes behind us as we go, teamwork gets the job done. If the grandchildren are around, they help, unwrapping chocolate kisses and possibly snitching one or five when they think no one is looking. Their chubby fingers shape cookie dough into balls for snickerdoodles, putting their playdough-honed skills to good use. They then plop them into the cinnamon sugar and shake enthusiastically. By evening, the house smells wonderful, and the freezer is stuffed with containers of cookies, ready to serve and share throughout the holiday season.

A few days before that Christmas Eve, I unloaded box after box of cookies from my freezer, loaded them into my car, and headed to Mom's. She had festive containers ready to be filled. She had also made and cut out little cards that said, "Merry Christmas from the Cookie Fairy."

"That's it? You don't want anyone to know where the cookies came from?" I asked. She nodded, clarifying her earlier comment about not wanting her neighbors to smell cookies baking.

Late that night, like Santa making his deliveries, she tiptoed up and down the halls. She placed a package of cookies by each door, including a decoy by her own. Then she went to bed, happy and proud that she had accomplished her goal, and confident that none of the early-to-bed crowd had seen her.

In the weeks that followed, there was plenty of chatter and speculation about the identity of the mysterious Christmas Cookie Fairy. Mom was publicly accused but steadfastly maintained her innocence. She thoroughly enjoyed being the anonymous spreader of a bit of holiday cheer. She intends to take her secret to her grave.

Since that initial cookie delivery, Mom has continued baking and blessing her neighbors, pulling us into her joyful endeavor. When her grown grandchildren happen to be here for Thanksgiving, they pitch in too, rejoining the baking ritual that endures from their childhoods. Occasionally, we make cookies in February, too. "Happy Valentine's Day from the Cookie Fairy," reads the note that accompanies each decorated, edible heart.

Several years ago, the activities director of the retirement community coordinated an effort to collect recipes from residents. She compiled a cookbook of personal and family favorites. The Cookie Fairy generously slipped an envelope under her office door. Inside were two of her favorite cookie recipes. When the cookbook was published several months later, Mom's recipes were not included. Apparently, anonymity is not universally appreciated.

Despite the snub, she determinedly and anonymously presses on. A few days after her Christmas 2020 delivery, she noticed a heartwarming sign posted near the mailboxes.

"To the Cookie Fairy. You didn't just wish us a Merry Christmas and give us cookies. You lifted our spirits and brought us joy during a very dark time. Thank you."

That heartfelt note, anonymously written and posted, and the first public thank-you the Cookie Fairy had ever received, brought joy to her heart.

I think, when I grow up, I want to follow in her footsteps.

— Capi Cohen —

19

Random Acts of Christmas

*I love Christmas, not just because of the presents
but because of all the decorations and lights
and the warmth of the season.*
~Ashley Tisdale

Christmas has always been my favorite holiday. I love everything about it — the music, the movies, the festivities, the food. All things merry and bright make me happy. When I met my husband Paul and discovered that he was a fellow Christmas fanatic, I was in holiday heaven.

Over the years, Paul and I have created many holiday traditions for ourselves: Corgi-themed Christmas parades, tea with Santa, frequent shopping trips to the mall to see the beautiful Christmas decorations, special holiday dinners at our favorite restaurants. These traditions always make Christmas a fun time of the year for us.

However, 2020 was a year unlike any other. By December, we had already been in quarantine for nine months and we knew that the holiday season would be much different from years past. We would have to forget about most of our Christmas traditions. But the most difficult tradition to set aside was spending quality time with family. For us, these gatherings were one of the merriest parts of the holidays. Unfortunately, because of their age, many of our family members were considered high-risk, so we had to make the difficult decision to isolate from all family for the holidays. Needless to say, we were much in need of some alternative holiday cheer.

One weekend, I suggested that we drive around one of our favorite neighborhoods to see the Christmas lights. This suggestion lit up Paul; he grinned with excitement as we enthusiastically planned our route for the night. We made ourselves a quintessential seasonal beverage — hot chocolate with a dash of cinnamon — and jumped into the car.

Unfortunately, as we drove past rows of dim houses, it became apparent that 2020 was indeed a dark year, figuratively and literally. As we drove past dark street after dark street, our disappointment grew. It appeared that this Christmas was not going to be very bright either.

We were almost ready to call it a night when we saw them. Four houses were lit up like the most dazzling festival of lights we'd ever seen. Each home was decked out like an illuminated winter wonderland. We marveled at all the whimsical Christmas decorations: adorable snowmen, noble nutcrackers, jolly Santa and his sleigh, trusty reindeer, majestic trees, gorgeous snowflakes, and beautifully wrapped presents. We saw every gloriously illuminated display of merriment one would expect to see during the most wonderful time of the year. We were completely blown away by this amazing sight.

I had never seen anything like it before. By my estimation, it must have taken at least eighty to a hundred hours to construct and put up all those decorations and lights on each of those houses. It was so awe-inspiring that we had to pull over to take it all in, and we weren't at all surprised to see that we weren't the only ones who were blown away. A couple on a walk stopped to take several selfies in front of the houses. I must have snapped over a dozen pictures myself.

Those houses literally brightened our day and made us remember the joy for which the season is known. As Paul and I drove away, we couldn't stop gushing about how impressive they were. We wished we could tell the homeowners how much we enjoyed their light display — and that's when I got a bright idea. (Pun intended. Sorry, I couldn't resist.)

We had a lot of Christmas cards left over, and I thought it would be cool to write a Christmas card for the inhabitants of those houses to let them know how much joy their light displays had brought us. Judging by Paul's grin, I could tell he liked this idea, too.

That night, I pulled out my box of unused holiday cards and sat down at my desk. At first, I wasn't sure what to say. But eventually an intriguing thought began to crystallize in my mind. Throughout this unprecedented year, I had been looking for any signs of normalcy that I could find to help me get through the uncertainty of it all. That's when I realized that those dazzling displays showed us that the miracle of light could still shine through the darkness. Seeing those beautiful lights gave us a real sense of hope that the magical spirit of the holidays was still all around us, even during a pandemic.

That's when I knew exactly what I needed to write. I wholeheartedly thanked those neighbors for giving us the gift of hope and normalcy. I told them that, against the backdrop of darkness, their winter wonderlands shined even brighter. I had never written Christmas cards to total strangers before, but it felt surprisingly natural to write to these people as if I were having conversations with friends. And in that moment, I felt truly connected to people I had never met. I felt comforted, as if my circle of Christmas enthusiasts was virtually unlimited.

A couple of days later, Paul and I returned to the illuminated winter wonderland and left a Christmas card at the front door of each of the four houses. As we drove away, I joked that this was our first "random act of Christmas."

A few days later, that first random act inspired us to commit a second one. Since we couldn't spend time with family for the holidays, I had assumed there would be no gift exchanges as well. But suddenly I had an out-of-the box idea — a quarantine-style Secret Santa idea to be exact.

Recently, my sister and nephew had begun cooking together, attempting to recreate my late mother's delicious pho (traditional Vietnamese noodle soup). So, Paul and I ordered two customized aprons for them to further encourage their culinary adventures. I placed those aprons inside a Christmas gift bag, and we secretly left it in front of their house, driving away like sneaky, little elves. Once we were out of sight, I texted my sister to tell her that Santa had left them a package. When she opened her door, she was delightfully surprised. Later, she told me that they absolutely loved their aprons, and they would proudly wear them on their next pho-making project. Making them happy made us happy.

When I think about all the wonderful things that embody the spirit of Christmas, one of the things that comes to mind is being open to new possibilities. Looking back at 2020, it was definitely filled with new possibilities, especially in the form of the random acts of Christmas that we decided to commit. They taught us that the Christmas spirit still lived on, no matter what, and with a little creativity, we could still make the holidays merry and bright.

— Kristen Mai Pham —

20

Free-Ranging Turkey

But ask the animals, and they will teach you,
or the birds in the sky, and they will tell you.
~Job 12:7–10

There was a chill in the air that morning a week before Thanksgiving. Upon waking, I staggered out of bed and poured myself a cup of coffee. Still sleepy, I plunked down in my recliner to warm up in front of my electric fireplace.

Sipping my coffee, I thought of all the preparations I needed to make for our traditional holiday at my sister's house, but I couldn't seem to muster up any holiday spirit. The dancing flames took me back to the carefree days of my childhood when cozy holidays were spent by my grandparents' red brick hearthside, and neighbors stopped to greet one another.

Maybe it was the lack of sunlight that comes with the long winter days or the heaviness of the divisiveness our nation had seen in recent times. Whatever the reason, I needed to shake this mood, so I pushed myself to get started on my holiday cooking in hopes that would spark some cheer.

I headed out into the cold November air and drove toward the village of Williamsville, New York, for baking supplies. As I approached the corner of Paradise and Klein, I saw ahead of me a procession of taillights lined up bumper-to-bumper. Slowly, cars began creeping closer to the traffic light. Suddenly, just ahead, tires screeched, and the car ahead of me came to a halt. What could be the hold-up?

Then I saw it whirling across the intersection like a Tasmanian devil. I gasped at the sight of the culprit. Pausing underneath the stoplight, he stood there like a traffic cop on duty. It was a wild turkey.

The traffic remained gridlocked. The turkey surveyed the situation, spotted my red Malibu, and slowly moved toward me. Stopping and looking every few steps, he darted right to my driver's side door.

With a tilt of his head, he gazed up at me through the car window as if to beckon me. Our eyes met.

Having enjoyed birds as pets, I found him to be a handsome creature with sleek bronze feathers mixed with iridescent tones of green. His brightly colored head indicated it was a male turkey. We seemed to make a connection, and I almost wanted to open the car door and take him home. Strangely, there was something endearing about this bird.

The light turned green, and the traffic finally proceeded. Eager to move with the ongoing flow, I rolled down the window and waved my hand in a shooing motion. Still, he did not move. Finally, I honked my horn, and he nonchalantly waddled away from my car. Relieved that he had moved on, I quickly grabbed my cell phone and shot a piece of photographic evidence as I was sure nobody would believe me about my strange encounter with a turkey. I left the scene intrigued by such a presumptuous creature but also feared for his safety.

Later that evening, after baking two pumpkin pies, I excitedly shared a Facebook post about my experience with the turkey. Shortly after posting, someone commented that they were familiar with the turkey in the picture. Upon some research, I found several articles about this bird pecking at tires and "playing chicken" with moving vehicles. It seems Calvin was well known by the community. Throughout the week of Thanksgiving, posts were made from people who went to see him. People fed him, children adored him, and he was a friend to many, young and old.

The locals gave him many names. Some call him Gus, others Tom, but I call him Calvin after the clothing designer Calvin Klein because of his fine, luxurious feathers and his Klein street location.

I eagerly awaited a sighting of Calvin whenever I drove by the corner of Paradise and Klein. Someone even caught him on video running after a moving postal truck like a dog chasing the mailman! Another person posted a picture of him standing in the rain at his intersection like a watchman on duty, seemingly unaffected by the storm. I couldn't stop laughing at his vigilance. Sharing this connection over Facebook with the community gave me a much-needed sense of unity that had been so desperately missing in the world today.

With all the excitement of my new turkey friend, I no longer felt down. Who would have thought a wild, traffic-chasing turkey would chase away my blues?

Then one day, Calvin was nowhere in sight. I hadn't seen him near Paradise and Klein when I drove by. My heart sank. Could he have been hit by a car? I later read in the newspaper that he had become such a public-safety concern that somebody had taken him to a wildlife refuge. Officials had relocated him once before, and he managed to find his way back and reclaim his territory, but this time he did not return. Calvin's community of Facebook followers mourned the loss. I would miss him, too.

As Thanksgiving approached again, the holidays were wrought with restrictions, political division, and the uncertainty of the pandemic. But no matter how tumultuous the times, I count my blessings and found comfort in the unity of belonging to a community of people who were touched by a free-ranging turkey.

—Lori Carpenter Jagow—

The Miracle Coat

*To give and then not feel that one has given
is the very best of all ways of giving.*
~Max Beerbohm

A few years ago, I was having dinner with some good friends from work to celebrate the upcoming Christmas holiday. As we were finishing up the evening, one of my friends told us a very sad story about something that had happened the day before. Her son's friend was in his mid-twenties and self-employed. He lived on the second floor of a house nearby. Someone who lived on the first floor had been smoking and fell asleep. The house burned down. All the occupants escaped, but the house was completely destroyed with everything in it.

All this young man had were the clothes on his back and his pickup truck. He had no family in the area and nowhere to go. My friend was putting him up for a few days until he could decide what to do next.

Those of us sitting at the dinner table were horrified. Everyone started opening their wallets to contribute money. My friend put up her hand and said, "He will not accept money. We tried to convince him, but he thinks it is charity and won't take it. All he wants is a warm coat and some used clothing if anyone has some."

We were all more than happy to fulfill this request and were told that he wore a size 2XL. None of us knew men who wore that size, so it was going to be a bit of a challenge to take care of this quickly.

It was a typically cold New York Christmas, and I couldn't imagine him without a coat. I shed some tears on the drive home, a combination of grateful tears for the many blessings I had in my life and sad tears for this poor, young man and his troubles.

I went to bed and woke up in the middle of the night with a very clear thought in my mind. I was to visit a nearby thrift store and find this young man a coat. I had trouble getting back to sleep. For some reason, I felt very compelled to make this happen. I was not used to things like this happening to me, and I could not figure out why I was so obsessed. After all, this was a very sad story, but I did not know the young man. Why should I feel obligated to do anything else if he wouldn't accept money? However, I could not put it out of my mind.

Two days before Christmas, I had many things to do for the holiday. I had fifteen people coming to dinner on Christmas Eve, and I had no time to run around on a wild goose chase looking for a coat in a size that was difficult to find.

But I got dressed and went to the thrift shop the next morning. I was there when it opened at nine. I went through every coat and jacket but found nothing even close to what I needed.

As I headed toward the exit, I considered trying to find something in a department store, but it would be expensive, and I had no time to shop! Suddenly, a lady came out of the back room, so I stopped to ask if she had anything in the back in that size. I explained the story and how important it was to find a coat for this young man.

She went in the back and returned a couple of minutes later saying there was nothing else. I was crestfallen. However, a moment later, another woman came out of the back with what looked like a brand-new down parka in her arms. She walked toward me and asked if I was the woman looking for the jacket in 2XL. When I said yes, she said, "This was dropped in our overnight bin. Someone left it here between the time we closed last night and opened this morning. I just took it out. It was the only thing in the bin. Is this what you're looking for?"

It was perfect! I was stunned and could barely speak. Through my tears, I asked how much it was, and she said, "Please, just take it!" I gave her twenty dollars and left feeling like I had been part of something bigger than just finding a coat. This was divine intervention!

A Christmas miracle! There was certainly no other explanation for why I, a perfect stranger who had never even met this young man, was somehow charged with finding him a coat. Or why there just happened to be only one item, the perfect coat, left in the overnight bin of this thrift store.

My friend delivered the coat to the young man who was very grateful. He eventually got back on his feet with the help of other good friends.

I've told this story to many people who agree that we can be called to do a seemingly small thing that has a great positive impact on others. The story is so moving, and it reminds us why we are here, what's important, and why we should always live in gratitude!

—Jeanne Cassetta—

22

The Challenge

Kindness is igniting a light in someone else for no
reason other than to watch them enjoy the glow.
~Author Unknown

We were just grabbing a shopping cart when my youngest grandson turned to me and asked, "Grandma, can I have my envelope? I'll keep it in my pocket so that I am ready when the time is right." Reaching into my purse, I pulled out his envelope; it contained a twenty-dollar bill along with a small card that read, "Please accept this Random Act of Kindness." There were three other identical envelopes in my purse, one for each grandchild. Those yearly envelopes had begun appearing in my purse just a couple of years prior and had morphed from another annual ritual.

When they were little, my grandkids and I began a tradition. We would go Christmas shopping to purchase gifts for their parents. It had always been a fun excursion that included lunch or a treat afterward. The intent was to help them understand how important it is to think of someone else. I had selfish reasons, too. I got to spend quality time with my grandkids. On the agreed-upon day, we would head out with our shopping ideas and our budget, as well as a lot of Christmas spirit.

As my grandkids matured, it seemed appropriate to expand our annual excursion into an even more meaningful opportunity to practice sharing. Our shopping adventure morphed to include not just shopping for their beloved parents but also shopping for a stranger. The one rule of our added task was simple: Identify someone who looked like they could use a little extra cash or seemed to need a lift. The rest of the decisions were theirs to make. Would they hand the envelope with cash directly to their selected recipient or place it anonymously in the periphery of the intended's vision? I promised I would come armed with the cash and would not question their final decision. Thus began our Random Acts of Christmas Kindness.

The first time we added this to our annual holiday shopping fest, we had to help each other understand the ins and outs of what we were doing. Some needed encouragement to abandon shyness in favor of safely reaching out to a stranger. Some needed guidance to discern the appropriate receiver. Others were honest enough to question the true nature of our mission.

Over the past few years, the grandkids have given cash to store employees who looked worn out by the Christmas mania, people in line who seemed to be calculating the cost of the items in their carts, bell ringers who stood for hours in the cold to help others, busboys/girls doing a thankless task, and individuals who simply looked haggard and down on their luck. They have placed their Random Acts of Christmas Kindness envelopes in shopping carts, on seats near individuals, in people's hands, or left them for later discovery. When the envelope is not given directly to an individual, we linger near enough to enjoy the surprise that typically lights up the recipient's face. We have seen people go speechless, people who merely look stunned, people who deem themselves not worthy, and people who stumble over themselves to express their gratitude.

Regardless of a recipient's reaction, they have made an impact on all of us and been the catalyst for some great discussions about who they chose as the giftee and why. We speculate about how the receiver may have felt about the surprise gift and what they might do with it. Our sharing has led to discussions on whether it is our place to critique a person's lot in life or how they spend their money. Our outings have brought up discussions of need versus want. Our deeds have elicited reflection on what brings joy and whose responsibility it is to create it.

The COVID quarantine during the Christmas season of 2020

did not allow us to get together to shop or physically carry out our Random Acts of Christmas Kindness, but it did not deter us from continuing our tradition. The week after Thanksgiving, I contacted my grandchildren and proposed we continue our ritual by sending donations somewhere. They could all agree on one, or they could each determine a worthy recipient. All of them agreed they wanted it to be related to our COVID crisis but had different ideas of where it should be utilized. In the end, donations were sent to food banks, St. Jude's Hospital, and for COVID research. A pandemic was not about to stop our Random Act of Christmas Kindness tradition.

I am fully aware of the yin and yang that our sharing tradition has caused amongst my grandchildren: some wonderful feelings of doing good and some discomfort at being asked to look past our own emotional safety net. It has caused me to reflect on my own behaviors in terms of the times I am guilty of suppressing an urge to do good in favor of complacency or uncertainty. My one hope is that all of us, grandkids and myself alike, will learn that giving is its own reward, and no measurement can ever exist to weigh its value. We may never know what a difference one simple act of kindness made in the life of a stranger. But we've learned that sometimes we need to step outside our comfort zones and accept the challenge of sharing our blessings with others.

— Rose Robertson —

23

You Never Know

No one has ever become poor by giving.
~Anne Frank

When I was a child, the Salvation Army Angel Tree fascinated me, with the paper angels hung on the tree with age, gender and suggested gifts printed carefully on them. I wondered who the children were, what their families were going through, and whether they woke up on Christmas morning excited or sad. My family didn't celebrate Christmas, but I still felt empathy for those children.

Years later, as a single mother in my mid-twenties, I was working my way through nursing school with a part-time job at a high-end kids' clothing store at the local mall. As Christmas approached, the Salvation Army volunteers set up their tree and table on the concourse just outside our shop. The contrast between the children served at our store and the children served by the volunteers was poignant. I decided to pick out an angel.

His name was Billy, and he was nine years old, an only child, and had a short wish list — a pair of shoes, jeans, a warm jacket, and some games.

As this one child's simple needs taxed my nearly nonexistent budget, I enlisted the help of my roommate and co-workers, many of whom gave generously. My manager even added a store discount for our prize purchase — a thickly lined, leather-trimmed, baseball-style denim jacket — and we were able to check off all of Billy's requests, with a few extra gifts thrown in.

It was a fun time at the store as everyone working on the project got into hunting for just the right item at the best price, making our money go as far as possible and brightening our moods during the hectic holiday time.

Strangely, amid the excitement, there were naysayers, people who thought it was a waste of time and money to give to this little boy. "Surely," they said, "you realize his mother is probably a drug addict and will sell her son's presents on the street as soon as the wrapping is off, just for her next fix. That's the real reason people sign up their kids for a charity program."

These acquaintances had no more to go on than I did, just whatever clues were offered in Billy's name: age, size, and practical requests. And yet they had strong opinions and were sure they knew all about Billy and his family.

Thrusting these fears to the side, my roommate and I walked out into the mall and placed our little bundle of goods on the table. The volunteer placed the items in a bag marked with the child's ID number and name, thanked us for our donation, and turned back to her organizing.

We stood at the table, a little lost, wondering, *What now?* It seemed anticlimactic.

I took home Billy's paper angel and placed it on our tree, explaining to my five-year-old daughter how we had helped a little boy have a better Christmas. The naysayers had made me wonder, so I hoped that what I was saying was true.

A week or so passed, and the cheerful holiday rush turned into the chaos of post-Christmas returns. I was struggling with a sore throat and tired feet while working the cash wrap at the store. I survived by keeping my head down and working quickly, efficiently, and (hopefully) politely to keep the line moving.

Suddenly, I saw a familiar denim baseball jacket placed on the counter and looked up into the warm smile of a mother urging her son, "Go on, Billy. Tell the lady what you want."

Billy shyly whispered, "I need to change this jacket." The woman, his mother, went on to explain that they had received the jacket and some jeans as a present, but they were a little too small. They did not have the receipt. Could the clothes be exchanged?

The floor associates fell over themselves to help the little family find the right sizes and colors (while exclaiming softly to each other, "It's Billy! It's Billy!"). Soon Billy and his mom were back at my register. My manager worked more retail magic, and suddenly Billy had a small cash refund as well.

He turned to give the few dollars to his mother, who put up her hand to stop him, saying, "No, it was your present. You keep the money and buy something else for yourself."

I was stunned.

Here was proof in the face of this clean, polite, well-loved child — proof that our efforts had been worth it. Here was our paper angel come to life.

After they left the store, one of my co-workers came forward to say that she knew Billy and his mom. His mom had recently lost her husband, a police officer who died in the line of duty, and the family struggled financially without him. Their church was doing what it could to help the family but could not cover all their needs, so the congregation had given Billy's name to the Salvation Army Angel Tree program.

It was so moving to know these details, the untold story behind the flat information we had read on paper. We were all amazed at the rare chance meeting that brought the true meaning of giving to life.

I often hear people say, "You never know…" and it is true.

You never know why someone needs your help or how helping them might change you. You never know when something important is about to happen, when you are about to witness a little miracle.

You never know.

— Carrie Karnes-Fannin —

24

The Heart of Christmas

Seeing the world through the eyes of a child is
the purest joy that anyone can experience.
~Constance Zimmer

It was the Christmas season and Jack was five years old. A bright, precocious child, Jack struggled with social and emotional difficulties that would later be diagnosed as Asperger's syndrome, anxiety, and ADHD. Because of this, my husband and I were attempting to instruct Jack in appropriate behavior and to instill in him a deeper sense of empathy for others.

That Christmas, our church had assembled a live nativity scene, complete with real animals, a young couple with their newborn baby, and a backdrop resembling a stable. They had also recreated the town of Bethlehem as it might have looked on the night of Jesus's birth. Hearing that the church assembly hall had been transformed into Bethlehem, Jack begged me to take him to the evening's festivities. I was hesitant, as Jack tended to become overwhelmed by the sensory input generated by large crowds. But he was determined to attend, so I agreed to take him. We arrived early that evening, hoping to be in and out before it got too crowded.

As we entered the church assembly room, Jack caught his breath in awe. The large room was filled with wooden stalls and bustling characters dressed appropriately for Bethlehem long ago. It seemed we had stepped back in time as we strolled through the busy scene. Each small area held an interactive activity true to the time. Villagers in robes and sandals made candles, dyed cloth, and hand-ground grain for flour. Roman soldiers in their helmets, tunics, and scarlet cloaks patrolled the area. Sounds of joyous music filled the room as performers in colorful attire danced and sang to the rhythm of tambourines. Jack smiled as he was offered the opportunity to add his name to the census with a quill and ink, spin a dreidel, and help to weave a basket.

Perhaps the interaction was a little too real as Jack bounded ahead toward the inn where there was no room for Mary and Joseph to stay. A hurried innkeeper flew toward us, admonishing us, "Move along! There is no room in the inn. Move along!" She flapped her hands toward us in dismissal, and Jack doubled back toward me, tears forming in his eyes. He didn't understand she was merely acting out a part in a scene. To him, everything here seemed acutely real. I comforted him and led him back to another activity. As we walked, we passed a man dressed in tattered robes. "Can you spare some bread for a beggar?" he asked us, his hands outstretched. Jack answered solemnly, "I'm sorry, I don't have any bread, and I don't have any money either."

We engaged in a few more activities and then made our way to a corner where bakers were making traditional Jewish flatbread. The warm smell of fresh bread wafted toward us from a platter of flatbread recently baked over the fire outside the building. After showing us how to mix and roll out the dough, the baker took two pieces of baked flatbread from the platter and handed one to each of us. I smiled, waiting for Jack to taste the sample. But Jack had another idea.

"Oh, good!" he exclaimed. "Now I have some bread to give that man who was hungry." My heart swelled with joy as Jack retraced his steps to the beggar and offered his piece of bread. The man smiled and graciously accepted it.

Soon afterward, we ended our tour of Bethlehem with the live nativity scene. As Jack stood staring solemnly at the tiny infant sleeping peacefully in Mary's arms, I felt overwhelmed by God's gift of grace to us on that first Christmas, a gift available to us even now. Jack may not have tasted the flatbread that night, but he did engage tangibly in the heart of Christmas — self-sacrificial love.

— Jenni Clark Dickens —

Santa's Helpers

25

Mission: Undercover Santa

*Of course, there is a Santa Claus. It's just that no single
somebody could do all he has to do. So the Lord
has spread the task among us all.*
~Truman Capote

Date and time: Christmas Day, one in the morning. Our mission: Invade the back yard of our target home, deposit the payload, and escape without being discovered. My partner and I waited down the street in our warm pickup with the headlights off. Despite our best planning, a single lamp still burned in the house.

I envisioned a thousand different ways this caper might go wrong. At least, that's how it seemed. "What if a neighbor sees us sneaking over there?" I asked my partner (and husband), Dave, who had an answer for everything.

"Look around," he said. "No one is out. People have already gone to bed."

I glanced at the scattered, shadowy clouds covering the full moon and pointed skyward. "What if those part? We'll be more visible, and someone might call the cops."

Dave leaned toward the window, glanced up, and shook his head. "So what if they do? I just told you no one is out tonight. Will you relax?"

I checked the back of the cab to make certain the boxes hadn't shifted or toppled. Then I scanned the street again, just in case. *Come on, go to bed already,* I urged the home's occupants. As if I possessed magical powers, the light switched off.

"Let's go," I said.

"Wait," Dave said. "Give them about twenty minutes to fall asleep."

I rolled my eyes, but I also realized it was sound advice. I settled into my seat and hoped our plans weren't about to blow up in our faces.

From the moment Dave heard his friend and co-worker Bob mention how tough the holidays were going to be for his family, Dave knew he couldn't sit around and do nothing. Bob and his wife, Darlene, had three children. The two boys were six and four, and their baby daughter was just one. "What would you think about giving gifts to the kids?" Dave had asked.

"Absolutely. Let's do it," I replied. "But I think we should get a little something for Bob and Dar, too." But then I had another thought. "Thing is, though, I think they'd see this as a handout. Would they even accept the presents?"

"You've got a point. And Bob would probably feel even worse that he couldn't do more for his family."

So that's when we hatched the idea for Undercover Santa. Dave shopped for Bob — a basketball pole, hoop, and backboard. I bought a necklace and book for Dar, games and clothes for the boys, and a stuffed animal, a doll, and clothes for Sarah.

I wrapped the gifts (except for the basketball pole, of course), and we placed them in cardboard boxes to protect them from the weather. We slipped an unsigned Christmas card in one of the boxes before we packed them in the truck cab. After Christmas Eve service ended, we drove home to change clothes before heading out.

Now we were minutes away from the big moment.

Finally, Dave cut the engine. "Let's go."

We exited the truck and hauled out the boxes. The basketball equipment would require a second trip. It had snowed a few days earlier, but thankfully the streets were clear. As we moved off the sidewalk into the yard, the snow crunched with a sound that seemed louder than Santa's reindeer landing on the rooftop. I half expected the lights to flip back on.

Slowing our steps to try and make less noise, we crept behind the house. A wooden picnic table stood about thirty feet from the back door. We brushed off the snow and positioned the boxes on top. Then we retraced our footsteps and headed back to the truck to grab the basketball equipment.

I shivered as cold air seeped into my coat and gloves. When we approached the house again, the clouds drifted away from the moon. Now the snow glowed silver-white, and our shadows appeared. "Hurry," I whispered, my heartbeat accelerating. We deposited the last of the gifts and retreated to our vehicle.

Bob and Dar's house remained dark as we climbed into the truck and drove away. "I can't believe we pulled that off," Dave said as he turned up the heat in the cab. "I just hope someone looks out that back window in the morning."

A few days later, Darlene called and told me about finding the boxes and how excited the children were when they unwrapped their gifts.

"And you don't know who left them? Did they leave a card or anything?" I played along.

"Well, there was a card, but no one signed it. I can't believe someone did this!"

I hung up a few minutes later and smiled.

The next time we had dinner with Bob and Dar, they brought it up again. Darlene looked me in the eye and said, "Did you guys do this?"

Uh-oh, crunch time. And I'm a terrible liar. But lie I did, and she seemed to accept my answer.

We didn't speak of it again except for an occasional remembrance. Over two decades have passed since then. The family moved across town, and the kids are grown. Bob and Dar are grandparents now. We figured they probably solved the mystery way back when, but even now we're not quite sure.

Over the years, Dave and I collaborated on a few more secret Christmas adventures for other families, but none of those experiences compared to the year we accomplished Mission: Undercover Santa.

— Toni Wilbarger —

26

The Power of Kindness

Extend yourself in kindness to other
human beings wherever you can.
~Oprah Winfrey

A few days before Christmas, a girlfriend called me to see if I wanted to grab a coffee. As a new mom, I was always looking for an excuse to get out of the house, so I agreed immediately. I must have desperately needed some adult time because, two coffees later, I had barely let my friend get a word in edgewise.

A mother of two herself, she completely understood and gladly let me chatter on. About halfway through another story, I noticed my friend wasn't listening anymore. She was clearly distracted by something over my shoulder. Turning around, I noticed a frantic woman trying to get her debit card to work.

"Do you know her?" I asked my friend.

"I do. Give me a minute. I'm going to go and see if I can help," she replied, standing up to walk over to her.

A few minutes later, my friend returned to the table with the frantic woman in tow. The woman looked upset. Her eyes were swollen, as if she'd been crying all night. She looked pale, tired, and disheveled. After I was introduced, my friend asked her if she was okay. She admitted she wasn't and burst into tears. Alarmed by her sudden outburst, I quickly jumped up to grab her some napkins as my friend consoled her.

When I returned to the table, I could sense she was a little embarrassed by her emotional response. Wanting to put her at ease, I quickly told her not to worry. I shared that I was a new mom with raging hormones, and I'd already cried fourteen times that day. She laughed at my silly confession, but soon her tears were flowing again.

For the next forty-five minutes, my friend and I both sat and patiently listened to her. She revealed her humiliation after her husband had left her a few weeks earlier for another woman and her devastation when she discovered, days before Christmas, that he'd heartlessly cleared out their bank accounts and left her with nothing.

Through my friend's questioning, I was able to gather that she was a stay-at-home mom of two, didn't have any siblings, and wasn't close with her family. In one split second, her entire life had come crashing down around her.

We tried our best to cheer her up. My friend even tried to give her some cash, which she refused. When she finally got up to leave, she wiped her tears, thanked us both for listening, and walked out.

"Wow, can you believe her sad story?" my friend asked, shaking her head in disbelief.

"No, I can't," I answered, a little shaken by the entire encounter.

As I drove home, I couldn't stop thinking about how depressed she looked when she left the coffee shop. *No one deserves to feel that sad,* I thought, *especially right before Christmas. There must be something I can do to help.* I racked my brain for an answer.

Gladly, a solution came. I decided to make Christmas a little better for her family by buying them a few gifts. I knew it wouldn't solve their problems, but it could distract them from their pain for at least a day. As soon as I got home, I called my girlfriend and excitedly explained my plan. She agreed with me that it would probably be best if she delivered the presents and said they were from an anonymous donor. The woman felt humiliated enough, and the last thing I wanted to do was embarrass her more.

On Christmas Eve morning, I drove to my friend's house and dropped off a large hamper of food and a few presents for the three of them, all addressed from Santa Claus. I felt like a Christmas Elf and loved the feeling of being able to spread some Christmas cheer.

Once my girlfriend had delivered everything, she called to report that the kids had been overjoyed and excited to receive their presents. However, their mom seemed embarrassed to receive charity from a stranger and felt she couldn't accept the packages. My friend insisted that Santa didn't accept returns. Eventually, the mom accepted the kindness and thanked my friend for bringing them.

Months later, I asked my girlfriend if she had heard from her. Sadly, they'd lost touch, and she didn't know how to reach her. A year and a half later, as fate would have it, I saw the woman at the gym. I hardly recognized her. She looked so different — bright, confident, and happy.

She walked up to me and asked if we knew each other. I reminded her that I had met her with my friend the year before. Realizing who I was and that I had witnessed a difficult moment in her life, she apologized for her behaviour and said she was doing much better. I quickly told her there was nothing to be sorry for and agreed she looked amazing.

"Thank you," she responded politely, but then she seemed to be lost in thought.

"Are you okay?" I asked.

"Yes, I'm fine. You just reminded me of a significant moment," she answered.

"I'm sorry, I didn't mean to reawaken old wounds," I said.

She waved off my apology. She wasn't thinking about her upsetting breakup, she reassured me. Then, out of nowhere, she asked if I'd ever experienced one moment that completely changed the trajectory of my life.

"I don't know... I guess. Why?" I asked, a little perplexed by her question.

She explained that after she'd left the coffee shop that day, she'd sadly decided that once Christmas was over, she was going to take her own life. She really felt it was her only option. I asked her what changed her mind.

"Santa Claus happened," she answered.

Suddenly, I could feel myself blushing. Did she know I was the person behind the gifts? Apparently, she didn't; she just wanted to share her story. In detail, she told me about my friend dropping off the gifts I had wrapped as well as her shock and gratitude that a complete stranger would go out of his or her way to do something so kind for her family. Apparently, it had been the kindest thing anyone had ever done for her. The gesture had actually given her hope when everything had seemed so bleak.

Listening to her describe her awe-inspiring interpretation brought me to tears. I hadn't realized a simple act of kindness could change or, even bigger than that, save someone's life. I apologized to her for my emotional reaction and then thanked her for sharing her story, never revealing I was her Secret Santa.

From that day forward, I understood the power of kindness and never missed an opportunity to spread some around. A compliment to a friend or co-worker holds so much more meaning for me now. Holding the door or even smiling at a stranger on the street is acknowledgment that I see them. Going out of my way for someone helps me connect with people on a deeper level.

I may not be changing the entire world with these actions, but they can easily change someone's world when done from the heart, at Christmastime and all year long.

— Heidi L. Allen —

27

The Gifts Santa Forgot

Christmas, my child, is love in action. Every time we
love, every time we give, it's Christmas.
~Dale Evans Rogers

One Christmas morning, I lay in bed and waited, not so patiently, for my mother to tell my sister and me that we could come to the living room. Finally, she called out, "Girls, don't you want to see what Santa brought?"

We sprang out of bed and raced down the hall. There, under the wondrous tree we had decorated the night before, lay piles of beautifully wrapped presents. There was one pile for each of us: Grandma, Mom, Dad, my sister Betty, and me.

Since I was the youngest, I had the privilege of opening my gifts first. I grabbed the top package and tore through the paper. Books. Three of them. I went from kneeling to sitting cross-legged in a second and cracked open the first book. I was in heaven.

"Honey," Dad said, "there are a lot of other presents. Don't you want to see what else Santa brought?"

Already absorbed in the story, I barely heard him.

"Honey?" he asked.

"Huh?"

"Your other presents?" He gestured toward the pile.

"Oh, okay." I grabbed a scrap of wrapping paper, placed it in the book, and set my new treasure aside.

I worked my way through the pile of toys and clothes while

watching the other members of my family open their gifts. Although I was thrilled with everything, all I really wanted to do was get back to my book, *The Little Lame Prince*. But the prince would have to wait for me to rejoin him on his journey.

After breakfast, Betty and I dressed in our new Christmas dresses. Since Grandma lived with us, the whole extended family would come to our apartment for dinner later that day. My mother and father had a lot to prepare, so we were told to go outside and play.

"And don't get dirty," my mother said. "Remember, those are special dresses, and I want you to look nice when everyone arrives."

We both nodded our heads, knowing this was one admonition we had to take seriously. When the clan descended (all eight of my mother's sisters and brothers and their children), we were expected to set the example for the younger cousins. Being the two eldest in the family wasn't fun. I still can't figure out how my mother fit everyone into our tiny, one-bedroom apartment, but she always managed.

So, with her warning in mind, we went outside.

"You'd better stay with me," Betty said, grabbing my hand. "That way, you won't get into trouble."

Betty was three years older and a stickler for the rules. I, on the other hand, was not.

Some of the other kids who lived on the block had also been banished to the street as their parents prepared for family get-togethers. We all screeched and squealed about our gifts, and a few carried their new toys with them to show everyone. Although we were poor, our parents somehow managed to scrape together enough to put toys under the tree every Christmas, and Santa always came through.

While we compared our bounties, Bobby, a kid from around the corner, walked down the block.

"Let's go see what Santa brought Bobby," I said to Betty.

Bobby was shunned by a lot of kids. He was a raggedy wretch with two drunks for parents. They seemed more concerned with where their next bottle of whiskey would come from than what they would feed Bobby for dinner.

"Hi, Bobby," I said.

All smiles, Bobby asked, "Want to see what Santa brought me?"

"Sure."

Bobby pulled a small, dirty cardboard box from his pocket and gently opened it to show Betty and me his treasure.

It was a box of mismatched buttons.

"Aren't they pretty?" he asked. His face glowed as he fingered each old button. Betty and I looked at each other in wonder.

"Put your hand out," he said.

We stood there in shock as he handed us, one after another, each precious button and extolled the virtues of each one.

"Oh, I almost forgot," Betty said. "Santa left some of your presents at our apartment. Remember, Eileen?" She grabbed my hand again and tightened hers around mine like a vise. So, I nodded my head furiously, hoping it wouldn't fall off.

"He left a note and said he forgot them when he was at your apartment and would we mind dropping them off?"

I stared at my big sister, amazed she could lie like that. Betty was the paragon of perfection and honesty. Although I didn't know it at the time, she was transferring her allegiance from Santa to Saint Nicholas. So, maybe she didn't think what she said was a lie.

"You wait here. We'll be right back," Betty said, and she pulled me down the block into our building.

"Betty, Santa didn't leave anything for Bobby."

"I know, but we have plenty of toys. We'll wrap some old ones we don't play with much anymore and give them to Bobby."

"That's a great idea," I said, already mentally choosing the ones I wouldn't miss too much.

Inside our apartment, Betty explained the situation to our parents, and they stopped what they were doing to pitch in and help. Mom dug out some wrapping paper and Dad wrote out tags for the packages while Betty and I rummaged through the box in the bottom of our closet for toys. Betty even threw in some "almost new" stuffed animals she was too old for but knew Bobby would love since he was younger than us.

By the time we finished, we had an impressive pile of "forgotten" presents.

Dad put them all in a big shopping bag and helped us carry them outside where Bobby sat on the stoop waiting for us.

I don't think I've ever again seen such a look of wonder and joy as what came over his face that morning. He actually glowed.

"Can I open them right now?" he asked.

"They're your presents. You can do whatever you want," Dad said.

Bobby ripped through the wrappings, not even looking at the To/From tags. He oohed and aahed over each gift, which Dad placed back into the shopping bag for Bobby to carry home. After the last present was opened, Bobby said, "This is the best Christmas ever."

His smile stretched from one side of his face to the other and made me even happier than the precious books Santa had left for me.

— Eileen Joyce Donovan —

28

Operation Christmas Magic

*If we experienced life through the eyes of a child,
everything would be magical and extraordinary. Let
our curiosity, adventure and wonder of life never end.*
~Akiane Kramarik

I have always been a believer. I come from a long line of them, and I am raising my son to continue this legacy. I believe in the power of Christmas magic.

Admittedly, the older I get, the more the strength of that faith is tested. Yet I always find my way back to the certainty that the impossible is always possible. As I watch my son Alex grow up, his innocence and trust help to renew my optimism and the idea of "the spirit of Santa," not merely as a person but as a concept of goodness.

Last year, I told him to write a letter to Santa and ask for a gift that no one else knew he wanted. I managed to peek at the letter before we posted it. The last line of his letter read: "P.S. Santa, my mom told me to tell you and only you of one thing I want. So, if it's not too much trouble, I would like the 1998 S.H.MonsterArts Shin Godzilla."

I did not give it another thought, and I went about my holiday duties the next few weeks. I purchased some gifts I knew he wanted, and then I decided to get the secret item too, as that wasn't something that Santa could obtain at the North Pole. I was able to locate the Godzilla on eBay where there were only two for sale.

Finally, Christmas Eve arrived. We did our normal food shopping and cookie baking. But that afternoon, while Alex was up in his bedroom, there was a knock at the door. When I went to the front porch, I noticed a red-and-white wrapped box. It was addressed to my son, and the return address was simply a zip code and the words "North Pole." I figured it was from a friend or one of my siblings. But when I contacted them, they all had no idea what I was talking about.

An hour later, an even larger delivery box was left. It was also addressed to my son and, again, the return address was "North Pole." I carried the boxes upstairs.

Confused, I opened one of the boxes. Inside were ten more red-and-white-striped wrapped packages, all addressed to my little boy.

I went online and entered the zip code that was on each delivery. I was directed to a program called "Operation Christmas."

Basically, it is a program set up by the postal service where people collect letters written to Santa and volunteer to help Santa fulfill the wishes on the list. It's all done anonymously. To be considered, your original letter to Santa must include the zip code of the North Pole and your return address — things that my son had provided.

Santa's helpers drop off the gifts at the local post office, where volunteers wrap them and deliver them to the letter writer just in time for Christmas morning.

I was incredibly touched by this amazing act of generosity, but also overwhelmed by a sense of guilt. Alex is already very loved and never goes a day without. In fact, he might sometimes have too much. I worried there might be a less fortunate child who could have benefited from the actions of our benevolent Secret Santa.

But it was Christmas Eve, and there was nothing I could do except enjoy the remainder of the holiday.

A few days after Christmas, I went to the local post office. I told the manager what had happened and how touched I was by this amazingly kind gesture. I wanted to thank the generous stranger. Bound by their rules, no information could be given to me.

I decided to donate the gifts to our local children's hospital. To do so, I needed to bring them in unwrapped. So, box by box, I discovered that each item my son had on his list was amongst these treasures, even including the hard-to-find Godzilla. That reinforced my sense of faith.

As Roald Dahl once said, "Those who don't believe in magic will never find it." I will continue to have faith in the spirit of Santa and the magic of the Christmas season.

— Tara Flowers —

29

The House Call

Blessed is the season which engages the
whole world in a conspiracy of love.
~Hamilton Wright Mabie

When my boys were younger, going out with them in public was difficult. My heart sank during the holiday season every time I looked at the long line of kids at the mall waiting to meet Santa. This was not an activity our family could enjoy. The noise and crowds caused sensory overload for my twin sons, both of whom are on the autism spectrum. I had a younger son, too, who needed an extra hand. Waiting in line was out of the question.

I always hoped for the best but planned for the worst when I took the boys out of the house, but I knew that attempting to get a picture with Santa wasn't worth the risk. It was hard to change their routines. If we had attempted to stand in line for even a few minutes, I would have been chasing the twins in opposite directions, the youngest child would have experienced a meltdown, and my husband and I would have argued about why I had thought this was a good idea. It was easier to stay home.

On the afternoon of Christmas Eve several years ago, the phone rang. The voice on the other end of the phone said, "If you're going to be home this evening, I'd like to arrange for Santa to stop by." It was Denny, the friendly owner of a concrete-cutting company, who had helped us a few months earlier when our do-it-yourself project became too much to do ourselves. Denny's company primarily worked on big projects, but when I had called and left a message, he had returned my call and driven over to see what we needed.

In the short time he was at our home, Denny's kindness and ability to relate to our kids were evident. He wasn't annoyed by their behaviors. As Isaac screamed and Noah covered his ears, I explained that they had been diagnosed with autism. He didn't seem flustered. When I mentioned how comfortable he was with the boys, Denny shared that his wife had spent many years working with the special-needs population.

Denny called us a few times after that day to make sure we were able to complete the rest of the project. Fortunately, my husband was able to finish it on his own. Looking back now, I'm sure Denny realized we had our hands full—with the project *and* our kids.

I felt nervous and giddy about having Santa come to our home. Denny assured me it would be arranged. Would our kids even notice? Would they be overwhelmed by a stranger in a red suit? Would they cry?

A few minutes before I was planning to cook dinner on Christmas Eve, Santa tapped gently on the living-room window. Five-year-old Noah was speechless; his jaw dropped. Finally, he said, "Where is Rudolph?" Henry, two years old, waved and said, "Hi, Santa!"

My husband opened the door, and Santa stepped inside. He said, "Ho, ho, ho!" at a volume that didn't scare my sons. His long white beard and bright red suit captivated the boys. He quietly sang "Jingle Bells" and looked carefully at the stockings that hung near our Christmas tree. Santa took a seat on our couch. Each boy sat on his lap while I took pictures. Isaac, who has a difficult time communicating, hugged Santa. It was priceless.

Santa was at our home for only a few minutes, but the time was magical. As he left, tears streamed down my face.

Denny had only met us once before, but without my saying a word, he knew how much our kids would appreciate meeting Santa in our own home. That house call was the highlight of our holiday season. Even now, fourteen years later, it remains one of our most treasured holiday memories.

—Tyann Sheldon Rouw—

30

The Christmas Elf

*Christmas is doing a little something
extra for someone.*
~Charles Schulz

"I'm not putting up a Christmas tree this year. I just don't have the spirit." I never heard anyone as sad as my mother-in-law as she uttered those words over the phone.

I thought my family celebrated big, but until I married into my husband's family, I had no idea what an over-the-top Christmas looked like. Lights in the front and back yard, decorations hanging from the ceiling, candles glowing in each corner, wreaths and poinsettias adorning each window… And the tree — a freshly cut pine standing in the front parlor decorated within an inch of its life. Christmas Eve culminated in a visit from none other than Santa himself, followed by a huge dinner and the opening of gifts. It was amazing.

But this year would be different. With my father-in-law's passing late that November, it was understandable that Mom's holiday spirit was nonexistent. Christmas decorating had been something husband and wife had undertaken together for over fifty years, and she simply would not do it alone.

Still, it was heartbreaking to think not even a tree would adorn their home this year. Phone calls were made to Mom and conversations were had with her children and grandchildren, trying to summon even one small spark of her holiday spirit. Yet, there was no convincing her.

That season, every Christmas carol I heard and each trip I made to the glimmering shopping malls only made me sadder as I thought of the barren spot in my mother-in-law's heart. Grief was hard enough, but fresh grief so close to Christmas was an even bigger type of awful. Surely, I thought, there had to be something that could be done to bring some joy back into her life.

One afternoon, I walked to a nearby supermarket to purchase a few necessities for Christmas baking. On the way home, I stopped at a discount store and bought a package of holiday-themed dinner napkins. Then, as I stepped toward the exit, I saw them — a crate full of fresh green tabletop trees. I walked over and inhaled their piney fragrance. Then I got an idea.

I went back through the store and selected a multi-colored string of lights, a silver tinsel garland, and a bunch of the funkiest, most glittery decorations I could find. If I was going to do this thing, I was really going to do it! Then I grabbed the largest tree of the bunch, paid for it all and walked home with four bags in one hand and a tree in the other. I can't imagine what I looked like, out in the cold, toting a tree for half a mile. I only know I felt a boost in my own heart — a boost I hoped my mother-in-law would also feel when I delivered one fully appointed tree to her.

Only my husband Bill wasn't so sure. "I don't think this is a good idea," he said as I added a few pinecones from our back yard to the tree's boughs. He stood back and scrunched his brows. "It's so small." He shook his head. "I wouldn't give this to her. She's not going to like it."

I was not deterred. After all, I had literally dragged this tree home. "Oh, no," I countered, "she's getting it. Tomorrow."

That night, my husband's words echoed through my head. What if my mother-in-law really didn't like it? I didn't want to offend her; I only wanted to do good. I pondered solutions, finally coming up with another idea. *Well,* I thought, *Mom couldn't be unhappy with me if she didn't know I was the one who brought the tree, could she?* So, the decision was made that I would place a note on the tree that read "Merry Christmas from the Christmas Elf" and drop the tree on her doorstep late the following night while Bill waited for me in the getaway car. She would never know the identity of the Christmas Elf, and she would get a tree. Perfect.

Bill and I set out the next night on our mission. He shut off his lights as he pulled toward the curb of his mother's home. Then, I lifted the tree from the back seat, ran up the front steps, and leaned the tree against the railing.

Suddenly, the front door flew open. "What are you two doing out there?"

I looked back at Bill. I'm pretty sure his first instinct was to put the car in drive and rocket out of there, but instead he shut off the engine and followed me into the house. My mother-in-law had already placed the tree in the parlor and was setting it up on a small side table. She stood back and surveyed her gift. "I love it!" She took a closer look. "Only one thing is missing." She left the room only to reappear with a small, framed photo of my father-in-law in her hand. She placed it on the table underneath the tree and then took a step back. "There. Now it's perfect." Bill and I agreed; truly, it was.

That Christmas, the only thing my mother-in-law enjoyed more than that little tree was telling anyone who would listen about her daughter-in-law, the Christmas Elf, who walked half a mile hauling a tree so that her holiday spirit could be renewed. Sadly, we only had one more Christmas with Mom. Two years later, she joined her beloved husband in heaven. But each year, in her memory, the Christmas Elf seeks out and delivers one anonymous tree with the hope that it will bring someone else the same joy it brought my mother-in-law.

— Monica A. Andermann —

31

What Santa Has Taught Me

My idea of Christmas, whether old-fashioned or modern,
is very simple: loving others. Come to think of it,
why do we have to wait for Christmas to do that?
~Bob Hope

After I retired from the Army (thirty-seven years, four months, and nine days — and, yes, I was counting!), I grew a beard because, hey, I could! It came out white, which at my age was no surprise. My wife began hinting that I should try being a Santa. I was surprised by that suggestion, but over time decided that when she was eight years old, she must have decided she wanted to marry Santa Claus. So, if she was to become Mrs. Claus... You get the idea.

I auditioned for a local park, and to my surprise and more than a small amount of panic, I was hired. Now I was in for it. I began walking through the toy section of stores. I memorized "The Night Before Christmas." I speak various languages with differing degrees of proficiency, so I memorized how to say, "What would you like for Christmas?" in Spanish, French, Italian, and German. (The park gets a fair number of international visitors.) I didn't have to understand the reply. A smile and knowing wink are universal.

By my third day on Santa's throne I was pretty confident. It was actually kind of fun. As long as I didn't promise more than "I'll look into it" I was golden. After all, I wasn't the real Santa and was just filling in for him and passing on whatever information I gleaned from the kids.

Then life threw me a curveball. One of the young ladies serving as an elf came up to me and said, "Santa, you're about to see three kids. They've been orphans for the past year. The foster parents keeping them have just been approved to adopt them, and they want *you* to tell them!"

I took a deep breath, and there they were, three kids, ages twelve, ten, and eight. No pressure, right? Unsure what to say, I fell back on the old standby, "What would you like for Christmas?" They said something, but I didn't hear a word as I was too busy wondering what to say about the adoption.

Then it came to me. I said, "Those are great ideas. I'll look into them, but I have something for you today."

"What's that, Santa?" the oldest asked, obviously the spokesperson for the group.

"A family," I said.

They looked puzzled, but when I explained that they would not have to leave the foster family, that they could stay together, well, there wasn't a dry eye in the house. Yeah, I teared up just now, even though it was five years ago.

So, what did I learn? In the *Hero's Journey*, the hero comes back changed by his quest. Though I didn't leave my throne, I had just been on quite a ride.

I learned that I wanted to be Santa Claus more than anything else in the world. I fully embraced the role after that. Santa has made me a kinder and more patient man. With my beard, I stand out anywhere I go. I must be careful about what I say and how I act for I never know where or when a child might see me. I must be in tune with "the better angels of my nature" whenever I am in public.

When I put on my superhero costume and go forth to fight for happiness, I never promise a toy, but I always offer a hug. I have a photo of me taken from behind as I hugged an elderly man during a gift exchange at an Alzheimer's daycare center. Every patient got a gift bag selected by the staff. I handed them out and hugged each one.

Walter's face was beaming, and through a trick of the lighting perhaps, there was a small halo around his head.

I got the photo from his daughter who tracked me down. She said her dad had been abandoned by his parents when he was five years old and had never had a visit from Santa his entire life.

The next year, I was told that Walter had passed. His daughter told the director of the daycare center that the photo of me hugging him had become Walter's favorite. At his funeral, his daughter had that picture blown up and placed on an easel beside his open coffin.

That taught me how powerful even one moment can be in another person's life. Don't hold back. That moment may never come again.

The Greek philosopher Heraclitus once said that a man can never cross a river twice, for each time both he and the river will have changed. Every time I assume the role, it may be the first time for whomever I meet. I may define Santa for the rest of their life.

No pressure, right? But here's the thing: Just like Dumbo and his magic feather, the magic is not in the robe. It was inside me all the time. I just needed the license that the costume gave me to tap into it.

You may not wear a red suit, but I hereby deputize you to share love and joy wherever you go. You can do it. Find that better angel that has been inside you all along and let it breathe. You, and all those around you, will be the better for it.

— Bradley Harper —

32

The Holiday Cheer Bus

Christmas is most truly Christmas when we
celebrate it by giving the light of love
to those who need it most.
~Ruth Carter Stapleton

I was sitting at my desk surrounded by Christmas gifts. I was glad I had finished shopping and managed to procure some hard-to-find items. I was about to sort through everything when my phone rang. It was my friend Melissa. She is the director of Kids Need More, a charitable organization for which my family volunteers. The organization offers many services to critically ill and socially disadvantaged children.

"Hi, I need to ask a favor," Melissa said. "Can you add one more family to your route? It's near the other stops."

One of Kids Need More's most popular events is the Holiday Cheer Bus. It's a huge event. Last year, twenty-three buses visited more than 200 families and delivered toys to more than 500 children. The organization always fills sacks with donated gifts for the families on the Cheer Bus routes. Each bus is manned by a team of volunteers dressed as Santa and his elves.

My family had sponsored a bus and been elves for several years. But this year was different. Donations were down due to COVID. Many people, concerned about social distancing, were not comfortable going on a bus. I had a list of the families on our route and had gone shopping with my son to make sure each child had at least one special item from their list.

"Of course. Can I have some details?"

"There's a young mother, Leanne, and her two children. The only thing she requested was a call to confirm the Cheer Bus is coming to visit her family."

"That's all she wants? That's easy. I'll call her now."

After a bit more chitchat with Melissa, I called the young mom. I told Leanne I was calling from Kids Need More to assure her that a holiday Cheer Bus would be visiting her family.

Leanne began to cry. "Are you sure? Are you really, really going to come?"

I was moved by this young mom whose only request was for a visit from the Cheer Bus for her children.

"Yes, the Cheer Bus is really, really going to come — and Santa, too. Is there something special that your children would like?"

"My daughter is only one, so she won't even know it's Christmas. However, my son is three, and I can't let him play in the snow because he doesn't have snow boots," she said through her sobs.

"Snow boots? Is that all?"

"That's all he needs. He likes Spider-Man."

Now, I was getting somewhere. I wanted to do more for this young mom and her children. "What shoe size does your son wear? Your daughter needs gifts, too. It's Christmas."

"He is a size 9. Thank you. Bless you. Thank you so much. You're really going to come!"

"Yes, really. And I will have snow boots for your son." After I said goodbye and ended the call, panic set in. It was two days before the Cheer Bus was going on its run, less than a week before Christmas and three days after a major snowstorm had hit our area. I was going to need a holiday miracle to find Spider-Man snow boots in size 9.

"We have to go shopping!" I called out to my husband and son.

"More shopping? Didn't you finish the last time we went out?" asked my son, John.

"Didn't you say you had everything you wanted from the lists?" asked my husband, also John.

"I did have everything, but Melissa called, and I have one more special item to get." I told them about the call and the need for boots. The three of us set off. We went to a few department stores and scoured the shoe departments, to no avail.

At one store, my husband riffled through a cart of returns. He called out, "I found boots in the right size" as he held up a lovely pink pair of size 9 boots.

"Thank you, but we need boots for a boy who loves Spider-Man." We went to a few more stores — still no boots. We were tired. We were hungry. We were becoming disheartened.

"Mom, we are going to have to give Leanne a gift card so she can get the boots herself," said my son.

"I don't want to give up. I promised we would bring boots."

"Okay, one more store but then we have to give up and get something to eat," said my husband.

At our final stop, my son pulled up to the curb by the store and stayed there with his truck running as he anticipated my husband and I would be back quickly and empty-handed. Expecting defeat, my husband and I trudged to the shoe department. All we saw were empty shelves where the snow boots should be. As my husband searched in one area, I searched another. I looked down an aisle and saw a Spider-Man box. I ran down the aisle. As I got closer, I could not believe what I was seeing. On top of the Spiderman box were black-and-red snow boots. I carefully lifted the tag and saw the size — a child's size 9! Spider-Man had saved the day. We bought the boots along with some Spider-Man sneakers. It was a Christmas miracle.

Rejuvenated, we shopped a bit more and got some clothing for both children and an educational toy for the baby. I was relieved we would be bringing snow boots when we visited Leanne and her family.

Two days later, on a chilly December morning, we arrived at the Kids Need More headquarters. My husband was dressed as Santa. My son and I were dressed as elves. We were ready to spread holiday cheer to the families on our route. We sipped steaming hot chocolate to warm us as we loaded our bus with bags of gifts for each child on our route. We decorated the bus with bright holiday lights, tinsel, and a huge red bow. As the bus left the parking lot, a light snow began to fall as Santa and the elves practiced holiday songs. We were ready to deliver gifts and holiday cheer to the families on the route. We called before each stop to let the family know we would be arriving soon. I don't know who was more excited—the families or the volunteers. I was excited about Leanne's stop. She had won my heart with her sweet, simple request.

Finally, it was time for the young mom's family. I called and told her we were on our way and would be there in about ten minutes. She said she was ready, and her son was, too. As the bus pulled up to her home with Christmas carols blaring and holiday lights glowing, she opened the door, and her son ran through the cold, wet snow without boots for the last time. Santa and his crew of elves got off the bus. We brought the bags of gifts to Leanne's door and handed her the boots. We visited for a while and took photos with Santa and Leanne's son and daughter. When it was time to leave for our next stop, Leanne waved us off with tears in her eyes. As we walked down the driveway, I heard her son ask if he could go out to play in the snow in his new boots.

—Eleanore R. Steinle—

33

Santa Undercover

Every individual has a place to fill in the world,
and is important, in some respects,
whether he chooses to be so or not.
~Nathaniel Hawthorne

It was a gorgeous warm day in May when my bearded wonder of a brother Jeremy came to visit. We were living in Washington, D.C. at the time and thrilled to be headed out to watch a Washington Nationals baseball game for the afternoon.

Now, Jeremy is quite the attention-getter wherever he goes because his beard enters the room before he does. And walking the streets of D.C. was no different. His bushy, chestnut-colored beard hung to the middle of his chest, and in the spirit of baseball, he'd braided the bottom half of it and looped some of my red hair ties into it to make it extra festive. A bright Nationals-red shirt and pale khaki shorts completed his ensemble. For a final dash of panache, he topped off his look with a red bandana, tied a la Willie Nelson around his head.

Most people would've grown self-conscious under the awe-inspired stares and quick whispers. "Take a look at that beard!" But not Jeremy. He relished the attention and even stopped to take pictures with strangers.

As we boarded the Metro bound for Nationals Park stadium, Jeremy caught the eye of a very curious five-year-old girl. She stared at him with completely rapt attention, squinting every so often as if she were trying to figure out the world's greatest mystery. Slowly, inch by inch, she scooted over in her seat toward Jeremy, until she was within arm's reach of him and his magnificent, red-ribboned beard.

I nudged Jeremy and whispered, "I think you have an admirer."

He grinned. "I think you're right."

Jeremy is also a gentle giant and a natural with children, having a sweet seven-year-old girl himself. He tilted his head, wiggled his fingers at her, and in his deep, booming voice said, "Hello!"

At the sound of his voice, the little girl could no longer contain her curiosity and screamed with excitement. "I knew it!" she cried. "Santa!" She screeched again, clapping her hands and tugging at her mother's sleeve as she alerted a very embarrassed woman that Father Christmas was right there on the Washington, D.C. Metro.

Those within earshot stifled giggles, but Jeremy didn't miss a beat. He looked around conspiratorially and then leaned down to her and whispered, "How did you know it was me?"

"Oh, it was the beard. No one has a beard like that but Santa!"

Jeremy didn't have to try hard to give her his best ho-ho-ho chuckle. "Well, you're right — it is me."

Satisfaction quickly turned to concern as she eyed Santa up and down and became very interested in his wellbeing. A flurry of questions poured out of her.

"But, Santa, why isn't your beard white? And you look skinnier than the last time I saw you. And where is your coat?" As she looked around the train car, we sensed questions about the reindeer were coming next.

Quick on his feet, Jeremy was ready. "Oh! Well, Santa is very impressed because you have found out one of my biggest secrets. After Christmas is over, that's when Santa goes undercover, to see who's being good all year long."

The little girl squinted at him, still a bit unsure, so Jeremy continued. "I dye my beard from white to brown, and I leave my coat at the North Pole so that people won't know it's me."

"Oh," she whispered now that she was an insider.

"You see, that's what Santa does when he's not at the North Pole. I travel all over the world, so I can find out who's being good and make my Christmas list. But that's a lot of travel and a whole lot of walking," he explained. He quickly remembered to add, "And the reindeer, of course, don't like the hot weather, so they stay at the North Pole while I travel."

The little girl nodded with understanding, her eyes never leaving Santa. We noticed that the rest of the train car had quieted, too, as they listened to a surprise Christmas story.

"With my reindeer at the North Pole, I have to walk — except on very special days like today when I get to ride the train. But, you see, all this walking and travel makes Santa a little skinnier during the year," he explained.

"So, when Christmas comes again, that's why I am so happy when good little children like yourself leave me all of those delicious cookies!" he said, giving her a wink.

Of course! The little girl beamed ear-to-ear as she worked out Santa's story.

"But now you know my secret — that Santa goes undercover after Christmas, so you can't tell anyone — except your parents, of course," he said, tossing a wink to the very grateful mother of an inquisitive little girl.

Maybe it was the anticipation of enjoying a baseball game under a gorgeous afternoon sky or just a little Christmas magic that had arrived early, but as we arrived at the Nationals Park Metro stop, we watched as couples clasped hands, and strangers smiled with kindness at one another as we filed from the train.

As the little girl hopped off the train, she took one last look over her shoulder. Jeremy called out to her, "I'll see you at Christmas! Be good!"

"I will! Your secret is safe with me, Santa!" she called back, as she skipped away clutching her mother's hand.

We had a wonderful afternoon, and it came as no surprise that as the jumbotron scanned the crowd during the seventh-inning stretch, it found Jeremy and his magnificent beard. And as we waved and cheered to an unseen camera, we could've sworn we heard a familiar little voice screech in the crowd, "Look! It's Santa!"

— Kristi Adams —

Magical Mystery Pyjamas

The light in a child's eyes is all it takes to make
Christmas a magical time of the year.
~Author Unknown

To this day, people tell my mother, "I don't know how you did it raising four kids on your own. That's pretty amazing."

"You do what you need to do," she always says.

It wasn't just that she kept us clothed and fed. She sent us to piano lessons and art classes during the school year, and then theatre camp and soccer leagues in the summertime. Back then, I didn't realize what a feat that was, but I do now.

The first year after my parents' divorce was a huge adjustment, but Mom and us kids pulled together to make the household run smoothly. The older kids helped the younger kids. My mom braided my sister's hair in the morning, and then my sister got the youngest ready for daycare. A kind neighbour drove us to our various schools, and I picked up my brother after class. The household was frenetic at times, but the five of us felt safe and cared-for.

Our first Christmas after my parents were divorced was particularly memorable — and not for lack of anything. My mother always worked extra hard to make the holidays special, and she succeeded every time.

On Christmas Eve, we set off to visit my grandparents. Together, we played poker for pennies, ate Tim Hortons donuts, and drank countless pots of tea. That was our traditional Saturday night entertainment, but it worked well for special occasions, too.

When we arrived home, the step in front of our house was covered with boxes wrapped in Christmas paper. There were five boxes total, each with a name scrawled in the corner but no indication where they came from.

We didn't recognize the writing — or the paper, for that matter. There were no cards. Just gifts.

My mother reasoned the presents couldn't be from Santa because why would Santa leave things on the front step? He would come in through the chimney and put them under the tree like he always did.

Anyway, it wasn't Christmas morning yet. It was still Christmas Eve. These gifts couldn't possibly be from Santa.

As we brought the packages indoors, my mother seemed a little unsure about it all. We'd never received anonymous Christmas gifts before. But it had been an especially challenging year for all of us. Somebody out there must have noticed, and it had to be somebody who at least knew all our names.

We sat around the Christmas tree, and my mom opened her gift first, carefully slipping a fingernail under the tape so that she'd be able to slide out the box without ripping the paper. The box was shiny and white, with a store logo embossed in one corner. My mother lifted the lid, peeked inside the white tissue paper, and smiled.

She told us to open our gifts, and we did — though not with her level of care and finesse. We tore into the paper, creating a flurry of giftwrap. We received flannel pyjamas, each with a different wintery print — penguins skiing, polar bears on toboggans, red-and-green plaid, angels and stars, and serene snowflakes for my mom.

After Christmas, we asked around, trying to figure out the identity of our secret donor. Every time we saw a neighbour shovelling snow, we told them the story of the magical mystery pyjamas. They all smiled, nodded and said what a lovely idea that was, what a nice thing to do. But nobody 'fessed up.

We knew to look for that special sparkle in someone's eyes. The problem was that, when we told the story, everybody seemed to get that sparkle. All our neighbours, friends and family members seemed as moved by the story as we'd been receiving the gifts.

After we outgrew the magical mystery pyjamas, my mother kept them out of sentimentality. Some were threadbare by then or torn from being worn by rambunctious children. Any other pyjamas would have gone in the rag pile, but these ones sat folded beside it... until years later when my high-school best friend showed me the "pyjama quilt" she'd made. She'd cut old pyjamas into squares and rag-quilted them. The finished product was whimsical and gorgeous.

That gave me an idea to preserve the magical mystery pyjamas. My mother handed them over. She also contributed a pair of pyjamas that had belonged to my grandfather — the grandpa with whom we'd played poker that long-ago Christmas Eve — which she'd kept as a remembrance after he died.

With flannel PJs from all my siblings, I got quilting. My friend made sewing look easy, zipping everything off on her machine, but I wasn't quite so experienced. Anyway, I preferred hand stitching. She'd created her quilt in one day. Mine took seven years to complete. But it was a labour of love.

Telling family and friends about the quilt reignited the story of the magical mystery pyjamas, giving everyone in our lives another opportunity to admit, after all these years, that the gifts were from them.

Still, nobody has.

The magical mystery pyjamas were left for us almost thirty years ago, and we still have no idea who secretly snuck them onto our front stoop.

— Tanya Janke —

Brotherly Love

*How dreary would be the world if
there were no Santa Claus.*
~Francis Pharcellus Church

The colorful lights on the houses in the hills above our house sparkled with a fairytale promise of things to come. Every day, a couple of new presents showed up beneath the tree. The restlessness that stirs within a twelve-year-old girl as Christmas Day approaches had reached a fever pitch. The next day was Christmas, and I couldn't wait for it to come. Neither could my seventeen-year-old brother, Johnny.

When we came down to breakfast, the smell of bacon greeted us but there was no cheery "Good morning" from our mother. We saw her speaking quietly on the phone, nodding her head, her eyes shaded with concern. She studied Johnny and me thoughtfully as we pulled our chairs up to the table.

After getting off the phone, she silently walked to the stove, brought a platter of eggs and bacon to the table, and sat down to join us. "I have something for you two to do today," she began. "There's a woman in our church with four children who has no money, and she'll not be able to give her kids any presents for Christmas this year. I told the church secretary that we would help out and get them some gifts. I'd like for you two to go downtown today and pick out some presents for the children. They all need pajamas, and you can get each of them a toy." She reached for the paper she'd set beside her plate. "Here are their names, ages and sizes."

Johnny and I felt very grown-up and important that day as we drove downtown with a sizable amount of cash. With the sound of Christmas carols in the background, I felt an awesome responsibility as we picked out pajamas for each child and then headed to the toy store. Johnny chose Lincoln Logs for the older boy and a truck for the younger. I sorted through the entire shelf of dolls to pick out the perfect one for each of the girls. Johnny suggested we top it off with a present for the mom. He threw in a little money of his own that he made at the Safeway to make up the difference. Then we headed for home to do the wrapping.

I felt like one of Santa's elves. The happiness of four children depended on me and my brother.

Johnny obviously felt the same responsibility, and he took the lead in devising the plan for the evening. It unfolded as an event that forever changed my idea of what makes a happy Christmas.

After dinner, we had our traditional family Christmas Eve service in which we lit candles, read the Christmas story from the Bible, and gathered around the piano to sing Christmas carols. According to our usual practice, Mother tried to hit the right keys on the piano, and we tried to hit the right notes to match, but the occasional discordant sharps and flats added to the merriment. Our family celebration, like our family itself, was imperfect but full of grace.

When it was getting late, we bundled the gifts into the Chrysler and drove to the house. Johnny and I sat in the back with the presents on our laps. My parents were in the front. When my father got to the address, he pulled stealthily alongside the unlit end of the house. Johnny and I gathered up the presents, carried them quietly to the front door, and set them on the stoop.

Johnny rang the doorbell and then he and I raced to our waiting getaway vehicle and jumped in. My father took off, and we laughed and chatted excitedly about what had transpired.

Remaining anonymous was part of the fun. We felt a bit like Santa Claus. We hadn't gone down a chimney, and we didn't arrive on a sleigh, but we had a driver both lively and quick (my father), who took off as soon as the presents were left. And, in our hearts, we had the pure delight of making children happy by surprising them with gifts on Christmas morning.

That night, as I climbed into bed, I imagined that mother going to the door and discovering the presents, and the children finding them under the tree in the morning.

I'm sure there were many presents for me under the tree the next morning, too. And I'm sure it was grand. But I don't remember a single one. I only remember the dolls, truck, Lincoln Logs, and pajamas my brother and I bought for four children we'd never met. And I remember speeding off into the night, exhilarated by the joy in my heart over delivering those presents to that family.

A couple of years ago, my brother Johnny passed away in mid-autumn. When Christmas came around that year, this memory was never far from my mind. Johnny was a very generous person, and I've wondered if perhaps the first blushes of his gift of generosity began to blossom the year that we played Santa's helpers. That year, I think we both came to realize the truth of the old maxim that it truly is better to give than to receive.

— Linda W. Rooks —

Treasured
Traditions

36

Thank Our Lucky Peas

Normal is nothing more than a cycle
on a washing machine.
~Whoopi Goldberg

My dad is from the "Deep South" but I grew up in Michigan surrounded by my mother's family. Throughout my life I have always noticed that my dad has customs, idiosyncrasies, and turns of phrase the rest of my family finds peculiar. "Southern folks have their own way," he always says. "That's just how we do it." We smile and shrug and let him do his thing.

When I planned to get married on New Year's Eve in Washington D.C., my dad came to me with a concern I was definitely not expecting. "Oh, I don't know about this," he stammered, "If your mom and I are away from home on New Year's Day, how will I get my peas? I can't go without my peas!"

"What in the world are you talking about?" I was baffled, and with only about a month before my wedding, you can imagine my frustration. It's not like I was going to suddenly change the location because of his hankering for legumes.

He reminded me that every year on New Year's Day my mom makes him a pot of black-eyed peas. According to my dad, southerners are also quite superstitious, particularly in the Black southern community. Traditionally, eating black-eyed peas as the first meal of the

New Year is said to bring luck and prosperity. There was no way he was going to miss out on a whole year of luck and prosperity, so we had to figure out a solution.

Thank our lucky peas that my mom agreed to pre-cook his favorite food to start the year, freeze them, and bring them along from home. I made sure to book them a hotel room with a microwave. Then I warned my D.C. friends that if all else failed I would be over to heat up black-eyed peas bright and early on New Year's Day.

Crisis averted, and the night went on as planned. Everyone danced their way into the new year without worry about the "bad juju" that my dad would keep at bay for all of us by eating multiple portions of peas. After the party ended and we retreated to our hotels for the night, my new husband paused in front of our door. "Stay there for a sec," he said, making me stand in the hallway as he walked in the door and turned to come back out for me.

"What was that?" I said.

He shrugged and told me, "It's after midnight. A man has to go through the door first on New Year's Day. It brings protection. If I carried you through, it might mess it up."

"Where did you get THAT from?"

"Your dad."

—Rachel R. Perkins—

37

Three Kings Day

Remember, a book is always a gift.
~Sheridan Hay, The Secret of Lost Things

In our house, Christmas Day isn't the end of the most wonderful time of the year; it's just the beginning! It's the first day of Christmas, and our countdown to Three Kings Day begins.

If you are familiar with the Epiphany, or The Twelve Days of Christmas, you already know a bit of the story. If not, it goes as follows: The first day of Christmas is December twenty-fifth, when the Christ child was born. When the Three Kings (also called the Wise Men or Magi) heard news of his birth, they traveled to witness the miracle and arrived twelve days later, on January sixth, Three Kings Day!

On Three Kings Eve, children in Puerto Rico, Spain, Mexico, and other Latin American countries fill a box with grass and leave it under their beds. After the children fall asleep, the Three Kings come, riding their camels. Tired from the long journey, the camels eat the grass, and the Kings leave a few small gifts in the boxes as a symbol of love, faith, and hope.

My father is Puerto Rican and moved to the Washington, D.C. area when he was a young teen. I grew up very close to his parents: my "grandpapa," a retired government employee who adored poetry, and my "abuela," who shared with me her love of the sunny, faraway island of her youth.

I always celebrated this holiday at my abuela's house. I loved watching her bustle around the kitchen on Three Kings Eve, preparing delicious traditional Puerto Rican meals of chicken fricassee with red beans and rice, along with creamy flan for dessert. She would sit me at the table with a task to complete, which usually involved something kid-friendly like peeling oranges, but still made me feel like a big help.

After dinner, Abuela would take my hand, and together we'd venture into the wintry night. Pulling bits of grass from the snow-covered ground was a task I took very seriously. The shoebox had to be filled to the brim! Then we'd place the box, stuffed with my mushy concoction of grass, snow and mud, under my bed. When I awoke the next morning, the grass was gone! How did three enormous, stinky, hairy camels slurp grass from under my bed without me waking up? It's a mystery to this day.

Inside the box were candies from the island: juicy *pilones* (Puerto Rican lollipops), crunchy sesame-seed candy bars, and a little toy like a *güiro*, a noisy instrument with bumpy ridges one strokes with a stick.

Excited to share my unique holiday with my classmates, I wrote about Three Kings Day in the second grade and entered my essay in the school's writing contest. It was a very dramatic tale of the Three Kings and their epic journey through the blistering winds, all so they could make it to my house before sunrise!

After reading my entry, my second-grade teacher, Ms. Repass, pulled me aside to have a chat. I was terrified. These things never seemed to end well. Much to my surprise, she told me I was a gifted writer and she told my mother to encourage my passion for spinning tall tales.

Fast forward a few decades, and I had children of my own: twin daughters. My beloved *abuelos* had passed on. It was up to me to carry on the Three Kings Day tradition.

When my daughters were old enough to understand, I took them to the library in hopes of finding children's books on Three Kings Day. I came across dozens of Christmastime books but nothing about Three Kings Day. I knew it wasn't a common holiday, but I was still surprised. Through a quick chat with the librarian, I discovered there were only a handful of children's books published on the topic. They were available in other counties and would take a while to be delivered. Disappointed that I wouldn't get the books in time for the holiday, I told the girls about the holiday myself when we returned home.

The twins were delighted at the prospect of getting even more presents after Christmas and set off to find shoeboxes to decorate. As I watched, I began to reflect on my own Three Kings Day celebrations with my *abuelos*.

Looking back through adult eyes, it suddenly dawned on me that I didn't know nearly as much about my grandparents as I should. Why didn't I ask them more questions? I never bothered to ask my *abuela* what she got for gifts as a little girl. Other questions crept into my mind: What did it feel like to be my grandparents? To leave Puerto Rico in their thirties, come to the States, and struggle with the language and isolation? Were they terribly lonely that first Christmas, so far from home?

I didn't know the answers, and I never would. I always missed my grandparents during the holidays, but now that my children were old enough to appreciate our family traditions, the pain was deeper.

Slowly, an idea came to me. Maybe there was something I could do. I was trying to break into the world of writing professionally, so why not write my own book for children about Three Kings Day? Someone had liked my Three Kings Day story once, right? I had to laugh at myself. That's like saying, "Hey, I played on the all-star basketball team in middle school, so maybe I can go pro!"

But I couldn't quiet that little voice inside me that said, "Try, just try." Besides, what did I have to lose? If I wrote the story and no publisher wanted to buy it, I would still have a bedtime story for my kids.

So, I went for it. I worked on that piece for a year or so. I took it to writing conferences and workshops, each journey helping me to polish the book a bit more. Finally, I felt it was the story I wanted to tell. As I got ready to submit it to publishers, a wave of doubt washed over me. Maybe there weren't a lot of books on Three Kings Day because no one really cared. Perhaps this was a dying holiday, something growing dimmer under the long shadows cast by Santa and the Elf on the Shelf. Or maybe I wasn't as good of a writer as I thought. I took a breath and submitted it anyway.

Eight months later, I received an e-mail from a publisher. They loved my book and wanted to talk. Before I knew it, I had my first book contract. Not only had I accomplished a lifelong goal, but it felt amazing knowing that children who celebrated Three Kings Day could see themselves in a book, and children who didn't know about the holiday would learn something new.

I never imagined that I would be able to preserve my grandparents' memory in such a lasting way. I don't think they knew it at the time, but the best Three Kings Day gift I ever received wasn't a toy; it was simply them sharing their culture with me. I will carry those memories with me always, especially at Christmastime.

— Annette M. Clayton —

38

Half Jewish-Half Christmas

Hanukkah is about the freedom to be true
to what we believe without denying the
freedom of those who believe otherwise.
~Rabbi Jonathan Sacks

"So, what do Jews do on Christmas?" my boyfriend Rande asked me.

"Well, we go to the movies and eat Chinese food," I responded without a moment's thought.

"No, seriously."

"Really. Ask another Jew," I told him.

The next day, he called me after work, his voice incredulous. Rande had asked three friends at work the same question, and each had responded as predicted: a movie and Chinese food.

Rande and I had begun dating in September 1998. We met at a science-fiction convention. It's a rather convoluted story, but I'll try to keep it simple. My brother Peter and I were both getting divorced at the same time. We figured if we had to go through hell, we might as well do it together. My brother was an author of comic books and novels, and he did a lot of appearances at conventions as part of his work.

As for me, with my life blown to bits, I had nothing else to do, so I accompanied him. It was a win-win. He was not used to traveling alone, and I didn't want to be alone. One of his fans was a guy named

Joe. We met while he was waiting in line for my brother's autograph. I was seated behind the table, keeping my brother company.

Joe was very charming, and soon after meeting, we started dating. Sadly, Joe turned out to be kind of a jerk, and the relationship lasted only a few tumultuous months. The good news was that Joe had a really nice friend named Rande.

Now, Rande was on the other end of the phone surprised to learn that many American Jews spend Christmas going to the movies and eating Chinese food. In fact, if you throw in lunch at a deli, you have what Peter referred to as "the Jewish trifecta." The reason for this specific and odd custom is quite simple. They are the only places open on Christmas Day.

That Christmas, I discovered a few presents under the little tree in Rande's house with my name on them. We had only been together a few months. One box was fairly big, and I couldn't imagine what might be inside. It was brightly decorated with blue-and-white wrapping paper and ribbons.

I wasn't used to getting presents that were festively wrapped at the holidays. My parents were born and raised in Israel. They had explained to us that, in Israel, Hanukkah is a minor holiday. It had been hyped in America to compete with Christmas so Jewish kids didn't feel cheated. Each year at Hanukkah, my brothers and I would get a few small gifts — nothing major and certainly not wrapped in fancy paper.

So, to hold this beautifully wrapped present with my name on it was a special experience. The fact that Rande had wrapped it in blue and white, the colors of Israel, was not lost on me. I tore into the gift, feeling slightly bad for ruining the look of the box. I wanted to be like Darryl Hannah in *Splash* when Tom Hanks gave her a present, and she just hugged it. When I finally opened it, I discovered a golden menorah. It seemed a fitting way to start our new traditions.

By the following Christmas, we were married. Rande's mother lived close by, a mile or so down the road. She was kind of like Captain Christmas. She spent a few months getting ready for it every year. The idea of her oldest son having a new bride for Christmas was a momentous occasion that could not be ignored.

"So, what's the plan for Christmas?" I asked. To my way of thinking, it was his holiday, so he got to plan what we did for the day. Rande had other ideas.

"How about in the morning we celebrate the Christian way and, in the afternoon, the Jewish way?" I looked at him quizzically, and he explained, "The family will come over in the morning. We can have breakfast and open presents — the Christian way. In the afternoon, we can go to the movies and then go out for Chinese food — the Jewish way."

I was delighted. It was a perfect combination of us. It was just like our wedding cake. One layer was chocolate (my favorite), one was vanilla (his favorite), and the top layer was half-and-half. So, too, was our new Christmas tradition: half-and-half.

Two years later, Rande and I were looking forward to celebrating our first holiday season as a family of three with the addition of our daughter, Sarah. For our cards, we took a picture of our cherubic six-month-old posed under our Christmas tree in a red, green, and blue plaid outfit. She donned a baby-sized Santa hat and held a stuffed dreidel in her hands.

In subsequent years, a little sister, Emily, was added to complete our family. Our tradition changed through time. Going to the movies with a couple of toddlers was not a realistic option, so our tradition was adjusted. We rented movies and ordered in Chinese food. We explained to the kids that Daddy's family celebrated Christmas, and Mommy's family was Jewish and celebrated Hanukkah.

When Sarah was in first grade, she had to complete a worksheet about her family's holiday traditions. She wrote, in her best first-grade handwriting, "I'm half-Jewish and half-Christmas."

— Beth David Goodwin —

39

Lost and Found

What one loves in childhood stays in the heart forever.
~Mary Jo Putney

"What's that, Mommy?" My eyes grew wide as I watched my mother carefully open a corrugated brown envelope. A colorful picture of Santa Claus on the envelope's front had immediately caught my attention, prompting my inquiry.

Christmas was weeks away, but sugar plums were already dancing in my head. I was seven years old and impatiently waiting for Santa's arrival. My mother responded, "It's a paper template."

Completely puzzled, I answered, "It's *what*?"

As my mother unfolded what appeared to be a giant piece of paper with a plethora of perfectly drawn lines, she said, "Come, let me show you. Your father and I are going to make a life-size wooden cutout of Santa Claus for the front yard. This paper will help us. It's sort of like my sewing patterns. When I made your flannel pajamas, remember how I laid the paper on the material and used lots of pins and scissors to cut out an outline? It's sort of the same thing."

Still confused, I scratched my head and said, "Oh, okay. When are you and Daddy going to make this wooden Santa?"

With a loving smile, my mother answered, "Tonight, we will make the wooden Santa together."

Later that evening, I watched with excitement as my father laid the paper template on the plank and skillfully cut it out. My mother proceeded to paint an image of Santa on the wooden cutout, the exact image depicted in the template's instructions — with black boots, a red suit, a black buckle with a tinge of yellow-and-white paint, green mittens with black stripes, and a jovial expression. On the bottom left of the back of the wooden cutout, my mother inscribed in small black lettering our last name: "Rossi."

That December, with a spotlight cast upon him, Santa was firmly staked in frozen ground in front of our brick Cape Cod home. In the years to follow, for nearly half a century, Santa made his annual debut shortly after Thanksgiving. My father would climb into our attic to remove Santa from the rafters, dust him off, and bring him outdoors for the holiday season.

The mere appearance of that life-size wooden Santa made my heart race. It was the commencement of yuletide family festivities, a day certain to be filled with excitement and merriment. Every year, the long-awaited day began the same way: winter coats zipped up, snow boots buckled, mittens and hats tightly secured, followed by a race between my siblings and me to the front door. One of us would push open the door, and we'd all tumble out and gather around my father in the front yard as he strategically positioned Santa in place.

Once Santa had assumed his official post, we would unravel yards of colorful lights and haphazardly string them in the bushes and on the fence. Eventually, we would return indoors to decorate our artificial tree with too much tinsel, hang our stockings, and sip cups of hot chocolate with an abundance of mini marshmallows. Homemade pizza was eaten at the Formica kitchen table, which was temporarily relocated to the living room and accompanied by a stack of folding chairs that grew higher each year as our family continued to expand.

After dessert, my father roasted chestnuts in the fireplace, and my mother played Christmas carols on an old organ. Santa's annual appearance and our decking of the halls were inevitably captured on film, first on 8mm, and in later years on a VHS camera.

Throughout the decades, the wooden cutout of Santa retained not only a recurring role in our holiday home movies, but also served as the backdrop for still photographs, with each of us posing next to him. In due time, the next generation stood next to Santa and posed as well.

Certainly, Santa served as a holiday harbinger each year and a cherished lawn decoration for decades upon decades. But Santa was truly something more. He was an integral part of a holiday tradition that fostered quality family time and ignited a spirit of togetherness. In hindsight, the hours spent decorating, laughing, singing, and gathering around a table to share a meal were far more priceless than any of the gifts we exchanged.

Somewhere along the way, the annual holiday tradition was lost, and so was the treasured wooden Santa. Loved ones passed away, and our family home was sold. Every year in early December, I still find myself searching the Internet for the original paper template, hoping to stumble upon it or a close replica of the wooden Santa.

This past March, on a rainy afternoon, my husband and I cleaned out our garage. I made a pile of items to donate, which included an ornate wall mirror. I decided to drop the mirror off at a local thrift shop. I removed the mirror from the car and entered the store, which was packed from floor-to-ceiling with donated goods. The clerk thanked me for the mirror, and we chatted. On my way out, I turned my head and glanced at my wall mirror one last time. Suddenly, something caught my eye in the mirror's reflection: an array of randomly displayed items on the shop's opposite wall.

What to my wondering eye should appear but an old, wooden cutout of Santa. It looked just like him! Propped against some old cardboard boxes, weathered and tattered but exactly as I remembered him, he wore a red suit, jolly expression, and green mittens with black stripes. Could it be him? I immediately walked over to the wooden cutout, turned it over, and closely examined the bottom left for my mother's inscription. It was rather faded, difficult to ascertain, but it appeared as though something had once been written there. Perhaps my maiden name, Rossi? Possibly, but it was questionable.

I began to barrage the clerk with inquiries. Where did the wooden cutout come from? How long had it been in the store? Who dropped it off? At that very moment, I realized that answers to my battery of questions did not matter. Instead, I just needed to *believe*. I purchased

Santa, brought him home, and tucked him in the attic. This year, after Thanksgiving, Santa will make an appearance. My revered family tradition from long ago will be revived.

—Patricia Ann Rossi—

40

The Many Firsts
of Christmas

*Christmas is about giving from the heart
more than giving from the store.*
~Toni Sorenson

The year I gave birth to my first child was the first time I celebrated Christmas. My husband and I hauled in an impressive, six-foot pine tree and set it up in the living room. However, the tree looked bare and forlorn, presumably having an identity crisis much like its owners. So, we splurged on a kaleidoscope of multicolored lights and glittering ornaments, but the embellishments turned out to be woefully small and scanty for a tree that large. Then someone pointed out that the ornaments would look better if they were dangled elegantly on something called ornament hangers. The final indulgence came in the form of a velvet tree skirt that completed the look while cleverly concealing a confusion of wires underneath.

Through imitation, advice and exploration, I attempted to create my own bit of the holiday. You see, having grown up in a Hindu family in India, I didn't quite know how to celebrate Christmas. But now, for my eight-month-old son, I was keen to embrace the traditions of the country he would call home.

I wanted my son to have a balanced upbringing with a rich understanding of his Indian roots and a grateful appreciation for his American life. I wanted him to enjoy Christmas just as much as Diwali and belong in both worlds with equal heart. That year, we slipped his tiny hands and feet into a Santa outfit and posed for our very first Christmas card.

When my son turned two, I began hanging stockings over the fireplace. When he hit three, I started putting gifts under the tree. At four, when he came home humming Christmas carols that he'd picked up at school, I also memorized the lyrics and tunes. Together, we discovered the aroma of gingerbread cookies and tasted the novelty of cinnamon-sprinkled cream on hot chocolate. And when we saw people emptying their pockets to the ringing of the Salvation Army bell or handing a cup of Starbucks to Santa-capped volunteers, we learnt that Christmas was as much about people as it was about things.

Step by step, year by year, I was getting the hang of Christmas and the aura of its magic. After the arrival of my second child, my enthusiasm kicked into even higher gear. *The Polar Express* became a holiday favorite. Elfis the Elf started making annual visits from the North Pole, and reading *Santa's Sleigh Is on Its Way to Ohio* grew into a Christmas Eve tradition.

When I shared, through pictures and videos, all that we did for Christmas, my family in India also started experiencing the same tingle of excitement. Their animated questions included: "We understand the cookies, but who are the carrots for?" "Wait, so the elf reports back to Santa each night?" and "Why would you wear ugly sweaters to a party?" Their questions doubled the joy of our celebration. Even though we were far apart, our hoopla and their curiosity joined us in spirit.

Festivals have the power to unite people from distant lands and distinct backgrounds. They may be rooted in different histories and religions, but they carry a universal appeal. Be it Christmas or Diwali, they are celebrations of light, hope, new beginnings, and the innate goodness of humanity. They are times when we can set aside our differences and connect purely on the values of love, charity, and respect.

In my idyllic Midwestern neighborhood, the spirit of Christmas is contagious. When one house puts up its holiday lights, the others hurriedly get out their winter gear and hanging poles. When the first Christmas tree appears at one window, new trees pop up every day until the entire street is an enchanting row of bright and bedecked trees. Ours is a diverse neighborhood. With our unique accents and varied stories of immigration, we form a microcosm of the world. Within our homes, we say our prayers in different languages, but as a community we speak the secular language of Christmas.

After living in America for two decades, I thought I had perfected the art and joy of celebrating Christmas. There was nothing left to learn. But last year, when I saw an unusually large number of houses display wreaths on their front doors, I interpreted it as an unspoken symbol of bouncing back from the pandemic. If that wreath meant virtually holding hands with my neighbors and bowing to the profoundness of a common lived experience, I wanted to be a part of that collective expression of gratitude. And with that, I put up my very first Christmas wreath!

The quarantine cookies from a summer of lockdowns also made a comeback that Christmas as people went from house to house distributing the sweet flavor of hope. I noticed that some of my neighbors had hung sparkling foam ornaments with inspirational messages from trees in their front yards. Passersby could pick one and take the cheer to their own homes. I was struck yet again by the inclusivity of the idea and participated by bringing my first community ornament home.

I anticipate that there will be many such firsts for me, and I will never truly gain mastery over a festival that keeps evolving and growing in more and more imaginative ways. I know now that there is really no set way of celebrating Christmas. Christmas is as open to new ideas and new people as our hearts are to kindness.

— Yogyata Singh Davé —

41

Eighteen Reminders

I would thank you from the bottom of my heart,
but for you my heart has no bottom.
~Author Unknown

As intertwined as the red-and-white stripes on a candy cane, my birthday and Christmas are virtually inseparable. In fact, they are so entwined that I often need to remind people that they are separate occasions. It wasn't always the greatest growing up with a birthday on Christmas Eve.

"This gift is for your birthday *and* Christmas" was a common saying as I exchanged holiday presents with friends. I'll admit I harbored some jealousy of classmates as they brought in finely decorated cupcakes or cookies to share with the class on their special day, a day that didn't occur during our winter break.

My parents made a big effort to make me feel especially cherished every December twenty-fourth. For each birthday, they gave me a music box. And it was never just any music box. In the weeks and months leading up to my birthday, my mom and dad set out on a mission, searching store after store to find a music box that held particular significance to my life that year.

On my eighth birthday, they picked out an adorable dog with floppy yellow ears that hugged the sides of its face. It resembled our Labrador, Cooper, whom we had adopted earlier that year. For my thirteenth birthday, when I was captivated by all things ocean-related, they hunted down a stunning water globe with dolphins, turtles, and an array of other sea creatures. A shiny gold violin with sparkling rhinestones was the object of choice the year I began taking violin lessons. When I was in a very girly stage, loving all things pink and proper, they selected a beautiful carousel of horses, each finely painted with floral designs.

In my first several years of life, I was wholly unimpressed with this Christmas Eve tradition my parents so thoughtfully commenced. Quick to toss the delicate music box aside, I showed far more interest in my new Barbie dolls and stuffed animals. We have a family video that illustrates as much, showing me at age three opening my Christmas Eve music box. I was quick to move on to my next gift, a Barbie convertible. My dad made a comment as I opened my music box with disinterest: "Someday, these will mean something to you." He was right.

As I grew up, I learned to appreciate the beauty of each music box. From the little girl on her wooden rocking chair that I received for my sixth birthday to the intricacy of the piano I received for my fifteenth birthday, I was mesmerized by each box. But, even more so, I delighted in the thoughtfulness of my parents as they picked out each one.

I was excited to finally unpack my collection this past year after I finally settled into a permanent home. The eighteen music boxes had been carefully packed away for almost a decade as I bounced between apartments.

As I unwrapped the newspaper that carefully cradled each one, my tears fell. I was reminded of the love and effort that went into picking out the perfect music box for me each year. They are indeed my most cherished possessions.

When people remark that it's unfortunate to have a birthday so close to Christmas, I'm quick to correct them now. It's a gift. What a joyful time of year to have entered the world. And what a blessing to have been born to parents who were so dedicated to making their little girl feel special amid the holiday hustle.

— Emily Marszalek —

42

The Gaudy Star

*A Christmas tree teaches us that we can create magic
with happiness and unity of the loved ones.*
~Author Unknown

It was our first Christmas as a married couple. I was nineteen, and he was a twenty-three-year-old seminary student. We lived in a one-bedroom apartment in St. Louis where I worked as a secretary, deferring my own college degree. We never thought we were poor. We were in love and had very few material needs.

I'd always loved snow and the holiday season. So, when the first flakes of winter fell, we bought a tree at the Rotary Club, not remembering that we would need a stand, too. When we found a tiny store still open later that day where we could pick up a stand, we also splurged on a box of nine blown-glass balls in shades of blue and silver. And then there was one more item, a cheap, gaudy star made of plastic, tinsel, and yellow lights. My first reaction was "Never!" But my new husband pleaded that we had to have something special for the top of the tree. *Special* was not the word that came to my mind. But he was so sincere that I acquiesced, with the understanding that once he'd finished school and was also employed, we'd purchase something striking and beautiful.

We brought the star home, and when it was lit, I had to admit that it cast a warm glow on our sparsely furnished living room. After the holidays, we placed it back in its box, and I silently vowed to find an alternative the next year.

The years unfolded. One by one, the blue-and-silver glass balls succumbed to two children, a cat, a dog, and several cross-country moves. Each Christmas, we carried the boxes of our ever-expanding holiday-decoration collection up from the basement. After locating the strings of lights, my husband would begin searching for the gaudy star. Only then would I remember that I still had not found a replacement.

Not that I hadn't looked. I'd given serious thought to a punched tin star at one point but never placed the order. Then one year, my best friend gave me a delicate blue glass treetop spire. It was beautiful, and she knew that blue was my favorite color. But it just didn't seem quite right, so we removed it after a couple of days and stuck the gaudy star back on top of the tree.

Perhaps it was the look of relief on our daughter's face when we removed the blue glass spire. Or maybe it was the pride-filled way our son helped his dad string the lights and crown the tree, stepping back in delighted awe as the plug was shoved into the socket. Then again, it may have been my husband's obvious fondness for the star and the memories from Christmases past that it embodied. Somehow, over the years, that star had transformed from garish to radiant.

Twenty-four years later, the star refused to shine. Upon closer inspection, we discovered that the yellow bulbs were so outdated that no replacements would fit. Here was my final opportunity. No one would have blamed me.

So, on a snowy December evening, we stopped by a tiny store that was open late for holiday shoppers. We hurried home to perform delicate surgery on our star, an internal organ transplant that only my husband and I would ever know about — except for the Band-Aid of duct tape holding the new string of lights intact inside our radiant star.

Fifty years have passed since we were newlyweds. The transplant continues to pump life into our star, adorning a tree encircled by our children, their spouses, and our grandchildren. Invariably, before admiring the old and new ornaments, their eyes raise to the tiptop, making sure the gaudy star still shines its light on us all.

— Christy L. Schwan —

43

Traditions

*There's something about a holiday that isn't all about
how much money you spend.*
~Hilarie Burton

The idea of spending my first Christmas alone in New Mexico left me downhearted, and I didn't think watching Christmas movies was going to offer much consolation. One of my co-workers mentioned that the Pueblo people had a wonderful tradition of spending Christmas Eve and all of Christmas Day celebrating the holiday. Since I had both days off from work, I decided to make a trip to a nearby village to witness their celebration. Snow was in the forecast, so I put on my heaviest jacket and warm boots before heading out the door.

It was almost midnight when I arrived, and a full moon cast the only light on the path as I followed women in flowered shawls and men in ribboned shirts into a two-hundred-year-old church. The small church filled quickly. When the service began, I felt as if I had been transported to a different country. All the prayers were in a language I didn't understand, and instead of an organ, a single flute accompanied the hymns while raspy voices kept time to the beat of native drums and rattles.

At the end of the service, everyone remained seated as a line of dancers wearing masklike headdresses, bandanas, and brightly colored vests entered and approached the altar. As the scent of bonfires drifted through the church, the dancers removed the nativity crib and the infant child within it from their place of honor near the altar and carried them out of the church, across the road and up a hill toward a small adobe house.

Sand-filled paper bags lined the way between the church and the house. Tiny candles flickered inside the bags. As the procession moved through the village streets and up the hill, people began singing songs of praise and homage to the newborn child. It was a slow and difficult climb. Fathers carried their children. The young helped the old. Understanding neither the words being sung nor how to react, I tried to blend into the crowd.

An elderly woman must have noticed my plight and took pity on me. Whispering in my ear, she explained that every year one home within the pueblo is given the privilege to host the baby Jesus for the twelve days between Christmas and Three Kings Day. That particular year, the honor belonged to her son and daughter-in-law who had a home on top of the mesa overlooking the pueblo. The woman assured me that I would be welcomed there.

Following the procession into the house, I didn't notice any every-day furniture, just church-like benches and folding chairs. Instead of predictable Christmas decorations, the ceiling was covered with brightly colored shawls, pillows and tassels, while shimmering streamers, colored lights, paper flowers and tin ornaments decorated the walls. At the far end of the room, a simple pine altar adorned with candles, potted plants and native pottery stood empty until the dancers placed the nativity crib and infant upon it. Finding an empty chair close to the door, I sat down and instinctively bowed my head.

Throughout the night and into the next morning, people bearing gifts of food, candy and flowers came to keep watch over the beloved child. When new visitors arrived, they approached the altar, sprinkled holy water on the infant in the crib, and then blessed themselves and said a silent prayer. As the night wore on, the bonfires dwindled and the candles burned out, but the infant Jesus was never alone.

Sometime during the night, I moved to one of the benches and fell asleep until the following morning when the smell of freshly brewed coffee reminded me that I hadn't eaten for more than twelve hours.

Looking across the room, I noticed the elderly woman I had met on the procession. She was serving food to a group of bare-chested dancers painted the color of the earth and wearing crocheted leggings, evergreen boughs, and antlers. Smiling, she waved me over and handed me a plate of pinto beans, crisp bacon, eggs scrambled with green chilies, and two warm tortillas. She explained that host families always provided a hearty breakfast to everyone who kept vigil throughout the night. No one was turned away, and nothing was ever asked in return. Grateful for the meal, I returned to my bench, ate, and wiped my plate clean with one of the tortillas.

After finishing their meals, each of the painted dancers picked up two sticks and, swaying from side to side, left the house. The antlers on their heads and their cautious movements mimicked the appearance of deer. Curious about where they were going, I followed.

Outside, a gentle snow had begun to fall but quickly turned into a blizzard. With snow accumulating on their bare shoulders, the dancers continued down the hill toward the plaza. Leaning on the sticks, they tilted their heads and cautiously looked off in the distance as though listening. Did they hear something no one else could? Once in the plaza, they were joined by other dancers, and together they began to perform the Deer Dance, an expression of thanks to the animal that gives its life to sustain those of the village.

The dances continued throughout the morning. As the sun radiated off the red sandstone mesa walls, the snow quickly melted, and I wished for a lighter jacket. Villagers visited with family members from near and far, exchanging stories and memories. I was invited back to the host home for a lunch of bone soup. However, feeling worn out, I declined the invitation and headed home.

All of us have traditions, but when life changes, like moving to a new place, some of our old traditions change as well. Traditions reflect how we think and how we remember. Each culture has traditions that make it unique. Growing up, I associated Christmas trees, fruitcake and Santa Claus with Christmas. In the pueblos of New Mexico, all-night vigils, dancers, and bone soup connect villagers with their origins. Observing Christmas at the pueblo that year helped me appreciate my own traditions and accept that, whether alone or in strange surroundings, celebrating Christmas can be a beautiful experience.

— Margaret Nava —

44

Pint-Size Santa

The best way to see Christmas is through
the eyes of a child.
~Author Unknown

Like most parents, my husband and I wanted our daughters to understand the true meaning of Christmas. However, we were under no illusion about what put the twinkle in their eyes in December: Santa.

Traditionally, we spent every Christmas Eve with my husband's family. The much-anticipated event each year was the grand entrance of someone playing Santa Claus. Jingling sleigh bells would announce his arrival, and then Santa would stride into the room, greeting family members along the way. He knew everyone by name and never made a mistake.

I think I was more thrilled about Santa's arrival than my daughters the year they were three and six. My heart pounded as we heard sleigh bells and Santa's "Ho, ho, ho!"

Santa entered the room shouting, "Merry Christmas!" We couldn't take our eyes off our daughters. Both little girls tugged at my arms, jumping up and down while squealing, "Santa's coming! Santa's coming!"

I looked up, and my mouth dropped open in shock. Yes, Santa was wearing the red suit. Yes, Santa was jingling the bells. But Santa was not larger than life. Santa was pint-sized, not even full-grown. I recognized our eleven-year-old nephew's face under that beard. All I could feel was disappointment that our girls weren't getting the full

Santa treatment.

After the little man in red had handed out all the gifts, he departed with much fanfare. I walked around the room, picking up wrapping paper and ribbons that were strewn everywhere. The trash bag was full, and my heart was heavy, thinking that my daughters had been short-changed.

It was getting late. We gathered our excited girls and all their presents, hugged everyone, and said our goodbyes before stepping out into the frigid night.

Winter in Rochester, New York passed, and the first warm days of spring were upon us. One day, Harry and I peeked in on our children as they played in their bedroom and overheard them re-enacting the last Christmas Eve.

"Listen," Harry said.

The girls were giggling and imitating Santa. With a pillowcase full of toys slung over her shoulder, our older daughter turned to her sister. She innocently commented, "Christmas was so much fun! Wasn't it great that Santa's son came to give out our presents?"

Harry and I looked at each other in wide-eyed surprise. We exploded into silent, shoulder-shaking laughter. Out of the mouths of babes came a lesson for us.

We had been so wrapped up in our own vision of the perfect experience for our girls that we had completely missed what we were looking for: seeing Christmas Eve through our sweet daughters' eyes.

— Terry Hans —

45

Hidden in Plain Sight

It is Christmas in the heart that puts
Christmas in the air.
~William Thomas Ellis

It was two weeks before Christmas. School was out. I was behind on the holiday preparations, but the kids were grown enough to help more around the house. They were excited. This year, they would string the lights on the outside tree without adult supervision. Was that scenario going to result in an unbridled disaster or a miraculous feat? Four siblings, all two years apart with different personalities, would embark on a task they had never done on their own. Each year, my husband encouraged them to join him to learn the ropes, but being know-it-all children, they ignored his wisdom.

It was a beautiful Saturday afternoon, just a few hours before dusk. My children retrieved the boxes of lights from the shed without fussing. I listened attentively from the kitchen. Surprisingly, they were communicating and working well together. "We have to unravel each string carefully," said Nelson, the oldest.

"We should handle one string at a time and then hang it on the tree," suggested Tamara, my second child. Everyone nodded. A plan was formulating. In pairs, they strung the lights using long sticks with hooks attached at the end.

After an hour of hard work, I served my kids lemonade. "You're doing a great job, but hurry, please. There are about ninety minutes left of daylight." They swallowed quickly and jumped back in. They had promised the neighborhood kids a tree-lighting ceremony that night. They were motivated, completely full of holiday cheer and enthusiasm, to get the job done.

I was so proud of my children. They were growing up and becoming more responsible every day. Some days, I was an overprotective momma bear, still thinking they were babies. I had to accept that they could do certain things by themselves. My husband encouraged me to relinquish more tasks to them to build their confidence and strengthen their sense of responsibility.

"Mommy, we're done, but the lights won't work." I snapped out of my thoughts. Angela was short like me. Being the elf in the house never bothered her. As a mini-me, she was sassy, spunky, independent, and outspoken. We were two peas in a pod. Apparently, she was the only one brave enough to deliver the news of defeat.

I walked outside to the sight of gloomy faces. "Don't give up. Look carefully and identify the problem."

"We can do it for our friends," Angela said as she jumped up from the patio chair and examined the first string of lights on the bottom branch. "There are no cracked or loose bulbs." Her siblings joined her. They were back on task. As I entered the house, my mother appeared with her favorite CD player. Christmas music lightened the mood.

"Thanks, Granny." Tamara flashed the widest smile. Aretha Franklin belted out "O Christmas Tree." My children giggled.

"Granny, you are so funny," announced Aaron.

With four pairs of hands working diligently, they took twenty minutes to recheck every bulb. They didn't find any loose or broken ones. My husband had assisted by holding the ladder so Nelson could examine the strings at the top. "What needs to be done next?" he prompted.

"Dad, we have to check the connections to the extension cords." My oldest child took the initiative. "Guys, sit down. I'll find it."

"We want to help," offered Aaron.

"It's fine. Get ready. Our friends will be here soon." His siblings complied reluctantly. My husband continued to work with Nelson to solve the problem. The neighborhood children were already seated on the porch, eating tuna sandwiches, waiting for the lighting of the tree.

Ten minutes later, Nelson and his father were chuckling uncontrollably. They were surrounded by a group of clapping children, including mine. "What is it?" I asked, rushing to the porch. The beauty of the illuminated lights slowed my stride.

"Mommy, I found the problem. There were two strings that were not connected in the middle of the tree," Nelson explained proudly.

"Sorry, bro. It was my job. I messed up," confessed Aaron sheepishly.

Nelson hugged his brother tightly and whispered, "It's okay."

In that moment, I knew we had chosen the correct house. We lived in a small, suburban area. Each year, the neighborhood children looked forward to the lights on our home. Most families' incomes could not support higher utility bills. My husband and I were professionals. We were blessed to be able to withstand the financial burden. We also put many smiles on young faces. Those toothy grins were the reason we decorated the front yard and porch every Christmas.

That night, the true meaning of the season was demonstrated at my home. My heart was bursting with peace and contentment.

— Abishai Ambrose —

46

Remember the Mistletoe

Mistletoe. I surmount all obstacles.
~Vanessa Diffenbaugh, The Language of Flowers

Although my family lives in basically the same geographic area of New York State, we generally don't spend a lot of time together until the holiday season, Thanksgiving through New Year's Day.

During those few weeks, along with all the decorating, cooking, shopping and gift-wrapping, we participate in one of our timeless, annual holiday traditions: family disagreements.

Every year, my mom complains that the Christmas tree my dad picked out is too big. My cousins always blame each other for burning the Christmas cookies. My uncles predictably have heated political debates. My sister and her husband dispute the best way to avoid Christmas shopping traffic. And I don't want anyone to even mention what happens each December when I'm hanging the Christmas lights on the front of my house.

But in our family, Aunt Marion has found a surefire way to temporarily settle our Yuletide skirmishes at the annual Christmas Eve lasagna dinner at her house.

"Remember the mistletoe!" Aunt Marion declares.

She's not talking about the well-known tradition of kissing under the mistletoe. Instead, she's referring to an obscure, ancient Scandinavian legend that her grandmother told her when she was a child.

According to Aunt Marion, back in the bygone days of the Vikings, the Scandinavians believed mistletoe to be the universal plant of peace. Therefore, if two enemies met in the vast, untamed Scandinavian forests and found mistletoe growing in the branches above them, they had to lay down their arms and call a truce.

"Now, think about it," Aunt Marion insists. "If the Vikings, with their swords and their shields and those awful helmets, could set aside their differences and call a truce in the presence of mistletoe, don't you think our family could at least do the same on Christmas Eve?"

And Aunt Marion always has mistletoe. It hangs on her front door, from the lamp over her dining-room table, and above her fireplace mantel. I wouldn't be surprised if she keeps some back-up mistletoe in her refrigerator. Our family needs all the help it can get.

Fortunately, Aunt Marion's mistletoe musings seem to work every year. Squabbles, disagreements, grudges and grievances are all set aside, and, for one night anyway, peace reigns in our family.

— David Hull —

The Joy of Giving

47

The Can Opener

For it is in giving that we receive.
~Saint Francis

A s I shuffled through the postcards that had arrived by return mail, one in particular caught my eye. Unlike the others listing gift requests for children, this one included a request for Ashley, the mother. She wanted a can opener.

I was angry. *How dare she ask for a gift for herself!* I thought. *We are trying to provide gifts for children, and this mother wants something for herself!*

This was my third year working with Angel Tree, a ministry of Prison Fellowship. Every Christmas, Angel Tree provided gifts for children who have one or both parents in prison. The gifts were presented in the name of the jailed parent.

Requests for gifts came from the prisoners via their chaplains. Once we received the requests, we contacted the recipient's guardian to determine their need. For families without phones, we mailed letters explaining the program, asking that they return a card listing requests and sizes.

It was such a card that I held now. Each time I thought of this mother's selfish request, I got angrier. Not having a clear idea of how to handle this case, I decided to make it a matter of prayer.

As Christmas drew closer, I began to collect the Angel Tree gifts from donors. My living room was packed. There were floor-to-ceiling, wall-to-wall boxes ready to be shipped to children who were suffering the loneliness of an absent parent.

Piled across the dining room were shopping bags filled with local deliveries. I browsed through my cards, checking off what had been received, and which gifts had been wrapped and packed. The card with the can-opener request surfaced, and I stopped to consider it.

We had purchased sweatsuits for Ashley's children and had even gotten a remote-control car for the youngest. But we did not have a can opener. I decided that I would explain to Ashley that the gifts were only for the children; adults didn't get any. She would just have to understand and learn to be less selfish.

Suddenly, I knew God was going to require more of me. He spoke to my heart and told me I was the one who was selfish. Who was I to decide whether Ashley needed a can opener? Realizing that the best way to overcome selfishness is to invest in the lives of others, I determined that I would buy the best can opener I could find for her. I didn't really want to spend the money; it was an act of repentance.

A week before Christmas, I made my rounds to almost forty families in the area. Ashley's home was my last stop.

Bracing myself, I knocked on the door. I don't know what I was expecting, but I was surprised when a bright-smiled, enthusiastic woman opened the door. Finding out who I was, she grabbed me with a big hug. "Oh!" she said. "I have the most wonderful news! My husband is getting out this week, just in time for Christmas. I'm so excited!" She laughed and did a quick-step dance in place.

I handed Ashley the gifts. I emphasized that we don't usually give gifts to adults, but we did manage to get her a can opener. I felt bitterness creeping over me as I recalled spending $24.95 of my own Christmas budget on her can opener.

She clasped her hand to her heart. "You got me the can opener? Oh, thank you!" She told me that her can opener had broken, and the only ones she could find in the store cost almost two dollars.

Two dollars? A flood of shame came over me as I realized that she had only wanted a cheap, hand-crank can opener. She was so poor that her two dollars had to go for necessities. Even a manual can opener was a luxury.

Feeling embarrassed at my misunderstanding, I explained that we had gotten an electric can opener, and I hoped that would be okay.

Mildred froze momentarily, her jaw dropping. Tears welled up as her shoulders slumped forward. She covered her face with her hands and began to laugh and cry at the same time. "Oh, you don't know! You just don't know," she cried.

Trying to compose herself, she explained that she had severe arthritis in her hands. Every time she used a can opener, she was in pain for an hour or more. Having an electric can opener was more than she had ever hoped for.

After leaving Ashley's home, I thought about my selfishness. This woman was just hoping for a cheap kitchen tool, even though a more expensive one could have relieved her pain. And I had harshly judged her.

I learned a good lesson that day. And I realized that each time I work with Angel Tree, I receive far more than I give.

— Annette Glass —

48

One Last Good Deed

Nothing else in all life is such a maker of joy
and cheer as the privilege of doing good.
~James Russell

I t was a hectic day at the office. We were coordinating Christmas gifts for hundreds of needy children, a massive undertaking. Our Angel Tree deadline had passed, and colorful parcels were being dropped off by "Angels" for distribution to the recipients. The office looked like the North Pole.

When the phone rang after closing, I hesitated. I was exhausted, and the after-hours voicemail could answer. But with the holiday coming... Sighing, I lifted the receiver. "May I help you?"

The woman's voice on the line was tremulous. "I'm looking for an Angel Tree. I'm sorry... I need to put my grandkids' names on one."

I started to direct her to one of the local organizations that might be able to assist, but she was still speaking. "They're so little. The girl is seven, and the boy is only four. They're so excited for Santa Claus. But we live on Social Security, so there just isn't anything extra."

"I'm sorry, ma'am, but our deadline has passed..."

"Their mama just dropped them off without one word," she said heavily. "We're working on getting custody, but we can barely feed them as it is. My husband's health isn't good, and we hardly know which way to turn. I saw an Angel Tree at the library and thought..." A sigh. "Well, I do thank you for..."

"Ma'am, wait!" My hand groped for my pen. "Tell me a little

about them."

The little girl loved Barbie, crafts, and books. The little boy liked dinosaurs and trucks. I also had their address. We had already made our charitable contributions for the holiday, but I showed the list to my husband.

Tom, a retired naval officer, adored Christmas. Months in advance, he had planned a huge holiday feast and spent December practicing a jolly "Ho! Ho! Ho!" for his yearly stint as Santa Claus at his office children's party. But Tom was about to have a biopsy to confirm a lymphoma diagnosis. Although the doctor was optimistic, I was concerned that my husband might not wish to undertake anything extra. But his eyes crinkled merrily. "Let's go shopping before I start chemo. I'll handle the logistics."

On our shopping day, Walmart was bustling. Tom and I sang along with the Christmas music as we headed to the toy department. "Dinosaurs dead ahead!" Tom said. He moved efficiently down the row, frowning in thought. "T-Rex, of course," he said, "This one, I think — the one that roars but has a benign expression."

While I was still trying to determine what a dinosaur's benign expression might look like, Tom was on his way to the next aisle. He peeked around the corner. "Trucks!" he called. I reached him to find his arms full. A fire truck and a dump truck joined the T-Rex in the cart, followed by various puzzles, board games, and a set of Legos. "Little kids like Legos," Tom explained seriously. He checked his list. "Books next!"

Marching along, we passed the crafts, so a jewelry-making kit and a set of art supplies joined the assortment. Tom delegated the selection of chapter books to me while he found one about construction machinery that made alarming noises and again consulted the list. "Barbies," he directed.

"Over there," I waved. Tom strode down an aisle with floor-to-ceiling fashion dolls on both sides. He came to a halt so suddenly that I nearly collided into him with the cart. "These are pretty," he said, contemplating gorgeous holiday-themed dolls. "And these are exotic... Morocco and India and... here's a mermaid and a fairy... and here is a veterinarian with her little animals... and a teacher... and — it looks like a Lady President Barbie!" My erstwhile logistics expert stood looking about helplessly, list crumpled, totally overwhelmed by the folks at Mattel.

Laughing, I added a veterinarian doll and several gowns, joking that Barbie might wish to have both a career and a night on the town. We were a very merry pair as we loaded up our car. "We can drop the gifts off after my biopsy," Tom said. His eyes twinkled at me. "And we should get some treats."

"We can get treats before we deliver the toys, so they're fresh!" I agreed.

"I'm looking forward to it," he beamed.

We chatted and planned the next morning as they prepped him for the biopsy. Then I kissed him, saying, "I'll see you in a couple of hours!"

I did see Tom a few hours later, intubated and unable to speak or open his eyes. The "lymphoma" was actually lung cancer — a massive tumor — and the doctors couldn't extubate him after the procedure. Briefly, he held my hand one last time, squeezing it with all his strength. I knew what he was telling me. "I love you, too," I told him. "I have always, always loved you." With great effort, his head nodded before he fell into a coma, and the fierce grip on my hand relaxed.

The following days were a blur. I sent for our children, and we talked to doctors, seeking some desperate hope. But there was none. And after the children had a chance to say goodbye, I knew what my next duty would be.

That Saturday, I spent the afternoon wrapping gifts. Piling them into the car, I could hear Tom's excited "I'm looking forward to it!" Then I remembered my own promise to get treats before delivering the toys. I had no treats.

Impulsively I pulled into the grocery store. I picked up candy canes, cookies, Christmas cake — but I couldn't stop. Tom loved me; he loved bringing joy; he loved Christmas. Today, I was just his instrument. I piled in a holiday dinner, along with staples to help fill empty cupboards. And hot chocolate mix — Tom always loved hot chocolate.

It wasn't far to the small house, but it was nearly dark by the time I pulled into the drive. I told the elderly lady who answered my knock that I was the response to her Angel Tree request.

"The kids are out with their grandpa," she said, "Come in."

"This needs refrigeration," I said as I handed her the first box and continued unloading.

"Oh, my goodness," she kept repeating. "Oh, my." When I had brought in the last bundle, she clasped my hand.

"It's from my husband and me," I told her warmly. "Merry Christmas!"

"Thank you," she said, with tears in her voice. "I know the Good Lord put you here at this moment for a reason."

As I drove home, I said tearfully, "You were right, honey. It was something to look forward to." The following day, I made another trip. I went to sit beside Tom and held his hand as they switched off his life support. He quietly breathed his last with me at his side.

Tom's funeral was December twenty-third. The next night, Santa's gifts were under a tree in a small house where two children needed him. It was Tom's last earthly deed, and his first as part of the eternal spirit of Christmas.

— Loreen Martin Broderick —

49

In the Spirit of Giving

You give but little when you give of your possessions.
It is when you give of yourself that you truly give.
~Kahlil Gibran

When I was ten years old, we lived in an apartment complex in the heart of West Los Angeles. Dad, Mom, and I resided in a lovely two-bedroom just off the 405 freeway. Dad was an X-ray technician and wanted to be close to the veterans' hospital where he was on call most weekends.

Every Christmas, Dad would delight in decorating the apartment. We had a tall, gorgeous tree, trimmed with tinsel, blinking lights and colorful ornaments that had been lovingly handed down from generation to generation. He dotted our patio with poinsettias and holly. A green-and-red wreath always graced our front door. And inside, discreetly placed here and there, was mistletoe. My parents always stopped under it for a Christmas smooch.

As an only child, I knew there would be lots of beautiful presents under the tree Christmas morning. The wrapped presents I received from my parents were the most beautiful I'd ever seen. I always admired my dad and his ability to wrap gifts with patience, precision, and an innate sense and flair for beauty.

I knew this Christmas would be special and couldn't wait to open the gifts I'd requested: a Barbie sports car and Barbie Dream House.

Christmas morning came, and I wasn't disappointed. There were tons of gifts under the tree, and I was in awe. Gold, silver, red and green peeked out from under the tree with different ribbons tied on and decorations on top. Each one looked like a work of art. There was a large gift wrapped in a gold box with a silky white bow on the couch that I knew was for my mom. It was a pretty red coat she'd wanted.

I could hear my mom puttering in the kitchen, and smell the coffee percolating on the stove, and my excitement grew. "Kim, go sit on the couch. Daddy will be here in a few minutes," my mom instructed. I sat on the couch and waited. I glanced at the clock. Eight o'clock. My parents always had their coffee before we dug in and began opening our gifts, but usually we would start by 7:30.

"Where is Dad?" I asked as my mom came in with a tray of coffee, cups, cream and sugar.

She sat on the couch next to me. "Be patient, hon."

Shortly, I heard a noise and anxiously watched the front door. The knob turned, and in came my dad. He looked exhausted. His pants were dirty, and it looked like he had been kneeling in mud. "I'll need plenty of that coffee," he said as he dragged himself through the front door. I looked at my mom, but she was watching my dad with a look of pride.

"I am going to go clean up, and then we can get started," he answered. As he walked toward the bedroom, he leaned down and gave me a kiss on the forehead.

Years later, I found out what my dad had been up to that Christmas morning. Our neighbor, Dorrie, had lost her husband in a traffic accident the week before. She and her husband had bought bikes for their two young sons, and my dad offered to put them together for her so her little boys could have some joy on Christmas. It took him hours, he confessed, as they were boxed in pieces. I remember he'd come home exhausted. He wasn't that mechanical, so I can imagine the challenge he'd faced. But being the sweetest man on earth, he swore he'd get those bikes put together.

I look back on that Christmas Day and remember watching Tommy and Jeff ride their shiny new bikes all around the complex with smiles on their faces even though they'd just lost their father.

To this day, tears spring to my eyes thinking of it. I learned a lot

The Joy of Giving |

that beautiful Christmas Day. My dad taught me that the holidays weren't about the receiving of presents, or even about giving material gifts. I learned the best gift we can give is ourselves. By lending a hand, my dad was lending a piece of his heart.

— Kimberly Kimmel —

50

A Little Less Alone

Without a sense of caring, there can
be no sense of community.
~Anthony J. D'Angelo

While attending Rice University in Houston, I happened to meet the director of the Rice Student Volunteer Program (RSVP), and he challenged me to get involved in one of the many opportunities available. I picked the juvenile court volunteer program. I first participated in a weekend of training, and then I was paired with a girl at the juvenile detention center.

Julie was about thirteen years old. I never knew the specifics of why she was there, but she seemed like any other teen to me. I would visit her once a week in a little room made of see-through panels.

As more of an introvert than extrovert, I had initially been worried that we would spend our time sitting in awkward silence. However, this did not happen as she was quite chatty and obviously thrilled to have company. I heard from the director of the center that I was her sole visitor. For whatever reason (maybe distance, estrangement, or lack of transportation on the part of her family), she was completely alone.

As it was almost Christmas, I knew this would likely be a difficult time for her and the others in the center. From the training program, I knew that I wasn't allowed to bring gifts to her, but I thought that a card might be okay.

I had been making my own Christmas cards, a new design for every year, since eighth grade. It had started when I was sick for a week and unable to attend school. My brilliant mom had suggested that I use the time to make some Christmas cards.

Back at school before Christmas break, I handed out these cards to everyone in my class, and they were a big hit. It expanded to quite a production, and I made about 125 cards every year. I would start planning my card for the next year as soon as Christmas was over.

At the detention center, I asked the director if I could give a card to each of the children staying at the facility, and she agreed. I had expected to just hand my eighty cards over to the director, but she surprised me by asking, "So, when do you want to come give these out?" My inner voice spoke immediately and loudly. *Wow, I don't really! I mean, I want the kids to have them, but I don't want to hand them out myself.*

Thankfully, I overruled this stupid, scared voice and arranged a night when I could go and give out the cards. This turned out to be a beautiful time of reaching out to these lonely, scared, tough-on-the-outside kids.

I was allowed to go from room to room and personally deliver a card to each child. Many remarked that this was the only handmade card they had ever received. Most of them smiled at me and said a gracious, "Thank you." Some even wanted to chat for a while.

I was so grateful that I had overcome my fear to let these kids know that someone was thinking about them and cared about them. It was one of the purest celebrations of Christmas that I have ever experienced. I can't remember what I received as gifts from family or friends that year, but I remember what made me the happiest, and it was the interaction with those lonely, grateful kids.

— Margaret Lea —

51

My Christmas Angel

Love and kindness are never wasted. They always
make a difference. They bless the one who receives
them, and they bless you, the giver.
~Barbara De Angelis

It was Friday, December 23, 1994, and I still didn't have my shopping done. It wasn't like I hadn't tried, but this Christmas season had been even crazier than usual.

My mother suffered from emphysema. She was on oxygen day and night and unable to live alone and care for herself. I, being the oldest of her children, had decided — quite reluctantly, I'm ashamed to admit — to pack up my family, close our home, and move in with Momma.

I must admit I was feeling sorry for myself that day in December. It wasn't that I didn't want to care for my mother, but the selfish side of me focused on what we'd lose as a family — all those wonderful family traditions my husband and I had started for our little girls — rather than on what we'd gain with my ailing mother. Self-centered, you say? Of course, you're right, but I didn't see it that way then. I didn't know that we had mere months left before Momma succumbed to the emphysema. I desperately needed a wake-up call, and I believe God lovingly intervened in the form of a Christmas angel.

With several gifts to buy, I bundled up my three little girls — LeeAnna, who was eleven, Karissa, who was only six, and our sweet Lexi, who was just a little over a year old — and we headed to Hills department store. I hoped to get what I needed and get out quickly.

I strapped Lexi into her stroller and headed for the store, walking briskly and with purpose while my older girls struggled to keep up. Once inside, I heard my middle daughter ask, "Mommy, can I get a toy?"

"Karissa, it's two days until Christmas," her sister answered even before I could. "Don't ask Mom to buy you a toy. You'll get lots of toys on Christmas morning."

"She's right, Karissa," I snapped impatiently. The last thing I wanted to deal with right then was a whiny child begging for a toy just days before she would be flooded with more toys than she could imagine.

The store was packed with shoppers just like me, rushed and frantic to find those last-minute gifts. LeeAnna and Karissa could barely keep up with me as I raced down one aisle and zoomed up the next.

"Excuse me, ma'am…"

I hate to admit that I almost ignored the speaker as I searched the shelves for a gift for my sister. Then I heard him again as I felt my oldest daughter tugging on my coat. "Excuse me, ma'am. Would you mind if I borrow your little one here?"

There in front of me was a kind old man with a white beard and a matching tuft of hair. Dressed in a worn overcoat and brown slacks, he looked a little like Santa as he bent over my daughter's stroller, with his eyes twinkling and a huge smile on his face.

"Pardon me?" I asked, sure I hadn't heard the gentleman correctly.

Patiently, he repeated his request. "I'd like to borrow your little girl." Sensing my concern and seeing a look of puzzlement, even fear, on my face, he continued, "My only daughter died in an accident a few years ago, and my dear wife passed away last year. I'm all alone this Christmas. Besides my family, what I miss most during the holidays is the chance to give a little something to the people who mean the most to me."

He paused, and then continued, "I was hoping you might allow me to give your little girl a small toy." Seeing my other two daughters standing close by, the old gentleman said to them, "You could all share it. Would that be okay?"

My little girls turned to me with hopeful looks on their faces.

Normally, I would have been overly cautious and perhaps even ignored this old man. After all, a mother can't be too careful. Something stirred in my heart, though, and I replied softly, "Of course you may, sir."

With a sigh of relief, he led us to the stuffed-animal aisle. After looking diligently, he selected a small, unassuming brown teddy bear, and we followed him to the checkout. He took out a few dollars from a worn leather wallet and paid for his gift. Out in the mall, he stopped and bent over to talk directly to my littlest daughter. "Here you go, sweetheart," he said, his eyes radiating pure joy as he handed the bear to little Lexi. "I hope you like it. Just don't forget to share it with your sisters."

Lexi hugged the bear to her chest. With tears in my eyes, I started to whisper my thanks, but the kind gentleman stopped me and simply said, "No, thank you. Thank you for letting this old man remember the joy that giving brings." He waved goodbye and was soon lost in the crowd.

I stood there in the middle of a crowd of people, stunned while my little girls beamed. We walked the mall that December day as I finished my shopping, hoping to catch a glimpse of that sweet, old man, but we never saw him again.

That day, my selfish, me-first attitude changed as that precious stranger's actions spoke directly to my heart. It was as if I heard God Himself speaking. "Sherry, you have forgotten what Christmas is about. It's about putting others first and giving the gift of your love. I gave My Son so that you might have life. This old man — my messenger — gave a gift from his heart to your little girls. Now, go and do likewise. Give your mother the gift of your time and your care."

And that's exactly what I did. I spent that Christmas showing my love to my precious momma. We still enjoyed our Christmas traditions, but that year they were extra special. On Christmas night, we loaded up Momma's portable oxygen tank in our van, grabbed some steaming hot chocolate from a local convenience store, and drove through the local Christmas light display. We sang "The Twelve Days of Christmas," trying to finish each verse before we drove past the next part of the display. We laughed until our sides hurt. It was definitely a Christmas to remember.

Some would say my girls and I met a nice, lonely, old man that day in the mall. I'm not convinced that's true. I believe we met an angel — be it a heavenly messenger or a mere mortal whom God used in angelic ways — whose job was to teach this young mother to treasure the time with her own mother.

Twenty-four years later, I still have that little teddy bear, and it never fails to remind me of the important lesson our Christmas angel taught me many years ago.

— Sherry Furnish —

Shopping with Mom

An effort made for the happiness of
others lifts us above ourselves.
~Lydia M. Child

I wondered how I was going to handle the holiday. I sat at my desk staring at the collage of my family that I'd tucked under the tall counter. Three weeks to Christmas, and all I wanted to do was crawl into bed and let the season and all its music and merriment pass me by. My mother had passed two months before and my heart was broken.

I took a sip of my coffee, trying to make the lump in my throat disappear.

She was not only my mother but my closest friend, confidante, ally, gentle critic, spiritual mentor, and teacher. She was my model of femininity, elegance, grace, beauty, strength, warmth, dignity, courage, total selflessness, and unwavering faith. And she was gone.

All I could do was put on the mask that said I was coping. But I wasn't. I didn't know how I was going to go through life without calling Mom and sharing my little victories. She had loved to hear about my life — the activities of her grandsons whom she loved so dearly, the successes my husband achieved in his career. She was endlessly filled with accolades, advice and unconditional love, and her absence left my life and my heart painfully and overwhelmingly hollow.

"Peggy, I have an idea for Christmas, and I need your help." My boss's voice startled me, and I looked up to see her leaning over the tall counter, her eyes bright with excitement. She leaned forward and said quietly, "I want to give everyone gift baskets for Christmas, and I want you to shop for them." She had no idea how unexcited I was about this. Maybe I could just pick up some pre-made gift baskets at Costco.

"I want each one to be personalized, not just any old generic basket." Well, there went my Costco idea. "I want each basket to represent the individual's taste, so they will be thrilled when they open it. I've budgeted $150 per employee."

Wow! That was a lot of shopping for twenty-three employees! I started to feel the pressure in my chest. When was I going to get this done? She must have read my mind, because she said, "You can do this on company time. I just want them ready by Christmas."

I realized this was just the distraction I needed. "Cheryl, that's so generous of you. I'm happy to help," I said, oh-so-ready to grab my purse and run out the door to get started.

"Great!" With a smile, she walked away.

How would I figure out everyone's taste and special interests? A personal survey would help me get to know everyone well enough to buy gifts for them. I grabbed my pen and wrote questions that would give me insight into their interests — sports, hobbies, books, food, etc. I was already having fun. Maybe there was some hope for me.

I printed the surveys and handed them to curious co-workers. "Just fill out the forms. This is not the time of year to ask too many questions." I winked at them playfully. The joy was beginning and it continued to expand as I shopped for items that would delight them. Each day for two weeks, my joy grew every time I found the perfect gift for a co-worker. It felt like I was being guided to each one.

The shopping was so easy that I felt like I was shopping with my wise mother again. It seemed like she was there with me, helping me find the just-right gift for each person. And I was so busy that I had stopped drowning in sorrow.

"Well, Mom," I said out loud, "next up is Dave, the former Marine who has a passion for wristwatches. I'm thinking we could add a nice military watch to his collection — something meaningful, as he is very proud of his service and his country. What do you think?" I headed to my friend's military surplus store. I walked in with the hopes that Murray would have what I envisioned at a price within budget. When I told him what I was looking for, he walked me over to a display case that housed a beautiful watch with a Marine insignia faceplate. This treasure was not only in the budget but also on sale. Perfect.

Next, I headed to the mall where I was saddened to discover a favorite store was closing its doors soon. For sentimental reasons, I walked inside for one last browse. A few steps in, I noticed a beautiful cherrywood watch display case, designed to contain six watches and intended to fit on a bedroom dresser. It was on sale, too. My heart nearly burst with excitement.

As the day of the Christmas celebration grew closer, I needed to locate twenty-three baskets in similar sizes. What store would carry baskets that were inexpensive, quality-made, similar in size, and large enough to contain all these different sized items? Then it hit me! Years earlier, my shopping-savvy mother had introduced me to a fantastic designer wholesale warehouse not too far from my home. I drove there expecting that what I needed would be waiting for me, since nothing on this odyssey had been disappointing. And there they were — twenty-three baskets, identical except that twelve were red and eleven were green, just waiting to be filled with Christmas joy! I grabbed some rolls of cellophane and festive plaid ribbon as well. I couldn't wait to see my co-workers' faces! I hurried home to fill the baskets.

When the day arrived to deliver the baskets I felt like a kid again. I arrived early so that I could place a basket on each person's desk, making it the first thing they saw. From my desk, I nonchalantly greeted them as they walked through the door, as if it were any other Thursday, and then giggled as I heard each reaction. I loved the glee from Stacy as she unwrapped the vintage *Star Wars* glasses in her basket, from Sarah when she saw the *I Love Lucy* memorabilia, and from Elizabeth when she lifted out the lovely porcelain box with the dolphin.

But it was Dave whose reaction touches my heart to this day. The former Marine walked over to my desk with tears in his eyes, with the military-faced wristwatch already strapped to his arm and holding the display case like a child clutching a beloved teddy bear. "Peggy, it doesn't matter what Lupe or anyone else in my family gives me. My Christmas is already complete," he told me. Overwhelmed with emotion, I smiled at him as he nodded and walked back to his desk.

Amazing. This holiday season had begun as the darkest and emptiest of my life, but now it was filled with warmth and joy. And I felt like my mother had been with me the whole time.

— Peggy Ricks —

Spreading Joy

*It's not how much we give but how
much love we put into giving.*
~Mother Teresa

This past Christmas season began for me as usual on the day after Thanksgiving, Black Friday. My mom, sister, and I had gotten up early to go shopping. As we were driving out of a store parking lot, we caught sight of a dreadfully thin woman sitting on a walker. She was clearly homeless, with bird feathers stuck into her filthy gray hair, and a dirty yellow raincoat.

That homeless woman got us thinking about what Christmas would be like for someone who has no place to call home. With no family to turn to and certainly no presents to open on Christmas morning, these people have nothing to look forward to but the cold and lonely place where they choose to camp. Even though we live in sunny California, the temperature can still dip below freezing on winter nights. Where would this woman sleep when the sun went down?

Sadly, homeless people are a common sight in our town. On our way home, we passed countless people pushing shopping carts overflowing with their belongings and people standing in the center dividers of roads holding cardboard signs with "Just Hungry" written on them.

The next day, my mom had a great idea. While we were out Christmas shopping, we purchased some blue tins of sugar cookies and a few boxes of candy canes. When we got home, I helped my mom carefully tie each tin with a festive red ribbon and tape a candy cane on top. Next, we wrote "Call 211 for Help" on index cards and taped the notes to the bottoms of the tins. "Not only will we be spreading Christmas cheer, but now the homeless people will have a number to call that can get them the help they need," my mom explained as we worked.

We put all the tins in the car and, whenever we went for a drive, we searched the streets for individuals down on their luck. Usually, the streets are bustling with people lugging sacks of bottles and cans and carrying sleeping bags, but somehow when you are looking for something, it always seems to disappear. Eventually, we found the woman in the Lowe's parking lot. She gratefully took the tin and whispered, "Thank you, ma'am" as my mom handed her the cookies. As we wished her Merry Christmas and drove off, the haunted look of her hollow eyes still seemed to follow us.

Over the weeks leading up to Christmas, my mom and I continued to hand out the tins to spread a bit of holiday spirit to those who clearly had none. We saw one young man sleeping on the ground next to a Starbucks coffee shop. I think homeless people sleep during the day to avoid having to sleep out in the open at night. My mom quickly got out of the car and placed a tin beside the young man. Hopefully, when he woke up, he found the tin and used a phone to call the helpline.

A couple of days before Christmas, we were driving around with our final tin but could not find anyone to give the gift to. As we started to turn back home, we spotted a police car parked at a deli. My mom and I walked in with the last tin, and after peeling off the "Call 211" index card I gave the cookies to a police officer who sat eating lunch with an older gentleman. The officer beamed when I handed him the present and said, "Merry Christmas." I had clearly made his day!

As my family and I exchanged gifts on Christmas morning, we were surrounded by love, joy, and happiness. We are so fortunate and blessed to have all the luxuries that we do, and Christmastime makes us realize how truly lucky we are. My mom and I were glad that we were able to possibly send a ray of hope to people without homes to live in, beds to sleep in, and families who care about them. After all, the joy of giving is what the spirit of Christmas is all about.

—Baylie Jett Mills—

Because We Get To

If you want to experience the true meaning of
Christmas, give something to someone who
can offer nothing in return.
~Toni Sorenson

I didn't grow up with much so I overcompensated for my children at Christmas. I knew what it felt like to wake up on Christmas morning and find very few gifts under the tree. Instead, for my children, I would pore over their Santa letters to make sure nothing was overlooked. But one Christmas, my son, Darku, bought the gift I forgot.

Each year, our Department of Human Services has an angel tree. When Darku was ten, we decided to start a new family tradition by selecting a child from the tree. The DHS crew made handcrafted wooden ornaments with each of the kids' ages, genders, and preferred gifts listed. Darku was so excited the day we got ours—a little boy his own age. I, on the other hand, wondered when I would find the time to shop for one more. I didn't need to worry, though. Darku had it all planned out.

Two weeks before the big day, we headed to the big-box store. Scouring the parking lot for a spot, waiting for a cart to be returned since all were being used, and generally dodging other shoppers did not put me in the holiday mood. But Darku wasn't deterred. He was on a mission. Somewhere deep in his heart, Darku knew that he was responsible for making it a merry Christmas for that boy his own age.

I checked the things off the list. Underwear and socks. "No, Mom. You can't get the plain ones. He'd like these SpongeBob ones. I just know he would." I had to smile. My son had envisioned the child we had never met, and he knew exactly what he would like. Same story with sweatpants and a hoodie.

When we went by the candy aisle, he reminded me that the child needed a stocking and he knew just the candy to fill it.

On to the toy section. Darku had memorized the list. Not knowing how much people had in their budgets for helping a child, the DHS had graciously listed wants from many price ranges. I was pulling for the lower end as I still had a lot of necessary gifts to buy for my two. "How about a puzzle?" I asked. "Says here he likes puzzles and model airplanes."

Darku just shook his head and continued his mission. He marched down the aisle, not looking to either side. There it was — a bicycle. All I could see was the price tag. It was going to throw a kink in my Christmas budget. I started to protest until I saw his face. "This is it," he said. "This is the bike he needs."

He put up the kickstand and started to wheel it to the checkout. I did some mental math and refocusing. I could cut a gift off each of my kids' lists to help cover the cost.

From the back of the store to the front, he wheeled that bike with a never-faltering smile. At the checkout, the man in front of us asked, "Are you getting a new bike?"

"Not me," Darku replied. "It's for my friend. He needs a bike for Christmas."

"He's lucky to have a friend like you to give him such a nice gift," the stranger replied.

Darku shook his head. "Naw, I'm the lucky one because I'm able to give it."

I did my best to cover up the tears that were welling up in my eyes as we paid for our purchases. The cashier probably thought I was emotional over the total. She didn't know I had just received the best

Christmas gift of all. Through my son's generosity, I was reminded of how we should all give — not because we must but because we are lucky enough to get to.

— Christine Jarmola —

55

The Kindness Project

Christmas is the spirit of giving
without a thought of getting.
~Thomas S. Monson

Until a few years ago, Christmas gift-giving in our house was over the top. Festively wrapped treasures used to spill from under the tree and well into the living room. And though we felt grateful that we were able to fill the wish list for our five children, it became clear that we were missing the real meaning of the holiday.

What changed? Well, a few weeks before Christmas, our local paper ran an article about a woman who had helped a homeless man. Instead of handing over money, she registered him in a two-day course that taught him how to drive a forklift and work in a warehouse. She helped set him up with temporary living quarters and gave him a food card to supplement his groceries. Within three weeks, this man had a job. And within two months, he was no longer homeless.

We realized her generosity was no simple random act of kindness. It took a lot of time, resources, and money to put it all together. But what if this could be done on a simpler scale? And what if it were encouraged from our own home? My husband and I found this article so inspiring that we felt moved to adopt it and use it with our grown children. As young adults, they had neither the resources nor the time to devote to this type of service. But what if they were given what they needed and the insight to motivate them? It was our hope that, individually, they could somehow make a difference.

That year, each child received just one gift and an envelope containing one hundred dollars and this letter:

> *Our gift to you this Christmas is cash — but it has to be used on a random act of kindness. It is your choice, as long as the recipient is in need. It can be used to buy materials, resources or even pay your wage. Some suggestions: donate some time at the food bank or a shelter; help a homeless person, refugee or needy family; or be creative by donating your skills. You have a year to decide. Enjoy the joy of giving!*

Over the next few months, we witnessed some remarkable outcomes. And not one of our children went for the obvious suggestions we had provided.

Our oldest son, an actor and web designer, created a demo reel for a needy artist, free of charge. Soon after it was sent out, this actor had employment.

Our second son had had a storage unit full of freeze-dried food. Most of the products had a twenty-year shelf life. When Bohol, an island province in the Philippines, was devastated by a major earthquake, he contacted the relief fund and donated the entire lot. He later received a letter stating that his generosity had helped feed many families.

Our daughter purchased wool with her gift money and knitted scarves and tuques for several homeless people over the next several months.

Our next son, a musician, gave piano lessons free of charge to a boy whose single mother could not afford to pay for them.

And our youngest son, a plumber, donated five hours of free service to a women's shelter.

Not only did all these recipients benefit, but doing these random acts of kindness brought joy to each of our children. And, for us, that was the greatest gift of all.

— Jane Cassie —

56

A Lesson in Sharing

If you really are thankful, what do you do? You share.
~W. Clement Stone

After my kids' dad and I separated, I was broke. I didn't have enough money to buy food let alone decent Christmas presents for my four children. It was a sad and depressing time.

My oldest daughter, age ten at the time, was the only one who understood a little of my struggles. She hugged me and said it would be okay. I scrounged around the house, sold what I could, and then shopped at consignment shops. For the first time in my children's lives, they wouldn't get anything special for the holidays. I couldn't afford even gift wrap, so I wrapped what little I had for them in plastic grocery bags.

The kids drew a tree on a big cardboard box, which we cut out and taped to the wall. We made decorations from leaves and pinecones and cut snowflakes from paper. Glitter was our best friend. As Christmas closed in, I pawned my wedding ring. We were getting a divorce anyway and helping the kids make the transition was more important to me.

Christmas Eve came, and we drove around looking at lights and admiring every house. Occasionally, I would shout with excitement, "Look, there goes Santa!" and the kids began copying me. "Mommy, look, there he goes!" they'd shout, pointing to the sky and laughing gleefully.

We went home and listened to holiday carols, singing "Jingle Bells" and other popular Christmas songs as loud as we could. The kids had chocolate cookies and milk, and then scurried off to bed in anticipation. Once they were asleep, I pulled the bag of gifts from the trunk of my car and went to bed for a few hours just in case the kids woke up. When I got up at about 4:00 A.M. to place the presents under our "tree," there were two black garbage bags of toys with a note from my ten-year-old:

Dear Santa,
We know many kids don't have anything, and we have all we need.
Please take these toys and give to those who don't have anything.
P.S. You don't have to leave us presents.

All the children had signed it. Even the two-year-old had scribbled on it. I bawled like a baby. What a sweet, heartfelt, grown-up thing my children did. I had never felt so sad, yet proud. I went through the bags, expecting to find old items like dolls with tattered hair or books that the little one had scribbled on. But, no, they had put their favorite items in there — my daughter's dolphins, my son's new basketball, my other daughter's drawing books, pens, and coloring books. They even threw in some toys my two-year-old used frequently.

I knew I couldn't afford to replace the items, but I couldn't put the items back in their rooms after their heartfelt gesture of kindness. I dragged the bags to the garage and hid them under tarps to take to the consignment shop later.

That Christmas ended up being one of my favorites because I realized my kids were the kind souls that I had hoped they would be. I learned from them that it's what's in your heart that matters, not the stuff you have.

— Pam Lindenau —

57

Christmas Present, Christmas Past

Dwell on the beauty of life. Watch the stars
and see yourself running with them.
~Marcus Aurelius, Meditations

"Silver Bells" played on the radio and I sang along. On the two-lane road in front of me, I could see only a handful of cars. Everyone, it seemed, was already where they needed to be at 4:00 in the afternoon on this Christmas Eve.

Minutes before, I'd pulled out of my sister's driveway after spending most of the day celebrating the holiday. Being with my family, the best people I've ever known, always makes me get teary eyed. That day, my brother had limped in wearing his signature cowboy boots. He'd suffered an ankle injury that would likely lead to surgery, but even that wasn't enough for him to give up his boots. My sister, all glittery in red and green, was the embodiment of the season. When she laughed, it felt as if the walls around her rejoiced. When she smiled, it felt like you were being hugged.

I had never felt luckier, but I had never wanted to leave more.

What waited for me less than five miles away was the Little Free Pantry, a movement started by an Arkansas woman who'd taken the idea of the Little Free Library and turned it on its head.

The idea was simple. Take all the food you need. Or leave all the food you can.

I'd fallen in love with the idea, donating often. On my birthday, I'd filled the pantry to the brim. It stood next to a busy convenience store on the main road in my little town of approximately 6,000 people. I didn't usually see anyone while I dropped off food, but I'd often drive back by, and the pantry would be empty.

Now it was Christmas Eve, and in the back of my car were bags of groceries. I had the idea that I'd stack the cans of vegetables, the jars of spaghetti sauce, the pasta, French bread, and all the rest, and maybe someone would stop by that night and feel the love of Christmas.

What I didn't expect was that there would be people waiting in the parking lot. But there they were, with the engines off on their cars and trucks, and the cold seeping in.

As I unloaded what I'd brought, several people got out and stood behind me while I filled the pantry.

A woman in a plaid flannel shirt, her auburn hair streaked with gray, approached me. "Do you have a can of tomato sauce?" she asked. My heart sank. I didn't. I did have a can of tomatoes, but that was not quite the same thing.

I offered it to her anyway. As she reached for it, she said, "I took my nephews in recently." She waved her hand. "Trouble at home. I have deer meat at home, but not much, so I thought I'd stretch it by making chili."

"I have other things," I said. I tried to hand the woman the sack I hadn't yet unloaded. "Here," I said. "Take this."

She shook her head. "Other people need it more," she said and turned to walk to her car.

Her kindness broke my heart.

After that, an older man walked up with a hitch in his step and his gray hair combed straight back and falling on his shoulders. "Any soup?" he asked, and I handed over the three cans of Campbell's I'd brought.

"God bless," he said.

When I'd finished unpacking the rest of the groceries and gotten back in my car, three more people approached the pantry.

I hadn't brought enough.

I drove to the closest market and bought fifty dollars' worth of food. I went back, filled the now-empty pantry, and started home. But something told me I wasn't finished. I drove back to the market just before it closed and loaded my cart again. Instead of heading to the pantry, I went home. I had a stash of presents on hand — costume jewelry, scarves, hand lotion, knit caps, gloves. I also had a basket of small toys I'd gathered throughout the year when I'd gotten kids' meals for lunch.

I took it all and raced to the pantry, which again, in that short time, had been emptied. A few seconds later, a woman in her thirties pulled up beside me in a car that rattled when it ran. It choked when she shut off the engine.

The sky was black by then, and the first stars glimmered.

I worked fast. In the back seat of her car were two kids in car seats. The light from the parking lot was bright enough that I could see the color of their hair and the superheroes on their pajamas.

The woman stepped out of the car as I shelved the last jar of spaghetti sauce. "Hello," she said.

I turned to face her. She had a look I recognized — not panic exactly, but that emotion beyond despair when one is close to giving up.

"It's been a hard year," she said.

"I'm so sorry."

"I've never come here before, but, you know, I tried to buy a little Christmas for them," she said, nodding toward her car. "And I got in a mess."

"I have a few things," I said. "Enough to get you through a few days." I wanted to tell her something that mattered, but I couldn't think what. "I don't know how you feel," I said, "but I know what it's like to have hard times."

I was thinking of my years as a single mom and how I'd had to plan carefully to make Christmas happen. The layaways. The scrimping on my food budget. I was thinking about Christmas the year my dad quit his unbearable job. I was thinking about our church Christmas play that year. Someone had bagged up hard candy, nuts, a Hershey bar, and an orange, and every child had gotten one.

There were other years when I received much more, but when I think of Christmas, it's always that one. The smell of that orange mixed with the scent of milk chocolate — it was heaven.

When she didn't answer, I said, "I have a few gifts too. Not much, but maybe something for their stockings. Something for you."

She sighed then, relieved. "You don't know what this means to me."

I touched her arm, feeling the roughness of her corduroy jacket. "You don't know what this means to *me*," I said. "You've given me the perfect Christmas."

On my drive home, I felt a million things, but the biggest emotion was gratitude — not merely for giving but for knowing how it felt to go without, to wonder if things would ever get better. While I hated it at the time, it was the thing that made me want to give now.

I live on a country road, so dark that the night sky gets to show off. I sat in my car once I got home, not ready for the day to end. I looked up. The stars were things of wonder. The stars were guiding lights.

— Marla Cantrell —

Chapter
6

Tales of the Tree

58

The Special Gift

Two souls with but a single thought;
two hearts that beat as one.
~John Keats

Every Christmas, my sisters and I would wait for that one special present to show up under the tree. Sometimes, we saw it arrive; other times, it would just appear. It was not a present for any of us children. It was from my father to my mother, and he did it every year.

The actual gift was not what we looked forward to. Sometimes, it was something special my mother wanted or a pretty bauble my father had found that he knew she would like. Occasionally, it fell into the useful category. The special part was the package itself.

My father was not the best gift wrapper. The paper was often wrinkled and the tape crooked. What he put on top of the gift was what we always looked forward to seeing. He would decorate the package with a message of love for our mother.

Christmas was always a big deal in our house. The tree, the decorations, the food and stockings—my parents loved the holiday. For some reason, my sisters and I never made the connection as to why until after they had passed.

My parents got married fifty-eight days after they met. Their anniversary was February twentieth. Doing the math, that means they met on Christmas Day or Christmas Eve depending on if you count their wedding day or not.

My father was a doctor, and my mother was a nurse. They were working in the same hospital. Neither had family in the city where they worked. They ended up working the holiday. They met and, after a whirlwind romance, got married. They were together fifty-three years until his death. He was in hospice as my sisters and I were taking my mom to an Alzheimer's facility to live. His last words to her as he held her hand were: "Fifty-three years." He carried a photo of her in her wedding dress in his wallet every day. We framed it and buried it with him when he passed. They showed us what love was.

Every year, he made his special package. One year, there was a small brass kettle filled with pennies. There was also a note saying she was the prize at the end of the rainbow. Another time, there were two little plastic Native American dolls with the sign, "To my squaw from her brave." (Funny since we are part Native American.) Our favorite was probably the row of four angels that was across the top of the box. On the backs of their wings were the simple words, "To Phyl, Love Don."

Some years, he really had to stretch his imagination. I don't recall the message that accompanied the walrus in a plaid coat and top hat. Trolleys, brass trains, a doctor, and more adorned packages year after year.

How do I remember all these gifts? Each year as we decorated, we placed ornaments on the tree that had been on packages in past years. They weren't just cute little items. They were new Christmas tree ornaments for my mother. She loved her tree, and they loved each other. Our tree was decorated with their love.

As my father's health was failing, he had us bring out the Christmas decorations and divide them up between us. He got joy from seeing which ones we chose.

Each year as we decorate our trees, we are reminded of our parents and the love they felt for each other from that first season when they met. We saw that expressed every year on top of the special gift from my father to the woman he loved.

— Traci E. Langston —

59

The Legend of the Spiders

Don't get your tinsel in a tangle.
~Author Unknown

"**B**ugs, Gamma," my two-year-old grandson squealed as he pointed his tiny finger up toward the eleven-foot vaulted ceiling. Maze loved finding bugs, so I wasn't overly concerned by his excitement.

Looking up from addressing a last-minute Christmas card, I tried to appease him. "Just a minute, honey."

But Maze wasn't giving up. His dark brown eyes were as big as saucers while he pleaded, "Bugs, Gamma! Look! Bugs!"

I glanced up to where he was pointing and gasped in shock. "Oh, my goodness, Maze!"

They weren't bugs. They were spiders — hundreds of itty-bitty black spiders covering the white ceiling! Not wanting to harm the little guys, I put the extension tubes and wand on the vacuum hose and gently sucked the spiders up one by one. Half an hour later, we took the vacuum outside and freed our little friends far away from the house.

I was surprised at the great number of spiders we'd captured since I'd cleaned the house thoroughly before putting up our Christmas decorations. I assumed they must have been scared out of their hiding places with the onslaught of deep cleaning.

When my son stopped by for a visit the following night, I noticed him squinting at the very top of our twinkling Christmas tree. He stood up and walked over to take a closer look before screeching, "Spiders! Mom, spiders are completely covering your angel!"

The multi-hued glow of the tree lights from beneath the angel's gown created a spectacular backdrop for the tiny creatures. As much as I would have loved to have stood and marveled at the awe-inspiring sight, Jeff quickly quelled that dream.

Grabbing a stepladder from the garage, he climbed up and removed the angel from the treetop. We counted thirty tiny spiders covering her white satin gown. We took the angel outside and gently brushed the critters off.

There were spiders on the branches as well, but we decided to leave them until they eventually made their way to the walls or ceiling.

My son guessed they'd most likely been nesting in the tree when we cut it down at the neighbor's tree farm. Once stimulated by the lights and warmth, they emerged from hibernation into our living room.

Maze and I honestly loved finding all the little spiders. They added a bit of unexpected joy to our Christmas. Setting them free outdoors was also a fun and rewarding part of the season, and a good learning experience for Maze on how to be kind to even the tiniest of God's creations.

The following day, after sharing my spider story with my good friend Jill, she replied, "Connie, that reminds me of the Legend of the Christmas Spider."

I'd never heard about the Christmas spider, but I was excited to learn more.

It didn't take me long to jump on the Internet in search of the story. It seems there are differing European folk legends about Christmas spiders from Finland and Scandinavia to the Ukraine and Germany. While some versions talk about the Christ child, others speak of Saint Nicholas, Father Christmas or Santa Claus.

All tell basically the same story about a mother who cleans her house thoroughly before putting up the Christmas tree. In doing so, she scares all the spiders into hiding in the attic. Late at night on Christmas Eve, the spiders, excited to see the tree, sneak down from the attic.

While exploring the tree, they leave their webs on all the branches.

Knowing that the mother would be disappointed to find her beautiful tree covered with webs, the Christ child — or Saint Nicholas, Father Christmas or Santa Claus — magically transforms all the webs into beautiful, shimmering silver strands.

From that day forward, tinsel has been used to decorate Christmas trees, and those who know the legend hang a beautiful silver or gold spider ornament on the tree as well.

After reading about the various Christmas spider legends, I wanted to surprise my children and grandchildren with a tinsel-covered tree, but sadly our local stores didn't have it in stock. Next year, however, I am determined to have a Christmas tree adorned in silver tinsel. And don't think for a moment that I've forgotten about the spider! I've already placed an order for a beautiful handmade silver-and-crystal-beaded spider ornament that comes with a copy of the German story, *The Legend of the Christmas Spider and Tinsel*.

Oh, how I love Christmas and tinsel — and spiders!

— Connie Kaseweter Pullen —

The Remembering Tree

Some Christmas tree ornaments do more than glitter
and glow; they represent a gift of love given
a long time ago.
~Tom Baker

The Christmas holidays were fast approaching, and I dreaded them. My husband had passed away this past year. Our family circle was broken. Our grown children and our grandchildren would be keenly aware of his absence.

For me, there would be no delight in decorating, cooking favorite dishes, and wrapping presents. I stared out my window and racked my brain for a way to help us through this first Christmas season without him.

Across our pond were some trees that Byron had planted for conservation purposes. One straggly evergreen caught my attention. It was squeezed between two mature trees. The top looked nice, but the bottom two-thirds had been starved of sunlight and water. I decided to cut down the tree, and use the top six feet as my Christmas tree.

I placed it in the corner of my living room. Wrapped in white lights, it emitted a warmth and feeling of peace. The next few nights, I plugged in the lights. Each night, it eased my troubled mind and my mixed feelings about the approaching holidays.

I hadn't mustered enough energy to haul up the ornaments from the basement yet. Maybe I would just be content with the warm lights. But I knew the grandkids would wonder why no ornaments hung on the branches. Maybe I could have them decorate the tree for me.

As I considered this, a different idea came to me. It might bring the family a blessing or just create a more difficult situation. Unsure if I should follow through, I prayed about it for a couple of days. A sense of rightness came over me, so I asked each of our children and grandchildren to bring an ornament to place on the tree that reminded them of Byron.

After our holiday dinner, we gathered in the living room. Furniture was arranged so the tree stood visible to everyone. The children quieted and sat on the floor.

I had scattered bright red apple ornaments throughout the tree branches. The apples opened the first story… my story.

"On our honeymoon, we came upon an apple orchard. Byron pulled in and suggested we grab a bag of apples. When we got back into the car, he asked if I wanted to try one of the apples. I said sure. He grabbed a Red Delicious apple, twisted it with his hands, and held out half to me. I'd never seen anyone twist an apple in two. I was impressed with his strength. Many times since that day, I'd ask him to split an apple. He always did. So, the apple ornaments remind me of his strength — not only with sharing an apple but his strength as a person."

One by one, someone stood to tell a story and hang an ornament on our remembering tree. Some stories brought tears, but many brought laughter. The grandkids heard some of these stories for the first time.

Byron became an integral part of our family celebration that day. He was no longer with us physically, but his memories were alive and being retold for future generations to know more about his life.

Next year, another tree will hold all the ornaments from this year. Plus, we'll hang new ornaments and tell new stories. Our family circle has healed and will remain complete.

— Kathy Boyd Thompson —

61

I'm Dreaming of a White Lie Christmas

*Never worry about the size of your Christmas tree. In
the eyes of children, they are all thirty feet tall.*
~Larry Wilde

There was a little boy who lived in our neighborhood. I'll call
him Pete. I don't know how to say this politely, so I'll just
come right out and say it: He was loud. He was annoying.
And it seemed like he was always around. He wasn't a bad
kid, and I really like kids, but he was always "in your face" and totally
obnoxious. And he talked and talked and questioned constantly.

Two weeks before Christmas, it was time to go and get our tree.
My husband and I walked outside to get in the truck, and there he was.

"Hi, Pete," we said as we kept walking to our truck.

"Where are you going?"

"We're going to go and get our Christmas tree."

"Are you getting a real tree or an artificial tree? How big is your
tree going to be? Can I decorate it?"

And on and on. We answered his questions with as few words as
possible. We were always polite but tried not to encourage him. We
kept walking to the truck. As we backed out of the driveway, Pete was
still talking. We waved. Bye-bye!

We drove to the tree lot and selected a tree. We decided to get
a four-foot tree so it would fit in the corner of the living room. We

found the perfect one. Luckily, we stopped and had dinner before we went home, so it was dark when we returned with the tree. Pete was already in his house by then. We set up the tree in the living room, gave it water, and put on the lights and a few ornaments, but that was it. We would finish the next day.

The next morning, we got up looking forward to finishing the decorating. But something was wrong. The tree looked droopy, even though we had filled the stand with water the night before. We could tell the tree hadn't taken any of the water. And now there were pine needles all over the floor. Something was not right with our poor tree.

Before we could figure out what to do, there was a knock at the door. My husband answered it, and there he was: Pete, the inspector. Really? He ran right in to see the tree without being invited. He was very excited to see that the tree was about as tall as he was and that he could just about reach the very top. We, on the other hand, were not that happy. After some encouragement and a little bribery, we got Pete to go home.

What were we going to do about our tree? We knew it wouldn't last until Christmas. At the rate it was dropping needles, it probably wouldn't last until the next day. And we usually left our tree up until New Year's Day. We knew it would never last that long. It was practically dead already.

We decided to take it back to the tree lot and see if they would exchange it for another tree. We undecorated it and got it back in the truck.

The people at the tree lot couldn't have been nicer. They apologized and told us that something like this rarely happens. They said they would be happy to give us another tree in exchange. We looked around and found another tree we liked. Although this one was bigger — about six feet tall — we knew it would still fit in our living-room corner. The tree-lot people wouldn't let us pay the difference in the price of the trees, and they helped us load our new tree into our truck.

We got the tree into the house with no interruptions from a little boy. We cleaned up the needles from the first tree, put the new tree in the stand, filled the cup with water, and started to decorate with the lights and ornaments we had removed from the original tree. We added more strings of lights because the tree was about two feet taller.

But before we could get out more ornaments and put them on the tree, we heard a knock on the door. We looked at each other, knowing full well who it was and wishing we could hide. That wasn't going to happen. We couldn't just ignore him because he would have seen us through the window on his way to the door, so he knew we were home. And he would just keep knocking and knocking until we answered.

My husband opened the door but didn't have to ask Pete to come in. He had already run in and come to a screeching halt right in front of the tree. He stood there with his mouth open, but no sound was coming out. How unusual! Pete was quiet. He walked from one side of the tree to the other. He really looked at the tree. He looked up at the top of the tree. He turned, looked at us and asked, "What happened to the tree? Yesterday, I was as tall as the top, but today the tree is taller."

My husband is a scientist and always has straightforward, truthful, and scientific answers for everything. His answer to Pete was scientific and thoughtful. With a straight face, he said, "Well, yesterday, when we brought it home, we put it in water, and it grew overnight." And me, not a scientist but an honest and trustworthy person, just said, "Yep."

I kept right on decorating that "growing" Christmas tree. Pete kept looking from one of us to the other and back again. For once, he didn't say one word, but the quizzical look on his face said it all. He turned and walked out of the house.

We listened to the quiet. How nice it sounded.

— Barbara LoMonaco —

62

The Miracle Tree

Miracles come in moments. Be ready and willing.
~Wayne Dyer

I t was Thanksgiving Day, and I was trying to focus on preparing my portion of the feast. However, in my mind, I was counting dollars more than I was counting my blessings. I knew it was a day to be thankful for all the wonderful blessings in our lives. But with the bombardment of commercials for all the latest toys and games new to the market — just in time for Christmas — I wondered what my girls would be wishing for this year. They were never greedy children, and that was one of my many blessings. But as their mom, I wanted to see the joy on their faces as they opened at least one fabulous gift from under the tree.

Oh, the tree. That was another expense. We had a tradition of cutting down our tree from a local tree farm. Perhaps it was time to consider an artificial tree. We'd have it for years to come, but pulling it out of a cardboard box seemed to pale in comparison to bundling up, loading the kids and the dog in the car, and fighting frostbite while my husband led the way through the snow, analyzing each and every blue spruce until he found the prize.

My thoughts quickly shifted back to the task at hand — finalizing the cooking and getting packed up to make the trip north to my sister's house in a neighboring town.

We set off, and on the way to my sister's passed a quaint, wooden country church. It was the typical little white church that dotted the countryside of rural Pennsylvania. A truck fully loaded with Christmas trees approached in the opposite direction. This wasn't a pickup truck; it was a truck used for hauling a load, and it was loaded to the top with, no doubt, the finest hand-selected Christmas trees money could buy. The recipients of these glorious trees would not have to ward off frostbite to get their perfect tree. The best had already been selected and cut, and — for top dollar — they could be purchased and possibly even delivered directly to their front door.

The truck seemed to be approaching faster than the 45-mile-per-hour speed limit on that rural stretch. The next thing I knew, my husband shouted, "Look at that! A tree fell off!" Sure enough, a beautiful, perfectly shaped Christmas tree lay in the road.

My husband pulled our truck to the berm and got out to remove the tree for the safety of other drivers. "They'll be back for that one," he said. "It's a beauty!" From the back seat, the kids began to rationalize why we should keep it. After all, the truck driver had lost it, and it would be sad that no one would be able to enjoy it if it were left to lie on the side of the road. I explained to them that the man may have worked hard to cut the trees, and perhaps the proceeds were to be used to buy Christmas presents for his family. My husband, on the other hand, was willing to compromise. If the tree was still there when we returned, it was meant to be ours.

We enjoyed a wonderful Thanksgiving dinner with family. As the sun was setting, we said our goodbyes and loaded into the truck for the journey home. The kids were tired but not too tired to remember the pact they had made with their dad. I truly didn't believe the tree would still be there. Even if the truck driver hadn't come back for it, someone else surely would have picked it up.

As the headlights shone ahead, I could see the little white church in the distance. I secretly hoped and prayed the tree would still be there. And it was! There were no colored lights or tinsel on it, yet it gleamed as bright as the Star of Bethlehem when the headlights shone on it. It was meant to be our tree!

The girls were thrilled when their dad pulled into the parking lot of the little white church and pulled some rope out of his truck. He hoisted the tree up to the roof and secured it for the short trip home.

I don't think a Christmas has passed since then when someone in our family hasn't brought up this story. It is a memory that I hope will be shared with future generations. A lot of people would say it was a series of coincidences. The tree accidentally fell off the truck on Thanksgiving Day, right by the little white church. We just happened to be passing at the exact time. The truck driver didn't come back. Many travelers had to have passed it during the day, but no one stopped to pick it up. I choose to believe it was a special gift that was shared with us from above. It was the perfect size for us, and free, but the wondrous way it came to us during a season when miracles abound is what we'll cherish above all else.

— Tamara Bell —

63

My First Christmas Tree

I may be biased, but even without all of these fancy
decorations, Christmas trees are special.
Cause they remind us this is the season,
that we should all love one another.
~John Loy

I am sixty-five years old, and today I did something I have never done before: I bought a Christmas tree. I was walking Todd, my fourteen-year-old Lab — which is something I find myself doing often these days thanks to a weak bladder (his, not mine) — when I noticed the sagging Christmas lights on my neighbor Jim's house. To be honest, I've noticed them before; Jim has never taken them down in the four years I've lived in this neighborhood.

Jim was in his front yard doing something that looked vaguely like pulling weeds. He was crouched over, moving slowly and painfully, clutching a plastic shopping bag with only one weed to show for his efforts.

"Doing a little yard work, Jim?" I cheerfully asked.

Jim looked up, his eyes squinting from the sun. He looked tired in a way that only someone very old can look.

"Bumper crop, for sure, Tom," he managed, forcing a smile.

"Say, Jim, the holidays are fast approaching, and I noticed that your Christmas lights are looking a little sad. How about I bring my extension ladder down and fix them up for you?"

Jim straightened, grimacing with the effort, and gazed at the lights on his house as if seeing them for the first time. "I suppose a little fixing up is in order, Tom. You handy with a ladder?"

I laughed. "I was a general contractor for forty years. I think I can handle it. As soon as I finish up with Todd, I'll be right over."

One thing I learned as a general contractor was that simple jobs were often not simple at all, and a five-minute fix sometimes ended up taking half a day. This was a lesson I was about to re-experience.

I lugged the extension ladder over to Jim's, having determined that a distance of three houses did not justify using my pickup truck. A sharp pain in my lower back said otherwise.

Jim held the ladder, or rather it held him as I carefully negotiated the steps and began reattaching the errant lights. "Hey, Jim," I called out. "You got any hooks? Several have fallen out."

Jim limped away and returned after what seemed like a long time to be searching for hooks.

"No hooks, Tom."

An hour later, after Jim and I had made a trip to the hardware store for hooks, with a quick stop for burgers and fries, I clambered back up the ladder.

"There," I pronounced, shoring up the last light. "You are now ready for Christmas."

Triumphantly, I descended the ladder while Jim admired my handiwork. "It's a celestial work of art, Tom, that's what it is. I'm going to switch them on."

Four lights were burned out.

"I guess we should have started with that," Jim sighed, stating the obvious.

Back to the hardware store for lights with a quick stop for frozen yogurt before I lumbered back up the ladder to replace the burned-out bulbs.

Success!

Jim was elated and insisted on helping me carry my ladder home. I reluctantly agreed, the pain in my back having been amplified by numerous trips up and down. It was a spectacle, to be sure—Jim at the rear, shuffling along, swaying back and forth, with me at the front, groaning in pain with each baby step.

With the ladder stowed away, Jim surveyed my house with a critical eye. "Where are your Christmas lights, Tom?"

"I don't put up any, Jim."

"Why's that?"

"I'm Jewish, Jim. Christmas lights aren't on the menu. But I will be displaying a Hanukkah menorah in my front window."

Jim puzzled over this, shaking his head in disbelief. "So, a man who spent half the day helping me with my Christmas lights, injuring his back in the process... doesn't even celebrate Christmas?"

"Do you pray, Jim?"

"Yes."

"So do I. Do you pray to God?"

"Of course."

"So do I. We're not so different, Jim. We just have different holiday displays, that's all."

Jim thanked me again and shuffled off, still shaking his head while muttering to himself, "Don't that beat all?"

For the next few days, I made it a point to walk past Jim's house on my nightly outing with Todd, admiring my handiwork and chuckling to myself at the ordeal it took to hang some simple Christmas lights. And then, one night, there was something else—something that made me recall the words Jim had spoken a few days before.

"Don't that beat all," I uttered to myself.

For there, shimmering in Jim's front window, bathing the yard and street in a lustrous gold light, was a menorah.

And that's when I decided to buy a Christmas tree.

I get some curious looks from the neighbors when they pass by my house. I expect Jim does, too. But maybe, just maybe, people will stop seeing our holiday displays as competing religions and start seeing that they share something in common: namely, brotherhood, compassion for others, respect for all religions and love of God. Until then, I say, "Merry Hanukkah" and "Happy Christmas!"

— Dave Bachmann —

Changing Traditions

You will do foolish things but do them with enthusiasm.
~Colette

The tradition in our house was to have a real tree at Christmas. It needed to be eight feet tall, with lots of healthy branches and the perfect shape. The only flexibility had to do with the type: Scotch pine, balsam and Douglas fir were all acceptable choices as long as they were freshly cut and smelled good. I'd always prided myself on being able to pick just the right tree. I had it down to a fine art, or so I thought. My wife and I could never understand why anyone would settle for anything less than real-tree perfection.

When we moved into a condominium, we decided to continue the real-tree tradition although we were aware that most condos did not encourage them. As we were in a new building, the condo board had not yet had time to set up any of the usual restrictions. We decided to continue until forced to make other arrangements.

The winter before we moved into the condo, I had been suffering from a particularly bad flu. When it came to tree picking, my wife decided she could go it alone. At the local market, she found a tree that looked to fit the bill. At the time, she remembers thinking, *What was hard about this?* She was a bit surprised by the high price she had to pay for her "vision of loveliness" but decided as it was the local market, it was worth the money.

The problem is that most trees are tightly bound when they are on display. This makes it difficult to tell exactly how they will look when

Tales of the Tree | 201

unwrapped. In my feverish state, I vaguely remember mentioning that I thought her choice might have looked better if we had left it wrapped. When she removed the netting around it, rather than expand into a decent shape, it seemed to flatten. I am sure that my second comment that it would have made a nice wall hanging didn't help much.

My wife good-naturedly put up with my tree critique because it was all true. No amount of decoration made that tree look festive. After that, we agreed that any future selection had to be a combined effort.

It was always the coldest day when we went to make our choice at the local tree lot. My method was to walk around the area and lock onto any tree that fit the nine-foot criterion. I would grab it with both hands and take it to the checkout as quickly as possible before I froze. The tree lot was run by a group of helpful volunteers because the sales benefited our local hospital. They wisely waited in a warm hut until it was time to take the customer's money, cut the bottom off the trunk, and help load it onto the car. It was so cold, though, that I turned down the trimming offer, saying that I would do it myself when the weather warmed up.

We smuggled the tree through the garage, into the elevator, and up to our eighth-floor apartment. It dropped several needles on the way, but I figured that was just part of the thawing process. To prevent it from dropping many more, I put it out on the balcony until I could deal with the trunk trimming. As soon as it was safely stowed, I rushed back down to the garage to clean up as many needles as I could to cover our tracks. Nobody would ever suspect that we had brought in a real tree.

A couple of days and a few thousand dropped pine needles later, I was ready to trim the excess off the trunk. I balanced the tree high against the balcony rail and lifted it in the air to saw the end. My saw wasn't exactly suited to the task. The sap in the tree jammed up the teeth at almost every stroke. The job was taking much longer than I had anticipated, and I was steadily losing patience.

I was almost finished when I must have raised the end too high in the air. I watched in horror as the tree tumbled over the rail, plummeting six stories onto my neighbour's patio. When I peered cautiously over the rail, I saw that the tree had come to rest amid my neighbour's expensive-looking patio furniture. It had also lost the last half of its needles in the fall. They were strewn all over the patio.

My overwhelming instinct was to deny ownership, but I finally worked up enough courage to go downstairs, introduce myself to my new neighbours, and collect what was left of my tree. Apart from my dignity, there seemed to be very little collateral damage, so I was able to clean up the debris and make my way back to the apartment. I finished my trunk cutting and at last installed the tree in its holder. Despite having lost most of its needles, I thought that with its lights, ornaments and baubles, it looked quite presentable. My cat seemed to think so, too.

Sometime in the middle of the night, we were awakened by a loud crash. Not knowing what to expect, we rushed into the living room just as the cat was making a hasty exit. The tree, complete with water container, decorations and the last remnants of needles, was spread out across the floor. That night of all nights, the cat had decided to see what it would be like to roost in the upper branches. He must have had quite a surprise when he discovered he was a lot heavier than the average Christmas ornament. We spent about two hours cleaning up the mess. Early the next morning, the tree remnants were wrapped in plastic and smuggled down to the garbage room. As I'm sure no one expected a tree to be dumped a week before Christmas, we managed to do it unobserved.

Sadly, this heralded the end of a longstanding family tradition. From that day on, a real tree would never darken our doorstep. We must stay flexible when following tradition, even at Christmas. Overnight, we became converts to the advantages of the artificial tree, and so began a new tradition.

—James A. Gemmell—

65

Chicken Soup for the *Soul*

Holiday Tradition Worth Keeping

*The best Christmas trees come very close
to exceeding nature.*
~Andy Rooney

On our way home from my mother's house in Sandy, Oregon, I pondered the events from the Thanksgiving weekend and what Mom had said. We had enjoyed a delicious dinner and planned to go out the next morning to pick out the annual Christmas tree, but my mother put an end to our longtime family tradition with an unexpected comment: "I don't want a tree anymore." After a short sigh, she continued with her reasoning: "The burden, care, watering, cleaning up the needles, even the fire danger if I forget to turn off the lights, not to mention getting rid of it when the season is over — it's just too much hassle now that I'm older and can't see very well. Sorry, kids, but I hope you understand."

No more Christmas trees! I was shocked, not to mention disappointed. What had happened? For years, ever since my family had moved to Oregon, we had cut a fresh tree for the holidays. Most of the ones at the tree lots were already dry, branches brittle, needles falling off. The fresh-cut ones, though, always lasted past New Year's Day. When Mom later followed us to Oregon from California, she liked our idea, too. It became our special tradition.

On the Friday after Thanksgiving, I would pick up Mom at her house and head to Lolo Pass to get our Christmas trees. Besides Mom and me, our tree-cutting crew included my wife, Laura, and our three children. On the way, I stopped by Zigzag Ranger Station to purchase the required permits for five dollars each. We were only allowed to cut trees underneath the power lines. No doubt our efforts provided free line maintenance for the electric company.

Our family made a whole day of it. Mom packed up turkey sandwiches, potato chips, a thermos of hot chocolate, and a few candy bars as a reward for completing the mission. We never missed a year, even when the road up the pass was snowed over. Having a four-wheel-drive vehicle made accessing it a snap, even in packed snow. Sometimes, we were the only individuals on the road.

One season, the snow was so deep I had to rent snowshoes to get to the designated cutting area. It was easy to imagine ourselves as part of the Lewis and Clark expedition, exploring Mount Hood, searching for a passable route through the snow-filled hills. Mom, of course, stayed in my Chevy Suburban while we hunted for the perfect tree. Actually, most looked like Charlie Brown Christmas trees, spindly with sparse foliage. However, we loved them because they were ours, handpicked, and cut the old-fashioned way.

To shorten the distance traveled, we later switched to a local tree farm in Boring. We still made a day of it, though, cutting two trees: one for Mom, one for us. Afterward, we returned to Mom's place for Thanksgiving leftovers.

Laura and I tried being as helpful as possible, making it easier for my mom to care for her tree. On weekends, we would stop by and vacuum up any needles that had dropped. When Mom mentioned that watering the tree was difficult since she had to get down on her arthritic knees, I installed a funnel and tube. I placed the device within the branches so she could water it while standing. Every holiday season, my wife and children helped Mom decorate her tree. My job was to string up the lights.

Now, all those efforts would be for naught. Laura and I discussed the alternatives, but nothing seemed like the right solution.

Then one day at the mall, a bright red box with a green Christmas tree pictured on it caught our attention. The front caption read, "Hi! I'm Douglas Fir, the animated talking Christmas tree. I look like any ordinary tree, but I'm not!" Large white print at the bottom stated that it talked, sang, and had an animated mouth and eyes. It was priced at only $24.99.

Smiling, I grabbed one off the shelf and flipped it over. The back caption said more: "Let me entertain you. Let me make you smile! I spring to life when someone walks by or makes a noise. I'll surprise your family and friends as I sing Christmas carols and holiday greetings. My eyes open, close, and light up. I am sound and motion activated."

Perfect! Just what we needed for Mom, and battery-operated, too. No cord to give it away. With a few changes, it would look like a holiday centerpiece. And unlike a poinsettia or other potted plant, it would not need watering or maintenance. No needles to clean up either. Mom would love it — or so we hoped.

Laura and I took it home and disguised it. We removed the Santa hat and decorated it with miniature red Christmas bulbs. It looked like a small artificial tree. Fortunately, its eyes and mouth remained hidden from view and only opened if activated. Mom liked her table decoration — or at least tolerated it for our sakes. To surprise her, we thought it would be fun to set it so Mom could enjoy some holiday music and a cheery greeting on Christmas Day. Since I had already installed the three C batteries, I only needed to flip on the power switch. We said our goodbyes and told my mom we would see her the next day for Christmas dinner and exchanging presents.

In the middle of the night or early the next morning, Mom must have walked into her living room, heading toward the kitchen. Perhaps she was thirsty, looking for a drink of water before returning to bed. Maybe she was having a sweet craving and wanted one of those chocolate donuts in her pantry. Apparently, something activated the tree. Her shadow probably crossed the light sensor. Opening or closing the kitchen cupboard might have made noise as well. Perhaps she sighed or mumbled a few words aloud. Any of those things would have set off the talking tree.

Suddenly, out of the stillness, a voice blurted out, "Merry Christmas, everybody!" Frightened, Mom looked over at the table and saw a pair of mysterious eyes glowing in the dark. She froze in place. Shock set in. Her heart rate jumped. Three holiday songs came in rapid succession: "Jingle Bells," "Santa Claus Is Comin' to Town," and "We Wish You a Merry Christmas." Each repertoire ended with "Happy New Year!" For a moment, she wondered if an elf or little green gnome had somehow appeared.

Then she moved... and the sequence started all over again. Rushing over to the table, Mom found the hidden switch and shut it off. Now wide awake, she plopped down into her kitchen chair, looked at her little Christmas tree, and started laughing hysterically.

After that experience, my mom said she was more than happy to go back to a full-size Christmas tree. It was, after all, a holiday tradition worth keeping.

— Charles Earl Harrel —

66

A Small Miracle in the Woods

Those who we have loved never really leave us.
They live on forever in our hearts and cast their
radiant light onto every shadow.
~Sylvana Rossetti

It was early January, another new year without Ryan. On my husband Michael's day off, we headed out to Quail Hollow Park to undecorate the tree we decorate for Christmas each year in honor of his son Ryan, who passed away seven years ago. It's just a little tree off a path in the woods.

Each year, we put a poster board sign there with the message, "Please sign here in memory of someone you miss this Christmas." People write their names, the names of their deceased loved ones, and brief notes.

This year, we upped our game. After decorating the tree, we took two wrapped copies of the *Chicken Soup for the Soul* Christmas book in which my story about the tree was published, and hid them for fellow woods walkers to find. We included a note about where they could find the tree.

That Thursday, as we trudged along the crunchy trail by the creek, I wondered what we'd find when we reached our tree. We'd had so much rain in December; I prepared myself to find the decorations lying on the ground and the sign ruined.

We reached the part of the trail that curves toward the tree. From the path, we could see many of our decorations still clinging to the branches. But instead of our sign, there was a baggie hanging on the metal sign holder.

Pushing through the dense branches, we made our way over to the tree. I plucked the bag off the stick. "Oh, look, it's the baggie we used to protect one of the books we hid," I said. I dug inside the baggie and pulled out a folded piece of wrapping paper. It was the paper we'd used to wrap the book. I opened it and realized it was a note. "I'm too excited to read it right now; let's wait until we get home," I said, sticking it back inside the baggie.

As we pulled the mini mittens and angel wings from the tree, I said, "I wonder what happened to our sign. Do you think it blew away?"

While I walked around to see if I could find it anywhere, Michael dug around in the snow with his boot and found it. He reached down and wiped the rest of the snow from it. Right away, we could see we had more names and wishes this year than we had the first year. I didn't take the time to read them all, but I noticed one dated January 1st. Our little sign had held up through the New Year.

The next day, as Michael and I sat sipping our morning coffee, we opened that baggie and pulled out the note inside.

The note explained how a woman and her husband had started off their walk stressed. They were grumpy with each other because they had taken a new path and the trail conditions were terrible. Finally, they gave up and returned to their regular trail, and that's when they found the hidden book. They thanked us for reminding them about the importance of the season. They ended the note by saying they were meant to find the note, and they left the park holding hands.

It made me tear up. I held that note close all day and then tucked it into the back pocket of my journal where I keep it as a reminder. As miracles go, the right person finding that book was a small one. But what she did with it increased its reach. By taking the time to find the decorated tree and write the note, two couples got to share in the magical moment.

Later, I read all the notes on our sign — some about loved ones who'd passed away, and some that were simply holiday greetings to Michael and me. Then, I stood up the sign on our kitchen island so I could look at it each time I walked into the room. It awed me that people would take the time to reach out to people they didn't know, on a sign in the woods, and wish them well. The sadness I'd been carrying inside the previous day was gone. Instead, I felt hope and anticipation for the new year.

As I watched the snow fill up the yard from our kitchen windows, I couldn't help pondering how that tiny tree in the woods had worked its magic — again. Spirits were lifted, and the evidence of a small miracle was shared, just because a few strangers cared enough to step off the beaten path.

—Amy Catlin Wozniak—

67

Seven Cats, One Christmas Mouse

Tree decorating with cats. O Christmas tree,
O Christmas tree, your ornaments are history!
~Courtney VanSickle

Every year, we buy one new Christmas ornament to add to our eclectic collection of tree decorations. Our pick for Christmas 1985 was based entirely on its cuteness factor. My husband and I found the mouse-in-a-Christmas-stocking ornament in a mall gift shop and made our choice on the spot.

The little mouse didn't have a body, just a fuzzy brown head poking out the top of a red, green, and white–striped Christmas stocking. He looked especially festive wearing a green felt elf hat. Two brown felt paws were glued to the outside of the knitted stocking, so it looked as if Mouse had pulled himself up and out of the stocking for a peek around.

I hung our little mouse on a medium-high branch of our tree. The next morning, we found the mouse in the kitchen, batted around by the only suspect in the house: Stanley, our two-year-old cat. I relocated the mouse a little higher on the tree, which, at first, seemed to be a deterrent. But we found Mouse on the floor just a few days later. None of the other ornaments had been knocked down.

Every few days, we'd find the mouse on the floor. Eventually,

Mouse started showing signs of mistreatment: a snagged stocking, a bitten nose, a soggy elf hat. We were determined not to let the cat curate our Christmas tree décor, so we kept returning Mouse to the tree. It was clear that Stanley had a deep-seated issue with the mouse ornament, however.

When Simon came along after Stanley left us, we thought our Christmas mouse problems would be over. They were not. When our tree went up, it was clear that Simon shared the same taste for Christmas ornaments as Stanley. In the same careful manner, Mouse was repeatedly plucked from the tree. It didn't seem to matter where we put him. The mouse would end up on the floor. Nothing else was knocked from the tree, not one other Christmas bauble.

In fact, over the next three decades, Squeakie, Charles, Milo, Ringo, and Victoria—all our cats—exhibited the same inexplicable obsession surrounding the Christmas mouse. Every year, at least once, Mouse would be removed from his branch. I even considered that we might have mistakenly purchased a catnip mouse. But after examining the ornament closely, it was clear that this was just a cotton batting-stuffed stocking with a Styrofoam mouse head. In recent years, we've started hanging the mouse lower on the tree, so if Victoria (now a senior cat with poor balance) wants to get the mouse, she can do it without destroying more fragile ornaments.

Last Christmas seemed like the end for our thirty-three-year-old stocking mouse. One morning, a few days after Christmas, I wandered into the living room to find the stocking on the floor once again. Notice I did not say "the mouse in the stocking." That's because the mouse's head had been gnawed off and separated from the stocking. Worse, I could not locate the decapitated head.

Victoria, our only cat, was the obvious culprit. I crawled around on my hands and knees, searching under the sofa, chairs, bookcase, and anywhere a mouse head might be. Nothing. "Did you eat it?" I asked Victoria. She meowed, but I didn't know if that meant yes or no. I found the head a few days later lodged in the air vent in our entryway. I was able to press out the dent in the mouse's cheek. Then I glued the head back onto the stocking, ready for next year. It seems our cats have adopted "The Bringing Down of the Christmas Mouse" as their very own Christmas tradition. Why end the fun now?

— Carol L. MacKay —

The Perfect Tree

When we recall Christmas past, we usually find that
the simplest things — not the great occasions —
give off the greatest glow of happiness.
~Bob Hope

Christmas was my father's favorite holiday. He would fully decorate the outside of our brick cape, including a giant tree shape made from strands of colored lights that he ran from the peak of the rooftop to the ground below. I'd watch him patiently untangle those lights for hours from the mangled mess they always seemed to become in the storage crate. Although no one touched the crate all year long, the strands of lights somehow managed to come out all twisted. My parents would joke that a gremlin had sneaked in and messed them up!

Inside, our family Christmas tree stood proudly in the parlor's big bay window. My mother would painstakingly separate the branches of the artificial tree and tie them together with black thread for the perfect look! The tree would then sit, dark and waiting, as the excitement around it mounted each day while we counted down to Christmas. On Christmas Eve, I could place one ornament on the tree before going to bed. While I was sleeping, Santa would come and decorate the rest of the tree before leaving presents under it. On Christmas morning, I would dash downstairs to find the tree in all its beautiful, twinkling glory! Oh, how magical Christmas was!

We eventually moved from the suburbs to the country, and our

Christmas traditions followed us. At our new home, lots of snow added a very special Norman Rockwell feeling to the picturesque Christmases.

Only a few years later, my father passed away quite suddenly, leaving my mother a grieving widow and me a very sad and confused teen. That year, Mom's joy for Christmas was nonexistent; it had left on the wings of my father's departure from this world. As Christmas Eve approached, there was no talk of putting up a tree. With moving, we no longer had the old artificial one.

I knew what needed to be done. I trudged through the snow to the woods behind our house. And then I found the most beautiful, perfectly shaped pine tree! I had found our Christmas tree. Even though I had never even so much as touched an axe before that day, I was going to surprise my mother by cutting it down, bringing it home, and decorating it.

As my dog circled around me, seemingly curious as to what I was doing, I began to swing the axe at the trunk of the pine tree. While in motion, it was much heavier than I had anticipated, especially for my skinny teenage arms! But many swings later, the tree came down! I hummed Christmas tunes as I proudly dragged it home.

Then I made a tree stand from pieces of wood nailed together in a cross shape and set it up on our back porch. Digging through our Christmas decorations, I found strands of lights and began untangling them as my father had done so many Christmases past. While the tree was not nearly as tall as our artificial one, and there wasn't much on it but lights, some garland, and tinsel, I thought it was one of the most beautiful trees I had ever seen. Having that tree kept my dad with us throughout the holiday season — our first without him.

For me, the best gift that year was seeing the expression on my mother's face when she saw the tree glistening in the dark. As tears streamed down her face, I said, "Merry Christmas, Momma." With that, she gathered me up in such a warm embrace that I can still feel it to this day. "Thank you, Doll. Your dad would be so proud," she whispered as we clung to each other.

In the spring, when all the snow had gone, my mother went about her annual gardening and stopped on the far side of our house to study the stump before her. Apparently, that perfect tree I had cut down at Christmas… well, it was one my parents had picked out at a nursery and planted! For years, my mother and I would joke about how I chose that tree!

Now, almost five decades later, that holiday still holds a very special place in my heart for I was able to bring Christmas home that year for both my mother and me. And what a wondrous gift it was.

— Dorothy Wills-Raftery —

Chapter
7

Around the Table

A Gumbo Christmas

The more you honor your spirit and soul,
the more that energy grows around you.
~Lion Babe

After my parents' divorce, my mother struggled financially. She didn't share this information explicitly. Instead, she explained over the telephone that she wasn't going to get a tree and would only buy small, token Christmas gifts for us. In the intuitive way siblings have, without discussing it, my brother, sister, and I decided that we would travel from Iowa, California, and upstate New York respectively, to celebrate the holiday with Mom in Chicago.

Our arrival galvanized my mother. She taped Christmas lights to the front windows. She found leftover red ribbon buried in a drawer and used thumbtacks to pin long strips of it from wall-to-wall, close to the ceiling. Then she hung icicles on the ribbons, so they danced and swirled over our heads. And "to spite the devil," she invited our extended family over for Christmas dinner even though it wasn't her turn to host.

Typically, Christmas dinner in our family was a potluck. As host, my mother was tasked with supplying the meat portion of the meal. Aunt Barbara would bring her sweet potatoes with marshmallows on top; Aunt Meme contributed a salad; Aunt Lil provided macaroni and cheese, Aunt Jane brought spiced peaches for dessert and so on until the table was laden with food. Those family members who couldn't cook were asked to bring napkins and soda pop. (If anyone has ever asked you to bring napkins to a potluck, now you know why.)

This year was different. My mother told everyone there was no need to bring anything. Dinner would be her Christmas gift.

It was a cold winter, so we were not surprised that on Christmas morning it was cold in the house. My mother turned up the heat from 68 to 72 degrees. After hot showers we all felt better, but it was still cold, and twenty-five people were coming to dinner. My brother went down to the basement and discovered the oil tank was empty.

The stove and oven used gas, as did the hot water heater, so those still worked. My mother would be able to make her legendary gumbo, which she had chosen instead of ham, turkey, or roast beef, because those would be way too expensive for a large group.

Gumbo is a stew served over rice. Like most stews, gumbo is mostly water and vegetables, in particular okra; in fact, in Twi, a West African language, gumbo is the word for okra. There is meat in the stew, but not prime cuts; the stew's long, slow boil tenderizes the lower quality grades. In my mother's gumbo, mixed with small chunks of chicken, beef, and Andouille sausage, are shrimp, crab legs, and oysters.

In addition to okra there are two other crucial ingredients. One is the stew's base called a roux, similar to a rich brown gravy. The secret to a good roux is to stir it slowly over low heat. The other is filé, a dark powdered herb made from the roots and leaves of the sassafras tree. The combination of roux, okra, and filé is what makes a good gumbo the color of Mississippi mud, and gives it the consistency of a stew instead of a soup.

Throughout the morning. accompanied by music from *A Charlie Brown Christmas*, my brother, my sister, her husband, and I shivered in thick socks and heavy sweaters chopping the "trinity" of garlic, celery, and onions, slicing okra, and peeling and deveining shrimp. While we worked, my mother told us stories about her father who had died before we were born.

Theodore Roosevelt Conrad had traveled on the City of New Orleans train up the Mississippi River from Louisiana to Chicago as part of the Great Migration, when over six million African Americans moved from the South for better jobs up north. My mother said that it was because of her father that she knew how much filé to shake into the pot and how to mix a good roux. The recipe for a good gumbo wasn't written down. It was in her blood, and ours too.

The ring of the white phone on the kitchen wall interrupted the food prep and storytelling. On the other end of the line would be the voice of a family member saying, "Ask your mother if I can bring anything." Or "Ask your mother if she needs me to stop at the store." We'd cover the receiver and giggle because we knew that what they really wanted was to know what Mom was making for dinner. Each time we answered, "Mom said she didn't need anything. Just bring yourself."

Unfortunately, to accommodate everyone in my mother's small open living room/dining room, we would need to squeeze some additional tables and chairs into the space. Mom knew that when Uncle Henry dropped them off, he was also supposed to find out what was for dinner. Then he'd report back to his wife, Aunt Barbara, Mom's older sister, who would then get on the phone, tell everyone else, and spoil the surprise.

Of course, my mother had planned for a way to block her sister's maneuver.

Mid-afternoon, Michael and Mo, my brother and brother-in-law, stationed themselves at the front window. When Uncle Henry's car arrived, they met him at the curb. They carried the tables and chairs to the porch—so as not to have to open the door and let the heat out, they explained—and then they told him they didn't need any help bringing it all in. Uncle Henry didn't get the opportunity to peek into the kitchen. Checkmate, Mom.

In our family Christmas dinners usually started around four o'clock. This time, as the grandfather clock in the dining room chimed its first "bong," we also heard car doors slamming. We welcomed our guests, took their coats, and then had them turn around so that their backs were facing us. "*Laissez les bons temps rouler*," we shouted, as we tied plastic bibs around their necks. We howled and laughed as their puzzlement turned to realization, and then relief, that Mom had made gumbo for dinner.

After dinner, there was ice cream — vanilla, and my mother's favorite, butter pecan. We played Dictionary, where you randomly pick a word out of the dictionary and guess its definition. My mother wasn't allowed to join us during that game. She taught high school English and knew every word in the dictionary plus its Latin root.

We also played Categories. My great aunt Lil' won the round for underwear because she was the only one who had girdle on her list. A couple of the younger cousins challenged her because they didn't know what a girdle was.

It didn't feel cold and I don't remember if anyone asked to turn the heat up. What I do remember is how much fun it was being together, full of good food and laughter. By the time the last guest left, my mother's gumbo pot was empty.

— Angie Chatman —

70

Feline Shenanigans

In a cat's eye, all things belong to cats.
~Author Unknown

"Did you take my fruitcake?" my mother shouted at me as she burst into my room.

"What are you talking about?" I replied. "Why would I take your fruitcake?" I loathe fruitcake, by the way, and my mother knew this.

"Well," she said, starting to calm down, "I don't know what happened to it then. I just bought it yesterday. I only had a little piece of it, and now it's gone. Have you seen it at least? It was a mini fruitcake wrapped in cute Christmas packaging."

"No," I laughed. "I haven't seen your fruitcake."

"Are you lying?" she quizzed, raising one eyebrow at me.

Now, I'll admit that I had done my fair share of "getting rid" of certain foods in the house. My mom had recently been diagnosed with diabetes and had to give up several foods that she loved, treating herself only occasionally, such as with a miniature fruitcake. This drastic change in her diet was hard for her to adjust to, so I "helped" her by making sure that certain unhealthy foods never stuck around long in the kitchen. My mom had deemed me "the food police."

All in all, I could understand why she might accuse me of throwing away the fruitcake. But this time, I wasn't lying.

Later that night at dinner, Mom started accusing me again. "Please, just tell me where that fruitcake is," she pleaded after we bickered back and forth for several minutes.

"Mom," I said, "I told you a thousand times. I have not done anything with your fruitcake, I promise."

Then I helped her search every possible place in the house that it might be.

When it still wasn't found, this only made her accuse me more. That was the end of the discussion. I had thrown it away, and that's all there was to it.

A couple of weeks later, I decided to do some cleaning in my room. As I was sweeping the floors, I swept the broom under my bed. The broom caught something a bit heavier than a dust bunny. I shined my flashlight under the bed to see what it was. Lo and behold, it was the fruitcake.

How on earth? I thought to myself. As I was thinking about how this might have happened, praying that my mom didn't open the door and catch me with it, my cat, Ella, strolled into the room.

Then it dawned on me: Ella. It had to have been Ella. Although she knew she was not allowed, she often climbed onto the kitchen counters. Under my bed was one of her favorite napping places. And I was constantly having to hide small things (earrings, bobby pins, paper clips, etc.) because she would snatch them and run away with them.

They were small things, though, not a fruitcake. But it had to have been Ella.

I burst out laughing at the thought of my sweet cat knocking that fruitcake off the kitchen counter and dragging it with her little teeth as she walked backward all the way to my bed.

Although it was starting to mold, I could tell that she hadn't eaten any of it. She could have been saving it for later. Or, more likely, I can add my cat to the long list of discriminating individuals who just don't like Christmas fruitcake!

—M.C. Manning—

71

Grand Slam

If at first you don't succeed, order pizza.
~etsy.com

Mom's Christmas dinners consisted of traditional turkey and dressing, mashed potatoes and gravy, heavenly yeast rolls, and an assortment of homemade pies. Our first holiday without her, I learned that preparing such a large feast wasn't as simple as she made it look.

On Christmas morning, I carefully kneaded the dough for everyone's favorite: her mouth-watering hot rolls. While I waited for the bread to rise, I baked desserts and washed, peeled and chopped the veggies. By then, it was time to cook the turkey. I slid the heavy roasting pan onto the middle rack. After setting the festive dining-room table, I hustled to the shower, confident I had everything under control.

A few hours later, I opened the oven door and gasped when I spotted the cold, white, naked bird. I'd forgotten to turn on the oven. Like a game-day rain delay, our meal was several hours late. Needless to say, I struck out that holiday.

Strike two occurred the following year. On Christmas Day, the sweet-potato-and-broccoli casseroles waited in the on-deck circle while the cherry and apple pies bubbled up through golden brown crusts. The smell of yeast wafted throughout the kitchen as the rolls doubled in size. All that was left to do was roast the turkey. Shock set in when I opened the refrigerator in the garage and found the bottom shelf bare. Oh, no! I remembered getting side-tracked by a phone call; the turkey was still in the freezer.

My family was fine with the baked chicken I quickly made instead.

The next holiday season, we'd just moved into a new home. I went overboard on decorations, thinking this would be the year I'd finally hit a home run. Trotting downstairs to the laundry room, I took the turkey out of the freezer and set it on the floor while I folded towels from the dryer. Lugging the basket upstairs, I made a mental note to add cranberries to my grocery list.

A few days later, armed with another load of dirty clothes, I walked into the laundry room to what looked like a crime scene. A stream of blood ran down the middle of the floor. My eyes followed the trail to a mound in front of the deep freezer — my thawed turkey. Strike three!

My husband witnessed me carrying the foul carcass to the trash and said, "Looks like we won't be making the playoffs again this year."

It occurred to me how silly it was to cook a huge meal on Christmas Day. After munching on cheeseballs, dips, and once-a-year homemade candies, everyone was too stuffed to enjoy the food that had taken hours to prepare. Besides, cleaning up the kitchen mess was time-consuming and postponed opening gifts and playing games.

My stats have improved tremendously now that we've traded our huge holiday feast for a much simpler meal — take-and-bake pizzas, a guaranteed grand slam.

— Alice Muschany —

72

The Best Christmas Eve Ever

*Love is what's in the room with you at Christmas if you
stop opening presents and listen.*
~Author Unknown

"Isn't it strange how Christmas has changed as we've gotten older?" I lamented to my dear friend Susan over lunch at the bakery. We were discussing our lack of holiday plans just days before Christmas. We were both going to be alone and were feeling down.

"When we were young, it was about the kids, family get-togethers and polishing that silver tray I only used twice a year," I reminisced. "But life changed. Our kids are grown. We're giving checks now instead of presents, and I've no idea where that old tray is."

Divorced, we found ourselves alone occasionally at holidays as our grown children lived hours away. Christmas as we knew it had changed. We missed those simpler family times when the season was filled with excitement as we shopped, wrapped presents, cleaned, polished, decorated, baked, cooked and entertained.

"I didn't even put up a tree," I confessed. "We celebrated early this year at Tim's since he and his family will be in Florida over Christmas."

"And mine aren't making the trip home either," Susan continued sadly. "I'll be alone, too. My son-in-law needs to be with his family since his mom is failing. It sure doesn't seem like Christmas."

While discussing our situations, we decided the two of us should not be alone. We hatched a plan where I'd prepare dinner, and we'd spend Christmas Eve at my house. However, while driving home, I remembered two other friends whom I knew were also going to be alone.

I called them, praying my last-minute invitation wouldn't be misinterpreted.

"I would love to have Christmas Eve dinner with you." It was Maureen, whom I had called first. "This will be great. It's tough being alone at Christmas, so joining you will help."

Next, I called Bill, a longtime, out-of-state friend who was spending the holidays at his nearby cottage. He, too, was going to be alone.

"Are you serious?" Bill, always the charmer, laughed when I asked him. "There isn't a bachelor like me around who wouldn't enjoy spending Christmas Eve with three beautiful ladies. You can count me in."

Hanging up the phone, I looked around my house, which I hadn't decorated at all, and decided that Christmas wouldn't be Christmas without a tree. I dragged my forty-year-old artificial tree out of the basement and spent the next seven hours decorating it and the rest of my house. It was well past midnight when I crawled into bed. But instead of feeling exhausted, I was exhilarated.

Early the following day, I shopped for groceries. I decided to prepare a Christmas Eve feast of beef bourguignon, mashed potatoes, and everything else that went along with that entree. I spent hours setting the table, using a full-length cloth and my finest tableware. It was absolutely stunning. I was even able to find my old silver tray. Not bad, I thought, considering that everything, including the table, came from either the local thrift shop or a garage sale.

Bill arrived first that night, dressed impeccably in a sport coat with pressed trousers. Since the ladies were a bit late, the two of us were able to sit and talk at the kitchen table while sharing hot cider. Finally, the ladies arrived. They were also dressed beautifully for our Christmas Eve celebration. In no time, we were in the living room, talking, laughing and simply enjoying the opportunity to spend this most special evening together. I'm not sure if it was due to that, or maybe it was when we all held hands and said the Lord's Prayer before eating, but somehow our dinner stretched into hours of conversation as we lingered around the table.

At first, there was the usual joking and laughter, but eventually it turned into a mutual sharing of life. We discussed Christmas memories, our personal situations, relationships gone awry, childhoods, a family situation not yet reconciled, and hope for a new relationship on the horizon. It was almost therapy, as tears and laughter were safely and openly shared.

"Hey, let's go to mass!" Susan said, looking at her watch. "If we leave now, we won't be that late."

Since the church was only two doors away, we all agreed. We grabbed our coats and headed out the door. Together, we settled into a rear pew while the choir sang in the loft. The church was dimly lit. We sat together, celebrating the birth of the Christ Child, and it couldn't have been more soul-satisfying. Secretly, we all felt the magic that only Christmas Eve can provide.

We walked home arm-in-arm that night. Reluctantly, we said our goodbyes on my front porch as we hugged. Although it was time, none of us was ready for the evening to end.

Bill stated it best: "This was the best Christmas Eve I've ever had, and I'll never forget it." Emotional and in tears, we all agreed that it was ours, too.

I went inside and looked around. The table was as we had left it. The sink was filled with dirty dishes waiting to be put in the dishwasher. My old tree was sparkling. Christmas carols were playing on the CD player. And feelings of love still lingered everywhere. *That's what Christmas is about,* I thought, *love.* Whether we're giving or receiving love, whether we're alone or with family or strangers, Christmas will always be about love. And starting with that little family huddled in a stable, it always has been and always will be.

Christmas never left. I'd simply lost sight of the bigger picture for a while. Family, I thought, isn't just relatives. Sometimes, family is a feeling, like when people are brought together around a table and share their love with former strangers. And it doesn't matter whether it's for a lifetime or for a few hours on a starlit Christmas Eve.

Indeed, love is what makes Christmas.

— Linda L. LaRocque —

73

The Pie Incident of 2005

Families are like fudge —
mostly sweet, with a few nuts.
~Les Dawson

At 4:30 P.M. on December 24, 2005, it was already pitch-black outside. From the window, I saw her walking up the driveway. I couldn't make out her face in the dark, but I knew it was her because she had already activated her battery-operated, blinking holiday-light necklace. And as if that wasn't enough for her grand entrance, she donned a second necklace made of sleigh bells that jingled loudly with every step she took.

My mom, Carol, had arrived.

When she took off her coat, the grandchildren giggled with delight to see her trademark red-velvet vest featuring a glitter-outlined Santa and reindeer. Standing in front of her fans, she showed off a bag full of presents in one hand and, in the other, a box from a local bakery that contained her dessert assignment: pecan pie. Carol had been a connoisseur of all things sweet since childhood. In fact, finding the perfect sweet for any special occasion was her superpower.

With no room in my refrigerator, I instructed her to put the pie in the garage. One of the few good things about Minnesota winters is the free refrigerator that the outdoors (or uninsulated garage, in this case) provides.

The evening went on as planned, marked by lots of laughter. After finishing dinner, we waited the customary five minutes to let our stomachs settle and then told Carol we were ready for dessert. She was on. This was her part of the show, and she loved it.

She retrieved the pie from the garage and marched in humming "Joy to the World" as she proudly placed the box in the center of the table. Oohs and aahs ensued, but from my vantage point I could see something was wrong: a semicircular hole in the side of the box. It looked like one of those mouse holes in old *Tom and Jerry* cartoons. As she opened the box to reveal the dessert, Carol was so pleased that she didn't notice the mouse sitting comfortably in the middle of the pie, using his little paws to hold his own piece.

Realizing she was oblivious to our extra guest, I shouted the only word of warning I could think of: "MOUSE!!!!" It took everyone a few seconds to comprehend what I was trying to communicate, and then there was a collective shriek followed by aunts, uncles, cousins and grandparents from the ages of eight to eighty running from the room, leaving chairs tipped over in their wake.

Swooping in to save the day, my husband slammed the box shut and walked out to the back yard. When he returned without the pie the real trouble began.

"Where is the pie?" my mom demanded.

My husband calmly explained that he had left the box and its contents outside. It was clear to him and every guest except for my mom that there would be no pie for dessert this year. But Carol continued, "What about the pie? Why did you leave it outside? Can't we just cut around the part where the mouse was sitting?"

Utterly speechless, my husband looked at me for help. "Mom... No... That's disgusting. We don't know how much of the pie the mouse actually touched, and we could all get sick," I explained, wondering why I even had to explain this to her.

Relentless, Carol looked at us and said, "But I paid $18.95 for that pie."

Feeling sorry for her nana, the youngest grandchild chimed in, "I want pie, too!"

Sobbing, another youngster pleaded, "What about the mouse? He will die out there in the cold! We have to let him back in!"

Regaining his ability to reason, my husband looked at the out-of-control crowd and addressed their concerns one by one. "I bet we have some Christmas cookies that will suffice for dessert tonight," he said to the youngest child. Then he gently explained to the young animal lover, "Honey, the mouse is plenty warm from eating all that pie. I am sure before tomorrow he will figure out how to get back in our garage the way he did the first time and bring lots of his friends."

Then his attention turned to my mom, but he could tell by the look on her face that she wasn't having any of it. Motivated by her sweet tooth and believing the amount she paid cancelled out any disease the mouse might spread, she once again firmly explained, "I paid $18.95 for that pie!"

At that point, regrettably, I lost my temper. "For Christ's sake, Mom, we are not eating that pie. I will give you $18.95 if it means that much to you!"

Awkward silence followed for what seemed like an eternity until a hard-of-hearing guest, who had apparently somehow missed the entire exchange, asked what was for dessert, creating an eruption of laughter.

Now fondly referred to as the Pie Incident of 2005, the story has taken on a life of its own. On Christmas Eve, it is a tradition for one of the original attendees to tell their recollection of the event — of course, right before dessert is served. It was the subject of a third-grade writing assignment aptly titled, *Mouse Pie*, and has been the impetus for my mother to receive mouse-themed Christmas ornaments every year since.

— Leslie Lagerstrom —

74

Recipe Magic

If baking is any labor at all, it's a labor of love.
A love that gets passed from generation to generation.
~Regina Brett

This holiday season, there are fewer gifts to buy and cards to mail. There are empty chairs at dinner tables and gaping holes in our hearts. In just over a year's time, I've lost my grandmother and two aunts. I am wondering what our holiday meals will look like this year — if my mom will host her annual Christmas Eve party, or if we will not feel ready to gather in the absence of those we have lost.

Last year, my mom asked me to bring a dessert to her post-Christmas dinner party. I flipped through some cookbooks that I've collected through the years that typically only gather dust. I considered a pound cake with a lemon glaze. I contemplated brownies with a caramel drizzle. I thought about a carrot cake with cream-cheese icing. Then I saw it: a dessert that my grandmother often made for my dad — Wayne's Favorite Apple Chip Cake. My mom had submitted the recipe to her church's cookbook a few years ago.

I knew I had to make it.

"I'm bringing a dessert," I told my mom over the phone. "I can't tell you what it is, though. It's a surprise for Dad."

"Okay," she said. "I'm making homemade fudge, so as long as your dessert isn't chocolate, it will be fine."

I read over the list of ingredients. It was a fairly simple recipe. As

I chopped apples and mixed dry ingredients, I wondered why it had been my dad's favorite. Once I poured the batter into the Bundt pan and slid it into the oven, I began to understand. The scent of nutmeg, allspice, and apple was intoxicating. I wasn't sure my dessert would last until the party.

I cradled that cake like a newborn on the way to my parents' house. Once we were there, I placed it on the table and waited for my dad to notice. It didn't immediately catch his attention, so I walked it over to him and asked him to guess what it was.

"You made an Apple Chip Cake!" he said. "That's what my mom used to send me when I was away at college."

He described the scent of the cake and how it made his hallmates flock to his room for a slice. The Apple Chip Cake was wrapped and placed inside a shipping box, but my dad's friends were always aware of its arrival.

After dinner, we nibbled on a variety of desserts, and we all had a piece of Wayne's Favorite Apple Chip Cake. At the end of the night, a bit of cake remained. I took a slice for myself and left the rest for my dad.

On the way home, I thought about how sacred family recipes are. Some are scrawled out in the handwriting of our aunts and grandmothers. They are smeared, stained, faded, and crumpled. Many are folded and stuffed into envelopes or slid inside cookbooks. But no matter how we find them, they can all tell us stories if we take the time to listen. We can imagine the flour residue on our grandmother's apron, hear her fuss about someone using the rest of the brown sugar, and watch her update her shopping list on the back of a receipt.

Recipes are magic, really. We gather ingredients, combine them in the prescribed way, and end up with the same tastes and aromas that generations before us have enjoyed. For a moment, we can be in their kitchens, standing in their shoes, and sharing their stories.

I still don't know what this year's holiday meals will look like — whether we will gather as an extended family or celebrate in our own homes. Either way, I'm going to spend some time going through my cookbooks and recipe collections. I want to follow one of my aunt's recipes for a holiday dessert and make something that helps me connect and remember. I'm going to try to share her story — one ingredient at a time.

— Melissa Face —

75

The Girl Who Came for Christmas

*Gifts of time and love are surely the basic ingredients
of a truly merry Christmas.*
~Peg Bracken

The girl was stunning, with sculpted cheekbones, liquid brown eyes, and a slim, elegant figure. But it wasn't her beauty that drew me. It was the haunted expression that swept across her perfect features when she thought no one was looking.

Together with sixty other background performers, we were on the set of a Christmas movie. Despite the overwhelming heat of the late August day, we were all clothed in wool jackets, down parkas, hats, scarves, and mittens.

Though we were all suffering, it was clear that the discomfort of being so overdressed in the scorching summer heat wasn't what had put that sad, empty look in the girl's eyes. A certain camaraderie often develops between complete strangers when faced with a common adversity. People chat together as if they were old friends, sharing stories they'd never dream of sharing with someone they'd just met.

Our mutual misery put us in just such an environment.

At lunch, I found myself sitting beside the quiet young woman, whose name was Alice. As we ate, I was overwhelmed by the sense that this young woman was hurting. After a few questions from me, she began to share her story.

It would take a few more days of working together for the story to unfold. I won't share details for the sake of her privacy, but I can say that she was twenty-three, the same age as my youngest daughter, and alone in a brand-new country. She had been displaced from her own for political and safety reasons.

When I learned of all she'd suffered at the hands of a corrupt government, and about the family she'd been forced to leave behind — a mother, a younger brother, and a girlfriend — my heart ached for her. She suffered from post-traumatic stress and depression, and she confided that she felt abandoned and alone.

I asked what she was doing for Christmas, which was still months away. "Oh, nothing," she said, with no hint of self-pity. "I'll just stay in my apartment. I don't feel safe going out on my own."

I couldn't bear the thought of this sweet girl spending the holidays alone. I didn't have to think twice. "Oh no you're not," I said with determination. "If you're interested, I'd love to have you spend it with me and my family."

Alice said, "Really?"

"Really," I answered, and showed her pictures of my two girls, my husband and our little Cocker Spaniel. I explained that each year we share Christmas dinner with friends who, like us, have no close relatives nearby. I assured her that they would love her just as much as I did.

Shortly afterward, I took my younger daughter and her best friend, whom we shared our Christmases with, to meet Alice. I hoped it would help her feel more comfortable if she met the girls before she came to celebrate Christmas with us. We gave her a bag of Christmas decorations for her tiny apartment and then took her for coffee.

The three girls, all the same age, had many things in common. Alice visibly relaxed as they chatted.

A few weeks later, a small wrench was thrown into our plans. My younger girl decided to head to Australia to spend the holidays with her new boyfriend.

Christmas without my baby girl? I was as horrified as she was excited.

Once I got over the shock, I realized that fate had intervened in the most perfect way possible. Here I was, a mother about to miss her daughter unbearably, and there was Alice, a daughter who was missing her mother probably just as much.

Life is so magical sometimes, isn't it?

When Alice arrived on the afternoon of Christmas Eve, I could tell she was a little overwhelmed. After all, she didn't really know us. But an extremely enthusiastic welcome by Pepper, our Cocker Spaniel, helped break the ice.

It didn't take long before Alice was smiling widely.

I took her to the guest room and settled her in, telling her to consider our home hers for as long as she wanted.

My older daughter and her fiancé arrived to help with preparations for Christmas dinner the next day. Alice chipped in without being asked, and soon we were all getting along wonderfully.

We explained that instead of dinner that night, we would snack on appetizers and spend the evening playing board games. Alice fit in well, having a blast as we played silly games and drank fancy Christmas cocktails. Watching her beautiful face light up eased the pain of missing my baby girl.

When I woke Alice in the morning, I gave her a hug and explained our family's traditions. Christmas mornings in our house have followed the same schedule since our girls were toddlers.

First, my husband puts on the coffee. Next, we pop our favorite breakfast dish, prepared the night before, into the oven to bake. Then we all head to the living room to check out what Santa has delivered in our stockings. When breakfast is ready, we take a break to eat and then return to the tree to open presents.

Alice was delighted to find that not only had Santa filled a stocking for her, but there were gifts for her under the tree. It brought me so much joy to see her laughing and joking with our family. The sadness in her eyes dissipated, at least for a while.

Our friends arrived in the early afternoon, bearing turkey and presents for everyone, including Alice. I don't think she expected that. But I'd let our friends know that I wanted her to feel like a part of our extended family, so of course they didn't dream of leaving her out.

We FaceTimed my younger daughter, who was basking in the heat of an Australian summer, and Alice told my girl, "Thank you for sharing your family with me."

Her comment brought tears to everyone's eyes.

After a long, joyful, and noisy dinner, we broke out the board games again, another tradition we've shared for almost two decades. We all laughed so much that my stomach ached, and my heart overflowed with love.

That night, I went to bed feeling particularly blessed, thrilled that we were able to make a lonely young woman's holiday a little brighter.

This Christmas, as we chatted about Alice and how I worried that she hadn't been answering my texts, my phone buzzed.

It was Alice — almost as if we'd conjured her by magic.

I was thrilled to hear she'd been reunited with her family and was spending the holidays with them. She'd contacted me to thank us for sharing our holiday with her and to tell me her mother sent her thanks, as well. She sounded so happy.

What a perfect full circle.

— Leslie Wibberley —

76

Heritage Cooking

Creativity is thinking up new things.
Innovation is doing new things.
~Theodore Levitt

"Where were Grandma and Grandpa born?" my ten-year-old son Jimmy asked as we were putting up the Christmas decorations.

"Here, in Canada," I answered.

Jimmy rolled a piece of masking tape, sticky side out, and fastened it to the back of a plastic Santa that decorated our basement door each year. "Where were their parents born?"

"Canada and England. Your dad's family has lived in Canada for centuries, in Quebec." Jimmy's sudden interest in genealogy surprised me. "Why do you ask?"

"Our class is making a recipe book, and we're supposed to give recipes for food that our ancestors ate at Christmas."

"I'm guessing that our ancestors ate pretty much what we eat at Christmas," I said.

"That's no good," Jimmy said. "It's supposed to be something different, something not from Canada."

"Our Christmas dinner at Grandma's is actually English," I said. "The turkey, the dressing, the pudding — they're English."

"Everybody knows about turkey and pudding. They're not different."

"You could take in the recipe for the *tourtière* we have on Christmas Eve," I offered. "Is that different enough? It's French-Canadian."

Jimmy scrunched his nose. "No, it's still Canadian."

"Well, I can't just pull a different heritage out of a hat," I said. "I don't think that's what your teacher wants."

"You don't understand. Jason's bringing in a recipe from Portugal, and this other girl's food is from Jamaica, and Steve's Ukrainian, and…"

"I didn't know Steve's family is Ukrainian," I interrupted.

Jimmy sighed.

"Wait a sec." I remembered a newspaper clipping I'd read years ago, which suggested that one of my husband's ancestors came from the area that is now known as Switzerland. "I might have something." I set a Santa snow globe on the bookshelf and reached for an album.

Jimmy joined me, and we knelt on the floor in front of the shelves. His finger traced the words Our Family Tree, printed in imitation gold leaf on a mock leather cover.

"I think one of your dad's ancestors came to North America from Switzerland." I leafed through the jumbled slips of paper with lists of ancestral names, which I had yet to copy into the album.

"Where's that?" Jimmy asked.

"Europe." I stood to find the *Larousse Encyclopedia of World Geography*. "I'll show you on a map." Jimmy didn't need to see a map. The word Europe sold him on a Swiss ancestor.

"What do they eat in Switzerland?" he asked.

I replaced the encyclopedia and found *The World Atlas of Food*. "They eat *rösti*." I read further and explained. "That's a potato cake. They also eat fondue. Tell you what. We'll make a fondue on the weekend so you can try it. You love cheese. You'll love fondue."

***

Christmas trees and menorahs cut from tempera-painted newsprint decorated the school gymnasium walls. A tinsel-laced basketball net hovered over the grade-six band members, who tuned their instruments while giggling phantoms shuffled behind royal blue stage curtains. I found a seat next to Steve's mom and hung my coat over the metal chair's back.

"Barb, can you believe it's been a year since the last Winter Festival?"

I asked.

"No, I can't." Barb gathered her coat onto her lap. "What recipe did Jimmy put in the class cookbook?"

"A cheese fondue." I pulled my camera out of my purse.

"What country is that from?" Barb asked.

"Switzerland," I answered.

The right side of Barb's mouth twitched. She nodded. "Steve gave a recipe for cabbage rolls."

"Oh, yeah. The Ukrainian recipe. I didn't know you guys are Ukrainian."

Barb leaned toward me. "Well, put it this way. We're about as Ukrainian as you are Swiss."

We both laughed. The lights dimmed, and the junior choir sang "Silent Night."

"Does this mean you won't be eating cabbage rolls for Christmas dinner?" I whispered.

Barb shook her head. "Are you kidding? Do you know how much work those things are?"

"Next year, you should be Swiss," I said. "Fondues are easy."

— Lynn Tremblay —

77

A Jewish Girl's Christmas

The fondest memories are made
gathered around the table.
~Author Unknown

I'll let you in on a secret: I love Christmas music. From *Rudolph the Red-Nosed Reindeer* to *Winter Wonderland*, I can't help but break into a smile, tap my feet, and hum along when I hear these songs being piped in at my supermarket.

I love Christmas décor, too. Even though I do most of my holiday shopping online, I still take a few trips to the mall during December just to see the decorations.

And Christmas movies are some of my all-time favorites. Even though I've seen *Miracle on 34th Street* and *It's a Wonderful Life* over a dozen times each, I watch them again every year. If I have time, I tune in to see *Frosty the Snowman,* too.

You are probably thinking that a lot of people think Christmas is the best time of year, and you are right. But what makes my situation a little unique is that I am Jewish.

When I was a kid, my mother would get grumpy during the holiday season. She hated seeing the decorations and hearing holiday classics everywhere she went. When she heard "Sleigh bells ring..." start to play, she would look annoyed and say, "I find it so rude. Not everyone in the store celebrates Christmas."

I think she was disappointed when I didn't nod my head and say, "Me, too. I hate it!" I guess it's hard when you feel so strongly about something as a parent, and your child does not agree.

Admittedly, I wished the stores had more than just one little menorah displayed because it made Hanukkah seem like an afterthought. It was the same with the holiday show at school; I wondered why the only song in the program for Jewish people was "Oh, dreidel, dreidel…"

But, unlike my mother, my heart had enough room for both holidays. I enjoyed our family's traditions of lighting candles, eating latkes, getting gifts and playing dreidel. I also liked seeing the splendor and fun of Christmas, even if it was not mine to celebrate.

Luckily for me, I met Andrea when I was a sophomore in college. She lived in my dorm, and although we were an unlikely pair, we became friends quickly. She was studying science and wanted to be a doctor. I was an English major with dreams of writing for a living. She was an athlete, and I was a klutz. Her record collection was legendary as was her giant stereo system. Conversely, I had six LPs to my name but plenty of books on my shelves.

Andrea was Italian and Catholic, so when she invited me to her family's Christmas celebration, I jumped at the opportunity. Finally, instead of looking through the window at the revelry, a place was being set for me at the holiday table.

My first Christmas dinner did not disappoint. Every inch of Andrea's was dressed up for the holiday with tinsel and twinkling lights. The food was plentiful and delicious. Her grandmother made homemade ravioli and gravy with meatballs and sausage. After we ate, her grandfather handed out songbooks, and we all sang Christmas carols. There was laughter, singing, and bickering — but mostly there was love around that table, and I was happy to be part of it.

Luckily, my first Christmas with the Mottas was the first of many. Christmas at Andrea's became a part of my holiday tradition. Even though life has changed a lot — we have moved, gotten married, changed careers, and had children — I still love hearing those Christmas carols when they start getting piped in at the mall. It reminds me that I will soon be sitting around the table sharing food, laughter, singing, and bickering — just like we have for three decades.

My family is Jewish. We love our religion and treasure our history, traditions and holiday celebrations. But, like me, my husband and kids love Christmas, too. We don't feel like outsiders when we join Andrea and her family because there is always room at the table. We don't need to share the same religion to share in a celebration.

It doesn't make us feel less Jewish to be a part of their Christmas. It just reminds us that, when it comes to love and ravioli, there is no such thing as too much.

— Randi Mazzella —

78

A Simple Strawberry Christmas Cake

*Baking is done out of love, to share with family
and friends, to see them smile.*
~Anna Olson

I am new at the whole stepmom thing. It feels awkward to even refer to myself as such. The kids already have two moms. Two amazing women raised them to be the kind and compassionate human beings they are today.

I wasn't there when they were sick or when they needed to be reminded to take out the trash. The last thing I want to do is step on anyone's toes or seem like I am slipping into a spot without earning it. I was there on the periphery as they grew up, an occasional visitor.

Their mom and I have been friends for almost two decades, but she and I were both well into our forties when we married, and her son and daughter were already in their twenties. I am not certain what I am to them, and if it's too late for me to be their stepmom. I'm not the type who imposes my presence on anyone, let alone two people who have a firmly established family that loves them abundantly. But I love them, too.

I'm not the best at showing my emotions. Although I can send heart emojis with the best of them, it's very different to say the words and wrap my arms around someone.

But I do want them to like me. I love their mom so much. Not only are they a piece of her, but I can see her in them. Their mom, Monica, and stepmom, Brenda, have lovingly reared them into two individuals whom I'm privileged to know. I'm not sure what I am to them, but I know that I want to be someone.

To Joseph, I am Donnasaurus. I'm not entirely sure how that name came about, but I like it. Izzy sometimes calls me a dork, and I can't help but love that. It always comes after I've displayed some type of cheesy verbal affection or after I've done something caring for her mom. Being a "dork" means I'm doing something right.

The holidays can be challenging with a blended family and multiple houses. The kids now have their own friends and family groups they're building. Joseph, who lives a couple of states away, usually spends the holidays with his new wife and her family, but we usually get to see Izzy for at least part of the time.

Because of the pandemic, last year was different. As we were unable to have our usual get-together, Monica decided she would make Izzy some of her favorite Christmas foods and take them over to her on Christmas Eve. I'm not the best cook, but I know my way around some fairly decent baked goods, so I offered to make Izzy a dessert to go with her mom's feast. She requested a strawberry cake with vanilla frosting, and I knew this was my time to shine.

After Googling about a thousand different variations on strawberry cake, I finally settled on what I hoped would be a beautiful and yummy Christmas cake. I was nervous. I wanted her to like it. Some would say that it was just a cake, but it was so much more than that. Not only did I want her to know that I put a lot of thought and effort into it, but I wanted her to feel that it was chock-full of positive energy and joy.

I don't know how to be a stepmom, but I know how to be a Donnasaurus who turns on some dorky Christmas music and bakes a cake that's filled with love.

— Donna Lynne Griggs —

79

Picking Up Strays

*Christmas is not as much about opening
our presents as opening our hearts.*
~Janice Maeditere

I "inherited" the task of hosting our traditional Christmas Eve
dinner from my mother when we moved into a house with a
big dining room. There was room for everyone around our long
table, and having a real fireplace in the dining room made it
even more special.

It was perfect for many years while our kids were growing up.
We usually had about twenty people around our table each Christmas
Eve. But, as the years went on, things changed. That number dwindled.
Our kids got married, had kids of their own and different obligations.
We lost some of our older family members, and others moved away. As
unimaginable as it seems, one Christmas Eve it was only going to be
dinner for two — my husband and me. Everyone else had other plans.

There was no need to set that big table in the dining room with
the Christmas tablecloth, good china, silver and crystal. We could
eat in the kitchen. It would be easier. No need to buy that huge roast
beef and all those pounds of potatoes to mash. We could each have a
steak and a baked potato. It would be much easier, with fewer dishes
to wash! No need for appetizers, fancy desserts or fine wine because
it was only dinner for two.

But wait… Dinner for two, I reasoned, should be just as special as
dinner for twenty! Maybe even more so. My husband and I deserved

something special, and so we would have it. It was, after all, a tradition, and we would carry it on even if it was a smaller version of the usual gathering. I had started to write my shopping list when the phone rang. My cousin and her husband had had a change of plans and wanted to know if they could come to our house. "Of course," I said. The next day, I received calls from a few more relatives whose plans had changed at the last minute. Our numbers were growing.

I learned that our neighbor was going to be alone for Christmas Eve. Oh, no, she wasn't! I wouldn't let that happen, so I asked her to join us. She was delighted. Then one of my sons called with the same story: Two of his friends had no place to go, so could he ask them to join us? We didn't even know them, but of course they could! And so it went, phone call after phone call. Our numbers continued to grow.

My husband put all the leaves in the dining-room table. It would be full once again. I got out the Christmas tablecloth, and we set the table with all the good things. My shopping cart was completely full when I did the shopping.

People started arriving. Some were family members; some were neighbors or friends; some were new friends we didn't know yet. Everyone told us how happy and grateful they were to share in our traditional Christmas Eve dinner. A warm fire was glowing as Christmas music played softly in the background. Then it was time to eat. I asked people to find a place at the table and sit down. My only request was that everyone sit next to someone they didn't know. Although apprehensive at first, everyone followed my directions. It was a little quiet at first, but soon the room was filled with laughter. Lots of laughter.

May I say that dinner was delicious? Absolutely scrumptious! I don't ever remember another Christmas Eve dinner that tasted as good as that one. Was it the food and wine, or could it have been the warmth and gratitude of the people around the table? Maybe a little of each? Who knows.

My grandmother called it "picking up strays." She had a habit of inviting people who had no place to go to her home for Christmas dinner — or for any meal. My mother did it, too, and here I was carrying on the tradition. It is a kind thing to do — both for the people who don't have a place to go and for yourself, sharing the warmth of your home with others. Picking up strays became our new family tradition, and I have passed it on to my children.

— Barbara LoMonaco —

80

Turkey and Foufou

A ship in harbor is safe, but that is not
what ships are built for.
~John A. Shedd

"Mom, is it okay if I invite a few of the mids for Thanksgiving?" asked my son Evan. "Mids" or midshipmen, are what Naval Academy students are called. Evan had been at the United States Naval Academy for two years. While it is an incredibly challenging school, he was thriving. We were very grateful that, after a lifetime of clothes left in heaps on the floor and vanishing homework assignments, our son had learned, not only to tidy up, but to polish and shine every square inch of, well, everything.

But with all the discipline and hard work, the mids were also forming lifelong friendships. It was a given that buddies unable to go home for the holidays would find a welcoming place at the table in any number of homes. We'd hosted Evan's roommate the previous holiday season and looked forward to meeting new guests.

"Oh, one thing, Mom," Evan continued. "These guys are exchange students. They're from Asia, Africa and Europe." I hadn't known that there was such a thing as a naval exchange, but there is — a limited number of foreign officers-in-training spend a year in Annapolis, learning the ways of the U.S. Navy. Our company this Thanksgiving would be Eldrick and Patrick from Cameroon, Costel from Romania, and Kanok from Thailand.

I was very excited about the international flavor we'd have at our dinner table. How best to roll out the red carpet for these special visitors? They'd probably love a traditional turkey and trimmings meal. But... couldn't we do more? I love to cook, so this was an excuse to haul out my wide variety of cookbooks and hit the food websites as well, to do a little research on the favorite foods of these three faraway lands.

I decided to roast a turkey, but then supplement it with sides from the other countries. I settled on Thai shrimp and lemongrass soup, and zacushka (a savory Romanian vegetable medley). Cameroon, though, was a stumper. The only recipe I could find from there was for something called foufou. Foufou turned out to be a very plain dish, similar to a corn meal mush. I ran it by Evan, who checked in with his African friends. "They are crazy about foufou, Mom! You have to make it!"

And so it was that Turkey Day morning found me in the kitchen, up to my elbows in eggplant, tomatoes, ginger and sesame oil. The bird went into the oven, and there was lots of jockeying for position in our oven with the other dishes. Luckily the Thai soup was a stovetop affair. I filled a casserole dish to the brim with the zacushka, and wedged it in beside the roasting pan.

But what about the foufou?

I followed the recipe (such as it was), stirring and stirring and tasting and tasting. The flavor never got any zippier, so I resigned myself to just making sure there were no lumps. Traditionally, cooked foufou is rolled into balls and dipped into a sauce, but there was no time for that. Our foufou would be just a little bit — different.

Meanwhile, in the family room, the young men were standing, ramrod straight, talking with my husband, mother and our other children. I was so used to the slouching teens who hung out with us during Evan's high school days that I was a little shocked. These guys had (much) better posture than me! It really was delightful to hear all the different accents — and lots of laughter too.

As I stood there, enjoying the festivities, I totally forgot that the foufou was still on the stove! For those who have never encountered boiling cornmeal — it's pretty intense. The scalding bubbles pop and spray all over. I was so worried about burning the dish that I snatched it off the heat, burning me in the process. I ended up scraping the unscorched part of the foufou into a serving dish and just hoped for the best.

First on the table was the spicy Thai soup. Kanok pronounced it authentic, so that was the first hurdle. As we launched into the turkey and zacushka, the friendly chatter continued, with the mids topping one another with funny, crazy stories about military life. Success! But wait — where was the darned foufou? After all that, I'd left it in the kitchen, and by now it had cooled down a good bit. I had a choice — reheat it into a mass of boiling cornmeal lava? Or just serve it as is? My blistered hand convinced me to go with Option #2.

I can't honestly say it was delicious. I can't say I'd ever prepare it again. But I'll never forget the joy on Eldrick and Patrick's faces as I put the dish on the table. "Foufou!" they exclaimed. "Just like home!" And at that moment, watching those young men, so many thousands of miles away from their families, I think the whole Thanksgiving gathering would have quickly identified the most important dish on the menu, for all of us.

It was the foufou.

— Elise Seyfried —

Chapter
8

Getting Creative

81

A Pandemic Office Party

The manner of giving is worth more than the gift.
~Pierre Corneille

I try to get all my holiday shopping done before the end of November each year so I can enjoy all the parties and festivities in December. In 2020, however, there wasn't much holiday excitement. We were experiencing the second wave of the pandemic, and my city was in another lockdown and would be well into the new year.

During the holidays, I normally looked forward to our office party, not only for all the food and games but for the tradition of Secret Santa. It was always fun drawing a name out of a hat and playing amateur detective to figure out a great gift for that person.

While the pandemic restricted any in-person holiday events in 2020, it didn't prevent us from continuing our celebrations virtually while we were all safely sheltering in place. And since this was a different year, our office Secret Santa worked differently, too.

Instead of picking a name and buying a physical gift for that person, my director Paul suggested that we select a name and donate to a charitable cause on behalf of that person. Everyone on my team jumped at the opportunity to participate. What a great idea!

If the pandemic taught us anything that year, it was that we should be getting back to what really matters. Material gifts for each other weren't important to us, but helping others and giving back, especially during such a challenging time, definitely were.

We arranged a virtual holiday party over Zoom. We ate our lunches in our respective homes while chatting about our scaled-back plans for the holiday break, including, of course, sharing TV recommendations with each other.

After eating, we took turns reading which charity had received a donation in our names, and our Secret Santas revealed themselves.

The person I selected had volunteered on Thanksgiving Day for the past two years serving food to community members in need. I made a donation for her to an organization that rescues fresh, surplus food (from places such as grocery stores, manufacturers, distributors, and restaurants) that would otherwise be thrown out and delivers it to social-service agencies around the city.

A colleague who had selected a dog lover on our team donated to a non-profit dedicated to rescuing dogs from unfortunate situations and finding them safe homes. Another co-worker gave to a foundation that funded education and research for a rare cancer because the person she picked had sat on their board for several years. And someone else supported a youth sport charity when she found out her chosen person was a big basketball fan.

Other charities to which members of our team contributed ranged from a children's hospital foundation to a regional community organization to groups cultivating young female leaders.

It was heartwarming to hear where each person donated and the reasoning behind it. People put a lot of thought and consideration into their choices. I think we were all more touched by these gifts of giving than any physical ones we would have unwrapped.

While I was initially disappointed that I was going to miss all the fanfare of our traditional office holiday gatherings, our virtual event in 2020 was definitely more meaningful. It brought us all together and celebrated the true spirit of the season. It also gave us the opportunity to create a new tradition that I hope we continue even when we return to our in-person holiday parties in the future.

— Debra Rughoo —

82

Creating a Christmas Tree

The perfect Christmas tree?
All Christmas trees are perfect.
~Charles N. Barnard

"**D**ress warm," my husband said. "It's time to get our Christmas tree." Tami, eight, and Ben, four, zipped up their jackets. I helped two-year-old Joel with his, wondering what Hal had in mind. Had he gotten a forest permit to cut down a tree? That would be a fun family field trip. Were we off to a Christmas tree farm? There were several only a half-hour from Portland. What had he found that we could afford this year with his business struggling and my part-time job at the community college put on hold?

"It's in our very own back yard," he explained as he led our little troop around the house.

Was he thinking about one of the hawthorns? No, they were too prickly. Surely not the cherry tree. What, then?

Hal stopped in front of a five-foot plant of questionable ancestry, possibly a fir tree some time back, but now more of a scraggly bush. Out of the base grew two spindly trunks, each supporting a few sagging branches with sparse needles. My heart sank as I gawked at it. Money or no money, we couldn't fool our kids into thinking this was a Christmas tree.

"You're kidding, right?" Ben asked.

"Think Charlie Brown's Christmas." Hal set his saw against the base. "When we get finished, it will be a beautiful Christmas tree."

"I want a tree like Nicole's." Tami folded her arms across her chest, tears misting her eyes.

Nicole was a new friend who lived up the street, and Tami was eager to make a good impression.

"Ours will be even better," Hal promised. "A homemade Christmas tree."

I'd seen Nicole's Christmas tree, a stunning, twelve-foot, perfectly symmetrical noble fir, lightly flocked like a fresh snow had blanketed it with soft powder. Decorated with large purple balls, it might have graced a window of Macy's or Saks Fifth Avenue. There was no way we could budget for one like it, but I didn't want to impose my financial concerns on the kids.

As self-appointed family cheerleader, I infused my voice with as much enthusiasm as I could muster. "Decorations will make all the difference," I promised as I hoisted Joel onto a hip, put an arm around Tami, and herded Ben in front of us toward the house.

While Hal finished cutting down the "tree" I handed down boxes of Christmas decorations from the attic. By the time the kids and I had stacked the boxes in the living room, Hal had the bush in the Christmas tree stand and was tightening the last screw. Beside him were clippers, a drill, and his pocketknife.

We watched as he clipped a branch off the back of the right trunk, drilled a hole on the side of the left trunk, whittled the end of the clipped branch to the size of the hole, and twisted and pressed the branch into its new position. "That's how my father did it," he said. "Not too many Christmas trees in New Mexico."

"Cool," Ben said.

"Very cool," I echoed.

When Hal had moved two more branches, the bush actually resembled a Douglas fir. I felt a stirring of hope, but worry lines still creased Tami's forehead.

"Lights, please." Hal took colorful mini lights from me, wound them around both trunks, and wove them through the sturdiest branches. We added red and gold balls wherever we could. "Not bad," Hal said, stepping back and studying the tree.

"It's still awful," Tami muttered. "What will my friends think?"

"It's getting better," I murmured, but my heart ached for my daughter. Eight years old is a tender age, and she didn't want to be embarrassed—especially not in front of Nicole.

"Everybody in the kitchen," Hal sang out. "I have a recipe for Christmas ornaments made from playdough. You can all create your own." He pulled flour and salt from a cupboard and was soon rolling out dough and parceling out cookie cutters, plastic knives and toothpicks.

Tami's face brightened as she shaped the dough into three round balls of varying sizes and created a snowman ornament. Ben made three cookie-cutter stars and then helped Joel cut out an angel. Hal fashioned a train engine and twisted two strips of dough into a wreath. Craft-challenged, I put on Christmas CDs and found sprinkles in the cupboard for the children to add to their ornaments. Using a straw, Hal punched holes for stringing thread in each ornament, placed the ornaments on a cookie sheet, and slid the sheet in the oven.

"Who wants to string popcorn while the ornaments bake?" he asked.

"Popcorn?" all three kids chorused.

I turned and kissed Hal on the cheek, although I still wasn't sure he could pull off a beautiful Christmas tree. "We have cranberries," I said. "We could string those, too."

We worked together, alternating popcorn and cranberries, although Joel mostly ate his popcorn. We made five strands, each about three feet long, and wound them around the tree. The effect was stunning. And my heart swelled watching all my chicks working so happily together.

The oven timer dinged, and I threaded the ornaments. "Hang them near the trunk; they're heavy," Hal instructed.

Tami's snowman, the stars, the angel, and Hal's train and wreath, hanging close to the center of our tree but clearly visible among the pine needles, added the final touch of magic. Hal placed his hands on Tami's shoulders. "What do you think?"

"My snowman looks good."

"He's perfect," he assured her.

The doorbell rang. Probably Nicole. I saw the concern on Tami's face, and my own breath caught as she let in her friend. "We've been making a Christmas tree," Tami said uncertainly. She took Nicole into the family room to see our creation.

"It's beautiful!" Nicole cried. "I wish we had popcorn and cranberry strings on ours. Where'd you get the train?"

The lines in Tami's forehead smoothed. She linked her arm through Nicole's. "My dad made the train. Our family made our whole tree. You really think it's beautiful?"

Nicole nodded and said, "Our families have the prettiest trees in the neighborhood."

Hal winked at me. My shoulders relaxed. To transform a backyard bush into a beautiful, homemade tree, we had worked together in love and the spirit of Christmas.

— Samantha Ducloux Waltz —

83

Not Giving Up on Christmas

What is Christmas? It is the tenderness of the past,
courage for the present, and hope for the future.
~Agnes M. Pahro

As twilight fell, I finished the note in my last Christmas card and placed it on the stack near the packaged gifts that were ready for mailing. I admired the twinkling Christmas tree and sighed with satisfaction. Thanksgiving was only days away, and I was ready for both holidays!

I loved having an entire month to relax and enjoy the Christmas season. It gave me time to prepare my traditional homemade assortment of chocolate nut clusters, fudge, and pecan pralines while enjoying my favorite Christmas CDs.

This had been my routine for over two decades, but things were different now. My house was empty. This was the second Christmas since my husband, Jerry, the love of my life for forty-seven years, had passed away. Our children, busy with their own family traditions, lived in other states.

That first Christmas, I had neither the heart nor energy to decorate and celebrate Christmas. Even spending Christmas with my children wasn't the same without Jerry. Maybe I was too distracted dealing with the sudden responsibilities of widowhood. One of them required quickly downsizing from our two-story, five-bedroom home to a tiny but adorable, more affordable place. I was resigned to the fact that Christmas would never be the same without Jerry.

Though my heart still ached, I decided sometime during my second year that I could not give up on my favorite season! Maybe the decorations would brighten my spirits. The warm lights, glowing on the tree and many indoor plants, might drive the darkness from the long, empty evenings and make it cozier for my cat and me as we snuggled in our recliner.

After my faithful handyman brought down the decorations from the attic, he staked the larger items into the ground, and I decorated everything I could reach. Keeping to our tradition, all the decorations were up and the lights were ready to go on the Saturday before Thanksgiving.

The only thing left to do was create the sweetest part. But why? What would I do with my traditional twenty-five pounds of homemade candies?

I had loved placing the tasty morsels in baking cups, arranging them in attractive Christmas tins, and giving them to people who had gone out of their way during the year to help us in some way. Special friends and relatives, of course, were always recipients. But here I was in a new neighborhood and had met only a few of my neighbors. Most of them worked during the day. Besides, Jerry wasn't here to eat his share.

"I know," I said aloud. "What better way of getting acquainted than by taking neighbors a container of my candies and introducing myself?"

Suddenly, the sweet voices of singing children interrupted my thoughts. After hurrying to the front door, I stepped outside and stood in the shadows beneath my roof overhang to quietly investigate.

About a dozen children stood on the sidewalk facing my brightly lit nativity set that was centered in the front yard. The large, colorful plastic figures, with lights glowing softly on the inside, represented Joseph, Mary, Baby Jesus, three wise men, and a camel. The children's cherubic faces, eyes wide in wonder, glowed as they sang softly "Silent night, holy night…" I saw no adult and assumed this was a spontaneous act by neighbor children. Moved by their awed expressions, I glanced around the yard, trying to see everything through their eyes.

Every bush bloomed with colored lights. A family of twinkling deer stood by a stream of glittering blue and white lights, simulating a creek. The fawn lowered its head mechanically as though drinking. Across the yard, a white mamma polar bear and her baby nodded their heads in approval. Glistening icicles clung to the eaves of the house as they crawled upward to a huge, brilliant star, the focal point of the gabled roof, and then back down.

When the singing stopped, I stepped out of the shadows, introduced myself and thanked them. "Your singing sounds like angels! Thank you so much!"

We chatted for a few minutes. Some children pointed to their house while others said they were visitors. As I turned to go inside, I regretted that I had nothing to offer them. If only I had made my candies!

Suddenly, I turned and called out, "Stop by after Thanksgiving for some hot chocolate and homemade candies. They will be ready by then." They all cheered, promising to come.

What began as a simple gesture that year became a popular Christmas tradition, one that quickly expanded to include the parents. To get better acquainted and deepen friendships, I began inviting one family over each evening. Now, even couples without children look forward to coming. Sometimes, it is just one person — a lonely widow, widower, or divorcee. To accommodate more guests, I extended the time until mid-January since my decorations stay up until the last weekend of that month anyway. Many adults who work and are extremely busy before Christmas look forward to a relaxing visit after the rush.

One year, I decided it would be fun to give each child a Christmas mug. The first Christmas that I set out a display of mugs and let the children choose one, I realized I had a winner! They loved the idea of choosing their own mug, knowing they could take it home. I soon realized that adults are still children at heart and also enjoy picking out their mugs. "I still have the one I got here last year, and I love it," one father commented, eyeing the selection for another.

I only select mugs that are unique and exceptionally attractive.

Because I am a thrift-store junkie, I pay very little for each mug. I discovered that if I wait until a day or two before Christmas, some thrift stores mark their mugs down to as little as twenty-five cents each! That way, I can stock up for the next season.

I also appreciate Christmas cards, especially those including hand-written notes. Because my cozy home lacks wall space to display the many I receive, I solved the problem by buying a small Christmas tree with lights at a thrift store. After placing the tree on an end table, I used a hole puncher and ornament hangers to attach each card to the tree. Not only were the cards beautifully displayed, but I created another unique decoration.

When it came time to remove the cards from the tree, I invited the next-door children over for a "Card-Removing Party." Afterward, I served them ice cream and cookies. They so enjoyed this that I had to promise they could do it again next year. *Voilà!* Yet, another tradition was born!

It's hard to believe that fifteen years ago, I almost gave up on Christmas.

— Kitty Chappell —

84

2020 Crazy Christmas Challenge

The best advice I ever received came from my mother:
"Do at least one fun thing every day."
~Clifford Cohen

The Emergency Health Orders of November 2020 were hardly a surprise, and yet I felt a dark cloud descend over me as I listened to our Provincial Health Officer on the news. British Columbians were being asked not to gather with anyone outside their household over the holidays. In that moment, it felt like Christmas itself had been cancelled.

In anticipation of a disrupted holiday season, I had already been planning some long-distance activities to keep the children of our extended family connected. But as the reality of the Health Orders sank in, I realized that *all* of us — adults included — needed something positive to anticipate. Winters on the west coast of BC are wet and gloomy at the best of times, but this year more than ever we needed something bright to lift our spirits.

Over the next few days, I went into overdrive, brainstorming fun challenges that each household could do on their own and then share virtually. When I had the framework in place, I sent out an invitation by group chat: "While we can't gather in person this season, that doesn't mean we can't have some festive fun. You are invited to participate in the month-long, 2020 Crazy Christmas Challenge."

Enthusiastic replies came back immediately: "Count us in!"

My fourteen-year-old daughter volunteered to be my "helper elf," and together we spent a busy weekend printing instructions, accumulating supplies, and packaging individual challenges in envelopes and brown paper bags. Over the next week, I scheduled curbside deliveries for the six other households on Vancouver Island that had signed on to participate.

There were twelve challenges in all, to be completed in order through December, as best suited each family's schedule. I set up a private 2020 Crazy Christmas Challenge Facebook page so that participants could post photos or videos of their completed projects for everyone else to enjoy. To avoid spoiling any surprises, each challenge had a tag with "Please Do Not Post Photos Before (pre-determined date)."

The first challenge was my favorite: What do Potato Heads have to do with Christmas? Each household received a bag with one potato per family member, along with grass seed, cotton balls, colorful pompoms, and large googly eyes. Participants were tasked with making and decorating a potato person or creature, and partially carving out the head to make room for moist cotton balls and grass seed. Points were awarded for completing a potato head, as well as for successfully growing "hair." I also set up a free survey account so that everyone could vote anonymously for the most creative and most attractive potato heads.

As the first photos went up on our private Facebook page, I knew the challenge was going to be a success. Every member of every household had participated, and the results were hilarious, from space aliens to a shark to a glamourous movie starlet.

The remaining challenges varied in time and the amount of creativity required. We made marshmallow igloos and "Yourself-the-Elf" Christmas ornaments. We completed customized crosswords, origami stars, cardboard reindeer models, and individual sections of a large jigsaw puzzle. We baked our favorite goodies, sang revised Christmas carols, and ticked off items on a festive scavenger-hunt list.

At the end of the month, the family with the most accumulated points was awarded a grand prize of a board game and fun treats.

Everyone else received a participation prize — already included in their challenge box — with soda, microwave popcorn, candy and a list of fun holiday movies.

The 2020 Crazy Christmas Challenge was just what we needed as an extended family. The individual activities gave us something fun to anticipate, along with a reason to connect and share on an almost-daily basis through the month of December. From ages two to seventy-two, everyone participated enthusiastically. It couldn't replace the joy of gathering in person, but the Challenge brought light and laughter to an otherwise bleak season.

While I don't anticipate that we'll repeat the entire Crazy Christmas Challenge, we may revisit a few individual activities in coming years. In particular, I plan to make grass-haired potato heads a new holiday tradition. Whenever I was feeling particularly low last Christmas, I would glance over at my festive potato man, and his big ears, red nose and goofy grin never failed to make me smile. I want to remember my Potato Head — and the hope it represented when I needed it most.

— Rachel Dunstan Muller —

85

Secret Santa

Christmas has come, and it's a time to have some fun.
~Author Unknown

I don't remember what brought me out, but as I stepped out of the car into the gently falling snowflakes, Christmas shopping seemed like a splendid idea. I searched the aisles, trying to find that perfect gift for my in-laws. What do you buy for someone who has everything? I had just about given up hope when I spotted a box at the end of the aisle. A nativity set. This year, we would give memories.

When I arrived home, I placed the nativity set on the dining-room table and gathered my supplies — boxes, brown paper, packing tape, a sheet of paper, typewriter, a book of Christmas carols, and my Bible. I opened the Bible and noted the passages that corresponded with the nativity set; then I found a related carol. I typed up five slips — each with a passage from the Bible to read and a Christmas carol to sing. I created a slip for Mary and Joseph, the animals, shepherds, Wise Men, and the Christ child. I packed each grouping with its paper slip, wrapped it in plain brown paper and attached a typed address label. My in-laws were in for a holiday mystery.

I sent the first box the following day, with no return address. I continued to ship them — one per week. The Christ child was not shipped; He would arrive on Christmas Day.

We spoke with Mom and Dad several times between the onset of the package shipping and our arrival for Christmas. No mention was ever made of the mysterious packages. On our Christmas Eve arrival, we noticed the figurines from the nativity set, some slips of paper, and the Bible resting beneath a lamp on the living-room table. Mom bubbled with excitement as she showed her granddaughters what her secret friend from church had been doing for them. (Bless them for not telling my secret!)

After Christmas Eve services and a cup of hot chocolate, everyone went to bed — except for me. I had one more plain-wrapped package to place under the tree.

When I descended the stairs in the morning and wandered into the kitchen, I found Mom and Dad arguing.

"What's a nativity set without the Baby?"

"Maybe it'll come in the mail today."

"Mail doesn't run on Christmas Day!" Mom shook her head as she tossed the dishtowel on the counter.

"Well, I don't know. I'm sure it'll be here." Dad slipped on his coat and went outside in a futile attempt to see if the baby had arrived.

I slipped back up the stairs. "Sweetie, maybe this wasn't such a good idea. Your parents are downstairs bickering."

"Everything will be fine," Willie said reassuringly. I prayed he was right.

The last present under the tree sat alone and forgotten. No bright paper or shiny ribbons. No glitter or sparkle. Just a plain, typewritten label. I nudged my daughter Rachael and encouraged her to give it to Grandma. But when Grandma told her to put it back, Rachael looked at me in desperation. "Mom, she won't even look at it." That got Grandma's attention. And as she took the simple brown package from her granddaughter's hand, she recognized the familiar parcel.

She looked at me. "It was you?"

Dad laughed. "I told you the baby would be here!"

Every Christmas, Grandma and Grandpa decorate things differently, but one thing will always be there under the lamp's soft glow: a beloved nativity set and some very special memories.

— Deborah Young —

86

Cocoa & Candy Canes

A well-balanced person is one who finds
both sides of an issue laughable.
~Herbert Procknow

When public schools closed in March 2020 due to the pandemic, my husband and I agreed that this pandemic was going to be a test of biblical proportions. With four children ranging from ages five to fourteen, there was never a dull moment in our house, and our calendar proved it. My father affectionately called me "Uber Mommy" since I was always on the go. But since extracurricular activities were postponed indefinitely, I started to relax.

Saying "I'm bored" was blasphemous in our house, so rest assured we were equipped with board games and books, social media and snacks. I encouraged the kids to pull out toys that were long forgotten. They rode bikes and rediscovered their imaginations. We painted works of art, built puzzles, and practiced yoga. We even wrote letters to friends and family.

Eventually, our children fell into a natural rhythm: wake up, eat, virtual school, lunch break, more virtual school, eat again, play outside until dinner.

Tyler, our eleven-year-old, resumed playing the piano. "Play Ariel's song," five-year-old Amber demanded, which was code for "Part of Your World" from *Little Mermaid*.

"Now, play *Aladdin*," Summer, our eight-year-old, commanded as if she were a queen and Tyler her royal subject.

Our daughters squealed with delight while Tyler played their requests. Eventually, they added choreography that Summer had picked up from watching *Hamilton* a dozen times. When I realized how happy this made them, I figured that others would enjoy hearing them play, too.

What should have been an enjoyable childhood memory turned into a mommy-fail in record time. Uber Mommy transformed into Social Media Mom! I started posting videos of the kids performing together all the time. The response on Facebook was overwhelming. Some of my favorite hashtags were #KingdomKids, #BrotherSisterLove, and #RonaRecitals. Nothing compared to #TinyBathrobeConcerts named in honor of NPR's *Tiny Desk Concerts*. Tyler had stopped wearing clothes around mid-May, opting instead for his bathrobe and boxers. It was a perfect fit.

Fast forward to the holiday season. Who doesn't like hearing Christmas carols? Who doesn't love hearing kids singing Christmas carols? I figured we could capitalize on the moment. People longed for a bit of nostalgia — nostalgia being last year. I came up with an idea: Cocoa & Candy Canes: A Tiny Bathrobe Holiday Concert. The kids would perform on Zoom and Facebook. It was a brilliant plan... or so I thought.

My husband watched with veiled amusement as I organized the program. You would've thought I was coordinating the Rockettes' Christmas show. Our house looked "lived in," the politically correct way of saying, "You're one step away from being on the television show, *Hoarders*." I hid our junk strategically behind the couch and used the Christmas tree as the backdrop. I practiced recording from my cell phone, careful to avoid the Lego landmine and Barbie wasteland that had become the living room. I consulted with no one; it was my event, and no one could tell me anything different.

"Babe, aren't you doing a bit much?" my husband hinted casually. He was a voice of reason on more occasions than I'd care to admit.

"You just want to steal my joy! Let *me* be great!" I snapped. If only I had listened to him.

I sent virtual invitations and publicized on Facebook. I chose an image with a cup of cocoa filled with marshmallows and candy canes. Even the font oozed holiday magic. I contacted current and former teachers, as well as coaches and classmates. I sent text messages to my entire contact list, sharing that my kids were performing, and all were welcome to join the festivities.

The children chose a few songs, but I had final approval. "Jingle Bells," the holiday classic, was an obvious choice, a great sing-along for the audience. I found Santa hats with bells at the tip. Amber didn't want to sing, but she agreed to ring the bells. She found every excuse to practice every day, all day. We couldn't get Amber to stop; she was dedicated. Needless to say, rehearsals were a bit challenging. "Silent Night," my mother's favorite, was the second selection, and "Mary, Did You Know," performed as a piano solo by Tyler, was third. Summer loved Mariah Carey's modern holiday hit, "All I Want for Christmas Is You," and "We Wish You a Merry Christmas" would be the grand finale.

Practice was every day after virtual school. "You practice like you play" was our motto. People continued to feed my ego. "Just think," they'd say, "your kids could form a band. They're so talented." I became obsessed with Summer's enunciation and making sure Tyler used the damper pedal at just the right time. I was determined that everything would be perfect.

Performance day arrived! My husband had rare time off from work. Due to the pandemic, his shifts at the hospital had increased.

You would've thought I was backstage at the Kennedy Center, barking orders in advance of curtain call. I enlisted the help of my older son, Hunter, to manage the Zoom virtual waiting room while I filmed the concert. He sauntered into the office with the speed of a sloth and the enthusiasm to match. In true teenager fashion, he plopped down on the chair and resumed playing on his cell phone, completely oblivious to everything and everyone.

I insisted that the kids coordinate their outfits. I looked in vain for matching holiday pajamas; alas, even Amazon Prime couldn't help me. Luckily, I found red tunic shirts with silver glitter for the girls at Kohl's. Tyler wore a long-sleeved red shirt we found in Hunter's closet. I brushed the girls' hair and greased their faces until they looked like shiny pennies. I inspected everyone's teeth and nails because the camera picks up on everything.

It was show time! I opened the Zoom link. Our family friend, Stephanie, wore festive holiday pajamas and an elf ear headband. My mother dressed up as if she were going to a bona fide professional concert, adding an element of sophistication to the event. Others started logging in, including Tyler's former orchestra teacher. I synced the Zoom with Facebook and began Cocoa & Candy Canes: A Tiny Bathrobe Holiday Concert.

That's when everything started to go wrong.

"What are you doing?" I whispered to Hunter. He wasn't paying attention to the Zoom. He was mesmerized by his game, expertly thumbing the screen. "Put the phone down and please do your job," I hissed.

I rushed the other kids out of the office and into the living room, pumped up with nervous energy. My husband sat squarely in the center of the couch; my ideal recording location was no longer an option.

"What are you doing?" I shrieked.

"I'm going to record. What does it look like I'm doing?" he asked coolly.

"No! You're in the way!" I was getting flustered. My family wasn't listening to me, but the audience was. I'd forgotten to mute the computer microphone.

I positioned myself in a corner with the mini iPad, trying my best to contain my excitement. Summer started to sing, and all was right with the world until she forgot the words. I almost dropped the device. Seriously, who forgets the words to "Jingle Bells"?

Thankfully, Tyler kept playing. Relieved that the moment was over, I motioned for Amber to ring the bells. Guess what? She didn't want to anymore! For weeks, we couldn't get Amber to stop shaking them, and now she refused. I gave her the "get-over-here-NOW" hand gesture usually reserved for the "don't-you-embarrass-me-in-the-store" moments. She reluctantly obeyed, but there was no joy in her jingle.

By the time they reached the finale, I was spent. We thanked the viewers, hoping they enjoyed the concert. I excused Hunter from his

Zoom duties and ended the recording. As if the experience couldn't get worse, it turned out that our Facebook friends never saw the concert! There was a software update that I failed to complete. People sent messages claiming they received my reminders, but nothing appeared on my page. I was devastated. All that work for nothing!

My grandma used to say, "God don't like ugly," and I had really shown my ugly side that night. When I reviewed the Zoom footage, the entire recording was blurry. I had practiced for weeks with my iPhone, which always produced high-quality videos, but I used the iPad at the last minute assuming it would be better. "Why didn't you just use your cell phone?" Hunter asked as he casually sought refuge in the kitchen, burying himself in the pantry. I glared at him, mad that he was right. I started bawling.

"What's wrong, Mommy?" the girls asked with genuine concern.

I moaned, "Everything." I went from Social Media Mom to Drama Mama in five seconds flat.

"Mom, were people happy?" Tyler questioned. I showed him the comments. The Zoom viewers enjoyed the concert.

He said, "Then what's the matter? You told us we were doing this to make *other* people happy." I explained that their performance wasn't seen on Facebook as I had planned. People looked forward to hearing them. My ego had gotten in the way. With wisdom far beyond his age, Tyler said, "Okay, then, let's do it again."

The next day, my kids went live on Facebook and did the entire concert again. No props and no fancy angles. Their outfits didn't match, but Tyler did muster the strength to wear clothes instead of his tiny bathrobe. Summer didn't forget the words. Amber opted out of her bell-ringing duties. Most of all, I stayed out of their way.

Okay, almost... You can hear me singing back-up vocals on "All I Want for Christmas Is You." Can't keep a Social Media Mom down!

— Miya Hunter-Willis —

87

The Christmas Card Challenge

I think the family is the place where the most ridiculous
and least respectable things in the world go on.
~Ugo Betti

My wife has this perfect cousin, Angela, in her hometown of Scranton. Angela has the looks and figure of a model, and she has two perfect little boys and one perfect little daughter. She has a gorgeous house that she got a tremendous deal on. In fact, she gets a tremendous deal on everything she buys, and she is very proud to tell you about each bargain. She is happy, bubbly, funny, generous, and so sweet that you just have to love her, no matter how imperfect she makes you feel.

We went for a visit from our house in Philadelphia, feeling like the Clampetts as we pulled our seldom-washed, wrapper- and crumb-strewn Subaru Outback into her driveway. Her house appeared to be professionally decorated for Christmas, but of course she had done it all herself. The outside was perfectly adorned with lights. There were angels and a nativity scene out front, a giant Santa on the side, and a two-story glowing snowman in the back yard for the kids to see from their bedroom windows.

I paused and thought of our house. We had half a bush lit up out front, along with a thick orange extension cord stretching across our walk and over our porch railing to the outlet. It was pathetic and probably hazardous.

I come from a long line of inferior holiday decorators. My father would take the tangled lights out of the storage bin and just hang them up in a messy ball. One year, the Halloween pumpkin above our door was still around months later, so he painted "Merry Christmas" on it in black paint.

Now we entered Angela's spotless home with our wrinkled clothes, stained with baby vomit and spilled yogurt. We were confronted with the bows, garlands and wreaths that filled every room. It was even more impressive than the perfect outside décor.

Angela showed Marissa and me the perfect Christmas card that she had made on her computer. She and her father were dressed as Mr. and Mrs. Claus, and her mother, children and grandmother were dressed as elves. She had made the costumes herself using discarded pool-table felt, cotton balls and old pajamas. She downloaded the image and printed out 100 copies. It had taken all of two hours and cost her $18.38, not including stamps.

After admiring the card, Marissa said that she was also going to make our own Christmas cards this year with our two-year-old Jesse and one-year-old Daniel on them. "I can't wait to see them," Angela said with just a tinge of sarcasm and a hint of a knowing smirk.

The next morning on the way home, Marissa told me she was going to prove Angela wrong. She wasn't upset. Angela was right. My wife, God bless her, thinks about and starts doing a lot of things, but somehow something comes up or goes wrong. And, like most of my projects, they usually end up half-finished.

That night, we dressed up the kids and tried to make them laugh, taking dozens of shots until we got the perfect one. Marissa bugged me for days to get the picture on a CD for her. After about a week of procrastinating, I finally got it to her.

The next day, she rushed off with the kids to the photo center at a nearby big-box store. There was no image to be found on the CD. She came home upset and confused but armed with the knowledge that she could take the memory card from the camera, which the picture machine at Target would be able to read.

She unloaded the kids from the car, took them into the house, and then grabbed the memory card. She loaded them back into their car seats and drove back to Target. Once there, she spent half an hour cropping and editing the picture until it was just right. All the while, Jesse screamed for a *Dora the Explorer* lunchbox he saw, and Daniel screamed to be nursed. The girl behind the counter told her to come back in twenty minutes for the printed photo.

Marissa decided to kill some time pushing the cart with the boys in it around the aisles, with Jesse screaming that he wanted this and that and Daniel frantically trying to lift up her shirt to nurse while she shoved Goldfish into his mouth.

When she returned to the photo center, she found that the picture looked like a fuzzy Renoir painting. If we squinted at it from about ten feet away, we could kind of make out Jesse and Daniel.

With the kids absolutely out of control, Marissa decided to go back another day to redo the thing. Two days later, she trudged back in, well-armed with Goldfish and cheddar bunnies, ever determined to show up Angela.

She didn't crop so much this time. She handed it over to the girl at the counter again. After spending twenty minutes saying to Jesse, "No, you can't have that. No, I'm sorry… No… No, maybe next time," while shoving food into Daniel's mouth, she finally got the picture back. It looked much better.

Now, how to dress it up? Being raised Catholic, she was initially drawn to the manger scene with the baby Jesus. But she decided to go non-denominational to be more inclusive and chose "Happy Holidays" as a theme. She placed her order and left with the boys, relieved that she was finally through the toughest part of the process.

The next day, she rushed back with the boys, who fell asleep in the car on the way. She reached out to me and asked if I could drive over to watch the boys in the parking lot while she ran in to pick up the cards. I wasn't too far away, and after I showed up, she walked back into Target and saw a sign over the counter that said, "SORRY, BUT WE WILL NOT BE MAKING ANY MORE HOLIDAY CARDS."

Frantic, she asked for her order, and the girl behind the counter said, "You got yours in just in time."

Relieved, Marissa paid for the order and started walking out to the parking lot as she opened one of the envelopes. There, next to the beautiful picture of our boys, it said, "HAPPY HANUKKAH." She screamed at the top of her lungs, "I can't freaking believe it!"

So, she sent me back in to take care of the situation.

After explaining several times to several levels of management that we weren't Jewish and this was an error, I was able to get us a refund, and we got to keep the cards. Doing them over was not an option. So, we sent them out. And surrendered to that perfect girl in Scranton.

— Richard McIlhenny —

A Crafty Christmas Beard

The most wasted of all days is one without laughter.
~Nicolas Chamfort

When my four children were young, my husband always dressed up as Santa Claus on Christmas Eve. After dinner, he'd mysteriously disappear and then show up at our front door, ringing his sleigh bells and carrying a big bag of toys.

One year, while my husband was getting ready for his appearance as Santa, I was busy in the kitchen baking cookies with my children. Out of the corner of my eye, I could see him peeking out from behind the bedroom door looking very upset. His beard was missing. It wasn't in the box with his Santa suit.

"You're the crafty one," he whispered, "so think of something quick."

My mind raced. What could I come up with that would look like Santa's beard? It was too late to run to the store and find a substitute beard.

"Hang on a minute," I said quietly. "I've got just the thing you need. Meet me in the bathroom ASAP."

I quickly scooted the children out of the kitchen, gave them a whopping plate of cookies, and sat them down in front of the television set. Then I ran to the bathroom to meet the bare-faced Santa.

"I hope this will work. It's got to," I said, pulling out a plastic bag of cotton balls along with a bottle of Elmer's glue. "We'll say Santa got a permanent and even glue some cotton balls onto your eyebrows. You'll look like a one-of-a-kind special Santa for sure.

We played with the glue to make it sticky enough to hold the cotton balls, but not runny enough that the balls would slide down Santa's face. In about ten minutes, the job was finished. It looked like a craft project gone wrong, but it would work in this emergency.

A few minutes later, the doorbell rang, and we heard Santa's voice.

"Ho ho ho! Merry Christmas! Have you been good little boys and girls this year? If you have, I have some presents for you."

Santa was smart. He diverted the children's attention to the toys in his bag and not his face. My daughter Vicki said that Santa's beard looked funny and needed to be combed out because it was too curly. My son Scott said his beard looked like a Poodle.

When Santa was offered a cookie that got stuck to his beard, he decided it was time to leave and bolted out the door with a hearty "Ho, ho, ho!" He left behind some cotton balls that had fallen off his face and onto the floor. The cat had fun playing with Santa's "beard" that Christmas.

— Irene Maran —

89

The Mystery of the Missing Jesus

The best of all gifts around any Christmas tree:
the presence of a happy family
all wrapped up in each other.
~Burton Hillis

To teach my children about Jesus's birth, I collected a variety of manger scenes throughout the years. We had a few plastic sets that we placed within reach of little hands, wooden ones for the floor, a special Grandma-made ceramic arrangement that we placed on the fireplace mantel to keep it safe, and a big, chunky, rubbery set in the bathroom right where the children would wash their hands. I even had a group of rubber ducks—kings, Joseph, Mary, and a baby Jesus—that floated in the tub.

The year Allie was six, Steven was four, and Martin was six months old, an odd thing began to happen. The children played with the sets, but the baby Jesus figures were constantly missing. During the week, I would find Jesus in the plastic-container drawer, stuffed in drying boots, in the garbage can, and on Hot Wheels car ramps.

The mystery was solved when I went to run a load of clothes in the washer and found what Steven had hidden in his pockets: the usual rock and melted crayon, but also three baby Jesus figures wrapped in a sock. Steven wanted to have figures of his own.

Feeling clever, I called the gal who ran our local religious-goods shop and headed down to the store. She had a few small, cream-colored, plastic Jesus figures. My thought was that I could give Steven his own baby Jesus wrapped in a soft flannel square, and he'd stop absconding with the others.

Like any mother of small children, I looked in the clearance section. A box of 100 small, glow-in-the dark Jesus babies, which had been mis-ordered, stared back at me. This was way more than I needed, but I bought them.

Steven loved his little gift of his very own Jesus and held it tight, but the babies were still on the move!

I cunningly replaced the missing baby figures in the nativity sets from my secret stash.

I kept replacing Jesus babies while still hunting for hidden ones during the coming days.

One night, while sitting in the dark with the family gazing at the beautiful, shining Christmas tree, Allison got up to get her favorite book. Her foot caught the cable connecting the tree lights, which pulled out the cord.

Immediately, the room became dark. For a moment, I thought I was having a problem with my eyes because little lights were glowing all around the living room!

They were all the baby Jesus figures Steven had hidden around the area.

I laughed and hugged him. Our Christmas joy surrounded us with a glow that I will never forget.

— Christy Piszkiewicz —

90

Reindeer Food

May you never be too grown-up to
search the skies on Christmas Eve.
~Author Unknown

I don't remember where it came from, but reindeer food appeared in our kitchen one Christmas Eve. I knew it was reindeer food because a label on the small brown bag said so. Glued to the other side of the bag were two construction-paper antlers, a fuzzy red nose, and a pair of moving button eyes — a reindeer face? The bag, though sealed, proved no match for my inquisitive prying. Once opened, the alleged food appeared to be nothing more than a couple of handfuls of oatmeal flakes and colored glitter. I soon learned, however, that this mix was magical.

Michael, four, and Tracy, two, knew what to do with reindeer food.

"Don't be silly, Daddy. We have to give it to reindeer," my son informed me.

"Of course," I said, but added, "You know that reindeer don't live around here, right?"

Ignoring my question, they happily reminded me that, later this same evening, a team of eight led by Rudolph would be transporting Santa Claus to our rooftop. Giggling with anticipation, Michael shouted, "Come on, Tracy. Let's go!" And off they went to prepare treats for the man in red.

Once upon a time, I'd left treats for the holiday gift-giving team, too. Eventually, I'd come to believe that leaving snacks for Santa amounted to nothing more than an act of bribery — a moral corruption committed with purpose to ensure the anticipated delivery of a plethora of requested gifts.

Of course, kids see it differently. Pure of heart and still untarnished by age or circumstance, my guys saw Santa as a kind man who happened to give away presents. Besides, if he was planning to travel around the world in one night, he'd surely need a snack. Milk and cookies for him and carrots for his reindeer, they decided, but the idea of leaving something extra greatly appealed to them.

And so, shortly before bedtime, preparations commenced. Tracy arranged some cookies on a holiday plate while Michael poured the milk. Next to Santa's treats, he placed some carrots and a note that thanked Santa for stopping by and told him about the reindeer treat in the yard.

When it was time to disperse the food, Tracy was ready. Wearing a misbuttoned winter coat over her yellow Dr. Denton sleeper, she stood waiting at the front door with the bag of food in her tiny hands. Michael remained inside, electing to spend his final moments before bedtime standing in front of the warmth of our real fireplace while mesmerized by the televised version depicting the ever-burning holiday Yule log.

Outside, the weather was nasty. A snow-sleet mixture was falling. Cautiously, I stepped across the treacherous ground with one hand holding the umbrella protecting us from the icy precipitation while the other held close my little elf. With her arms securely around my neck and her hands clutching the food, she held on tightly. Once we reached the middle of our frozen front yard, Tracy reopened the bag and began scattering small fistfuls of reindeer food into the chilly air. Suddenly, unexpectedly, there was magic. Once released, the food began to sparkle. The multicolored lights from outside holiday decorations reflected off the glitter as a frosty breeze captured tiny pieces of the mix — transporting them in gentle swirls above our heads and dispersing them throughout the yard.

After the bag was empty, we marveled as thousands of tiny, glistening specks twinkled from the frozen ground. And, as they did, the cynicism acquired during my years as an adult suddenly disappeared.

Eventually, the uncomfortable rawness of this wintery night began to permeate our heavy coats and reminded us it was time to go back inside.

On Christmas morning, after all the presents had been opened, Michael and Tracy remembered the reindeer food. Outside in the snow and all over the front yard were hundreds of footprints. Convinced the reindeer had thoroughly enjoyed their treat, my kids returned to their toys. For a moment, I considered the variety of local wildlife that could have enjoyed the reindeer's treat. I quickly concluded that, given the magic of the previous night, the tracks most certainly belonged to a particular team of reindeer — just as my kids had known all along.

— Stephen Rusiniak —

91

The Gingerbread Evolution

*The person who has a sense of humor is not just more
relaxed in the face of a potentially stressful situation
but is more flexible in his approach.*
~John Morreall

This was a mistake. I'd brought home a gingerbread house decorating kit, thinking it would be an easy, fun activity for me to
do with my three-year-old twins and two-year-old son while the
newborn napped. Fun? Yes, for the kids. Easy? Definitely not.

I felt like an octopus as I tried to keep three pairs of hands out of
the frosting and decorations while using that same frosting to construct
the house. My mad mom voice broke out a few (maybe more) times as I
sternly told the kids to keep away as I held together the pieces.

"No! Don't touch that!"

"Keep your fingers out of the sprinkles!"

"No, you can't lick the frosting bag."

"Don't touch the house! It'll fall over!"

Finally, I finished putting together the house and kept the kids away
long enough for it to set properly. Well, long enough. Then came the fun
part — decorating! It was a disaster for this neat freak. Globs of frosting
all over the place. Sprinkles everywhere except the gingerbread house.
Candy decorations "missing." While I frantically tried to keep up with
the mess, the kids were having a great time decorating and snacking on

the project.

The next Christmas I swore off gingerbread houses but found individual gingerbread men. They'd make a perfect project — small and self-contained, so that would limit the mess. The kids would each have their own cookies, frosting and decorations, so there'd be no fighting over who was using what and how much.

Nope. It was another culinary mess! There was frosting spread on everything and everyone. The individual containers of sprinkles were knocked over as one sibling reached for another's. Again, I frantically tried to keep the mess contained while helping the kids decorate their personal cookies.

"No, no, no. That's too much frosting."

"Yes, I can help you… whoa there, way too many sprinkles."

"Let's put some here to even it out."

"Stop eating the frosting straight from the bag!"

I walked away stressed and sweating. The kids enjoyed a sugar-filled cookie experience.

This past Christmas, I almost swore off decorating projects of any kind. But with the pandemic, we could do so few of our usual traditions that I couldn't cancel one of the fun things we could do at home just because I stressed myself out. So we continued with our tradition. I found a kit with four individual gingerbread cabins — perfect!

I constructed the little cabins, put each one on a plate, set out containers of sprinkles and decorations, then let each kid have at it. I helped a little when asked but mainly enjoyed watching how they chose to decorate and share supplies.

I'm not sure where or when my epiphany occurred, but I had finally realized the mess making was a large part of the fun. So I let it go. It would be okay if my kitchen looked like a sprinkle factory for a short while and the kids were covered in frosting. Hopefully I can keep this attitude through the year and next holiday season. If not, I can always tell my husband how much fun this was and outsource the project to Dad.

— Kristiana Pastir —

The Perfect Gift

92

Blended Faith

In family life, love is the oil that eases friction,
the cement that binds closer together,
and the music that brings harmony.
~Friedrich Nietzsche

I grew up in a Catholic home where my family was very involved with our church, the same church where I was baptized. I attended a Catholic school for three years and received my first Holy Communion and Confirmation there. Our faith was very important.

When I first met Harold in my freshman year of college, it didn't concern me that he was Jewish. We were young, had a lot in common, and had fun hanging out together. A serious relationship was the furthest thing from our minds. But, after a short while, it was inevitable, and we said those three magic words, "I love you."

My parents adored Harold from the very beginning. He was kind and respectable, and he joined us at our Easter and Christmas dinners. I was also welcomed into Harold's family and attended my first Passover and Hanukkah dinners.

We enjoyed learning about each other's religions and customs. The only obstacle we came across was my grandmother's disapproval of our relationship. She was a strict, old-school Italian woman who adorned her home with statues of saints, paintings of the Last Supper, and photos of the Pope. When Harold and I announced our engagement, she wasn't pleased. We wouldn't be able to get married in our family church because of our interfaith marriage and she refused to attend our outdoor wedding at the Brooklyn Botanic Garden. I was upset that she wouldn't attend, but I was more devastated that she didn't approve of our marriage or give us her blessing.

We settled into married life and enjoyed having family over to visit. My grandmother continued to refuse all invitations to our apartment. Although Harold came along when I visited her, she hardly spoke to him and made us feel uncomfortable. Christmas was right around the corner, and I was planning my first Christmas dinner. I had mixed emotions. I was excited, a bit nervous for everything to go well, and upset knowing my grandmother wouldn't come. I decided to visit her alone to have a heart-to-heart talk and convince her to join us.

As I walked up to her house, I felt like my heart was going to explode. I was already holding back tears as I knocked on the door. I hadn't told her I was coming and she was surprised to see me. She peered around the door and said in a happy voice, "So, you didn't bring Harold. Come on in!"

This was going to be harder than I imagined. My grandmother scurried to the kitchen and brought out enough food and snacks to feed a crowd. After some small talk, as I was munching on my fourth biscotti and drinking a second cup of espresso, I blurted it out. "I love you so much, and I'm saddened that you don't accept Harold because of his religion." She got up, mumbled something about washing dishes, and walked out of the room. Over the clanking of dishes in the sink, I could hear my grandmother's soft sobs. My tears started to flow as well.

I spent the next half-hour trying to convince her that Harold was a wonderful man and husband, and that her approval meant a lot to me — all to no avail. She was adamant and refused to change her mind. I told her I would love for her to come to our apartment to celebrate Christmas. I left her home more upset than when I arrived.

Christmas morning was a frenzy of preparation. Our parents would be coming in the afternoon along with our siblings. All the presents were wrapped and under our tree. The lasagna was in the oven, and the matzo-ball soup was simmering for the fifth day of Hanukkah. Everything was going smoothly, so I decided to take a break.

As we sat on the sofa, Harold sensed my sadness. "You know, your grandmother will eventually come around," he said. Then he added, with a goofy voice, "How could she not? I'm good-looking and charming!" He always knew how to make me smile and feel better.

The time came. Our family started arriving. The plan was to eat first and then open presents. The meal turned out to be a success. I was thrilled when my mother-in-law said the matzo-ball soup was delicious!

After dinner, we gathered around the Christmas tree to exchange gifts. We were halfway through opening our presents when the doorbell rang. We all looked at each other in puzzlement. "Who could that be on Christmas Day?" my mom said, bewildered, as I got up to see who it was.

There stood my grandmother bearing a gift. I couldn't speak, or I would have burst out crying. I held her hand and led her to the Christmas tree. The room became silent. We were all shocked to see her. The silence seemed to last forever until Harold broke the ice. He jumped off the sofa, offered my grandmother his seat and then placed her gift under the tree. We continued to open presents until there was only one left — the present my grandmother gave us.

I slowly opened the wrapping paper, not knowing what to expect. I thought perhaps it was a housewarming gift. All eyes were on me. The box was plain cardboard with no indication of what was inside. More suspense. I looked up at my grandmother, and our eyes met. I could see tears. Opening the box and pulling back tissue paper, what I saw took my breath away. It was the most beautiful menorah. Once again, I couldn't speak. No words were needed. I got up and hugged her. It was almost silent once again. The only sound was the sobbing from my grandmother and me. This time, it was happy tears. My grandmother had accepted my marriage and Harold. We had her blessing.

True to Harold's fun-loving personality, he announced, "Okay, okay, moving along. Let's have dessert!"

The dessert consisted of Italian pastries — cannoli and zeppole, along with Jewish pastries — macaroons and rugelach. My grandmother picked up a piece of rugelach, examined it, took a bite and announced, "This is delicious! I could get used to this." We all let out a roar of

The Perfect Gift |

laughter. And get used to it she did. She enjoyed many wonderful interfaith holiday celebrations in the years to come.

— Dorann Weber —

93

A Second Chance for a Second Chance

Love is the greatest gift that one generation
can leave to another.
~Richard Garnett

My mother had been reupholstering and reselling furniture for a year or so. Her gentle brown eyes would widen with the vision of how things could be as she scoured barn sales, yard sales and thrift stores for pieces that begged for a second chance. Sometimes, they needed to be reupholstered, and sometimes they were wooden and needed refinishing.

The chair she gave to me for my birthday not long before she was diagnosed with leukemia needed both: reupholstering and refinishing. It was designed in what is known as "mission style." It was crafted of lovely oak, and the seat was the only upholstered part. Mom chose a blue and white/gray checkered handwoven wool for my chair seat. She adored blue and white or blues and grays together.

I loved it, but when Mom was quite sick a couple of years later, I ran into some choppy waters financially. There was no way I would consider asking my parents for help due to all the difficulty they were facing. Instead, I contacted a man who bought household goods. When he came to my home, he wasn't interested in the things I was willing to sell. Instead, he looked straight at my "mother chair" and said, "I'd take that."

My throat tightened. It was one of the last things I wanted to see go, but I was desperate. I agreed, heavy-hearted. I watched him load the chair into his truck and tried to hide the tears filling my eyes.

Time marched on, and my mother passed away a couple of years after I had to part with the chair. She never admonished me for selling it. She knew me well enough to understand how much I loved her gift and that it hurt to let it go.

I missed her deeply after her death. Although I adjusted, many times over the next twenty-five years I thought of her and the chair that she had beautifully refinished and upholstered in her favorite colors. I kept wishing that I hadn't needed to sell it.

One of the things I inherited from my mother was a love of finding and repurposing old things that call out for a new life. I'd feel Mom move with me as I scoured yard sales and thrift shops. One day, I was exploring the back room of a thrift store when I spied something under a pile of boxes. It was the mere corner of some fabric on a chair, but it looked like the unique fabric my mother had used on her gift to me. I called to my husband, and he helped me remove box after box and some used drapes flung over the wood.

I gasped when I saw it. It was my chair!

It had been roughly used. The joining had dried and loosened, and it wasn't the sturdy piece it had once been. The fabric was filthy but unmistakable. "I can't believe it," I said over and over. "My chair! My chair!" I hurried to the woman behind the counter. "I don't see a price on that chair. How much?" She looked at the chair, looked at a list of items, and couldn't find any information on it. She shook her head and said she wasn't authorized to sell it without more information from her boss.

It was an odd business. I stopped by every chance I could, but I always found the place closed. I finally decided it wasn't meant to be, no matter how much I thought I wanted the chair. "It's just a thing," I finally told my husband. "I can live without it." My heart was telling me differently, but... it was a thing.

It was not long before Christmas, and I forced myself not to think of the chair and found other joys instead. On Christmas Eve, my husband asked me to go into the basement and grab an extra chair for our family gathering. I stepped gingerly down the steps and turned to where some extras were stored. There it was, my "mother chair," under the light with a bow on it. The wood had been repaired, and the seat taken apart and painstakingly cleaned and put together again. It looked nearly like the day Mom had given it to me. My husband had also kept stopping at that business until he found it open, told the employee the story behind the chair, and convinced her to sell it. He then fixed it himself.

It was the most precious gift I could have received. I took it as a message from my mother, too. After all those years, the gift of love found its way back to me as a gift of love again.

— Tanya Sousa —

94

The Mother of All Gifts

Family is like a Christmas buffet —
there is always at least one fruitcake.
~Author Unknown

A light dusting of Christmas snow sparkled in the morning sunlight. Family and friends were gathered around my mother's tinsel-covered artificial tree, awaiting the gift opening with anticipation.

By anticipation, I really mean trepidation because, when it came to my mom, one never knew what to expect. Sometimes, she would re-gift our presents back to us. Did she think we wouldn't notice?

Other times, her gifts left us baffled — like the *Beekeeping in Nova Scotia* guidebook she gave me for my twenty-fifth birthday. I have never lived in Nova Scotia, nor have I ever expressed an interest in beekeeping. So, I couldn't help but wonder what oddities awaited us that morning beneath the twinkling tower of plastic-kitsch greenery.

My mother had designated my seven-year-old son to hand out the gifts. His eyes lit up as he dove in to grab the largest box he could find. He grinned at me with flushed cheeks.

"I think it's for you, Mommy," he said.

I began to tear off the ever-so-familiar, recycled wrapping paper as Burl Ives sang, "Holly Jolly Christmas."

Suddenly, I froze — confused, stunned. All I could do was stare at the spectacle that lay before me. I was immediately reminded of a line from an infamous Christmas poem, but with a slight modification: "When what to my wondering eyes should appear; thirty boxes of tampons marked: 'To Daughter Dear.'"

Yes… tampons.

Thirty boxes.

In all shapes and sizes.

Thirty blue boxes of shame stared up at me. What was I to do? What was I to say? My brother-in-law fidgeted in his seat as his face turned the same colour as his ginger-red hair. My husband looked at me, looked at my mother, and then back at me. My friend looked down at her nails and then out the frost-veined window.

Was this a joke? Should we laugh? My mother wasn't laughing. If anything, she looked pleased, as if she'd given me the most wondrous gift ever. And yet, this had brought her gift giving to a whole new level of eccentricity.

I had been raised to always be grateful and show appreciation for whatever I was given. So, as the dutiful daughter, I thanked her while trying to keep the bewilderment from showing on my face. As I choked back a nervous giggle, I asked her how she had accumulated so many boxes of… well… "those things." Her reply was just as unsettling as the gift itself.

"Well, some of them I saved for you after my menopause kicked in, and some were delivered for free in my mailbox. So, I went around to all my neighbours and told them I was putting together a care package for my daughter, who lives way up north, and would they be so kind as to donate their free packages to the cause?"

No one spoke. No one moved.

The awkward silence was finally interrupted by my youngest son.

"What are those, Daddy?"

"Mommy will explain later," he said. (Oh, great.) "Here, open a present. Quick!"

As it turned out, the tampons were all unusable. My mom had stored them under her bathroom sink where a slow leak had made them all hard and crunchy — a leak she never knew about because my "gift" had soaked up all the moisture. Needless to say, they all ended up in the landfill. It was a shame, really, after all the work she had put into collecting them.

Although my mother's gift-giving exploits have long been the source of many inside jokes, I can't pretend that I understood or appreciated my mother's unorthodox tendencies while growing up. I also can't say that living with my mother was easy. Far from it. But for most of my life, I have felt compassion for those who are often misunderstood by society. Are the two things connected? I may never know. But I do think that my skewed upbringing made me a kinder, more accepting person — for which I am grateful.

Perhaps our life experiences are the real gifts, just waiting to be unwrapped.

And soaked up.

— Micki Findlay —

95

A Fruitcake Conversion

*Look at the world as a big fruitcake. It wouldn't
be complete without a few nuts in it.*
~Author Unknown

Until recently, neither my husband nor I would have touched a
piece of fruitcake at a Christmas gathering, even if it were the
only food offered. We'd been around fruitcakes for decades,
and if we had no other point in common, we would have
agreed that when it came to fruitcake, one taste was enough. How did
we become fruitcake enthusiasts? The only way we can explain it is
that the change came through a case of mistaken identity.

As couples, sometimes you come across another couple, and you
instantly know the four of you are going to share a lot of life's moments
together. That happened to us just after my husband retired. We'd
moved to Oklahoma and visited a church where we met Chuck and
Fran. They invited us to join their group at Kentucky Fried Chicken
for lunch. The camaraderie began.

After that, we four saw each other nearly every week. As the years
of conversations and life-sharing passed, we all thought we knew each
other pretty well. That's why Paul and I were totally surprised by the
excitement the McCarthys showed when they enthusiastically gifted
us with fruitcake a couple of weeks before Christmas.

Paul and I kept both our bewilderment and our cringes from

showing. But when we got to our car on that chilly Oklahoma night, we looked at each other and said in unison, "Fruitcake?"

The McCarthys had explained they had seen a billboard advertising a special fruitcake while traveling in Texas. Instantly, they'd thought of us because they knew, they said, we loved fruitcake. They backtracked twenty miles just to buy it for us. All the way to our house, we kept wondering how they could mix us up with another couple. We'd covered a lot of topics during our times together, but to the best of our knowledge, we'd never talked about fruitcakes.

At home, we set the fruitcake on our kitchen's island. How would I write the awkward thank-you note for something we probably would either toss or offer to someone else? If we could find someone who actually liked fruitcake, that is. We hadn't tried to deceive our friends before. We didn't want to start now.

Well, we thought, we might as well look at it. The lid was snug, but we pried it off. Five large half-pecans looked up at us. We do like pecans. We pulled the cake out of the metal tin and unwrapped it. The sweet aroma intrigued us.

We cut two small pieces, prepared to go to the sink if we had to. But, no, this cake was extraordinarily delicious! We savored the flavors. Wow! Suddenly, fruitcake became a highly ranked dessert. We'll never know who should have received the beloved fruitcake, but we were thankful it had come to us!

I did online research, thinking maybe we'd ship fruitcakes to loved ones for Christmas. Then I saw the prices. They were not in our budget. Our friends had given us a pricey gift, and they'd literally gone out of their way to buy it for us.

Having been raised to count the quarters, but also thinking fruit-cake would be an excellent gift, I finally found a promising "knock-off recipe" of that rather famous fruitcake. I bought ingredients and began baking. The knock-off passed our taste test.

Fruitcake is either a "can't-wait-to-taste-it" or a "don't-bring-that-thing-near-me" food item. Just for fun, my husband looked up what people thought about fruitcake and what they did with the ones they received but wouldn't eat. Some used them for doorstops or targets.

Knowing how good some fruitcake is, what might have been humorous a few days before about the "mistreatment" of fruitcake seemed insulting and uncivil now.

I thought of my Christmas gift list and wondered if maybe fruitcake might be the gift to give. However, I didn't want to waste the time, money, or precious fruitcake, so I did something I'd never done before. I called my would-be recipients and asked what they'd do with a fruitcake if we sent them one. Several offered a polite "No, thank you." Some were shocked I'd even consider sending them fruitcake because we'd grown up not liking it. I ended up offering "fruitcake counseling," explaining that not all fruitcakes would set your teeth on edge. After hearing our story, shipments were conditionally approved.

Homemade fruitcake became a welcomed Christmas gift that year. That wouldn't have happened without our close friends mistakenly thinking we were fruitcake lovers. As it turned out, they must have known us better than we knew ourselves because, in truth, now we are. At least, we thoroughly enjoy the kind they gave us!

— Margery Kisby Warder —

96

Two Turtle Doves

That's the thing with handmade items. They still have the person's mark on them, and when you hold them, you feel less alone.

~Aimee Bender, The Color Master: Stories

When I was a kid and I came running into the house all hot and sweaty from playing outside in the Florida heat, it was a good bet I would find my mom in front of her sewing machine. She, like her mother before her, made things: all our curtains and throw pillows; matching dresses for my sisters, dolls, Santas, bunnies, and birds.

She sold some of these creations in a local shop and did some by special order for weddings or showers. Old metal tins full of buttons and other sewing notions were stacked on the shelf above her machine. My dad, always handy, made a pegboard where she hung ribbon, thread, and other mysterious trappings of her craft like scissors with notched edges, bobbins, and colored chalk for marking patterns.

I would sit reading or doodling at Mom's feet, listening to the rhythmic buzz of the sewing machine as she worked. I imagined stories of British children named Simplicity and Butterick, named after the patterns that were filed in boxes under her table. We'd spend hours like this until she'd glance at the clock and see it was almost time for my father to get home. She'd push aside what she'd been working on and head for the kitchen to start dinner.

I never learned a single stitch. In junior high, I had a home-economics class where I had to make an item of clothing. My halter top was uneven and hung crooked, and that was after hours of tears, anger and frustration. The only thing I learned from my mother was how to sew on a button.

Twenty-eight years ago, we lost Mom to cancer in October. Two months later, it was Christmastime. I couldn't imagine family celebrations without her. I was mopey and depressed, angry that people had the nerve to just keep shopping, baking and decorating when, for me, the whole world had just come to a screeching halt. Joy to the world? No way.

My best friend was home for the holiday, and we ended up at her house. Then, we walked across the street to the Edlins' house to pick up some friends. I tried my best to be friendly, or at least civil, while we waited for everyone to get their coats on. I felt isolated and lonely, especially amid the happy crowd, and I wandered off to look at their Christmas tree sparkling in the corner.

Mrs. Edlin must have seen me there, and she came over to give me a hug. It was then that I noticed them. On her tree were two of my mother's doves — one red and one white. I was immediately transported back to sitting underneath the sewing machine, seeing my mother's hand-drawn patterns of little birds and the bin of wings just waiting to be attached.

"Oh!" I said. "My mom made those!" They were some of her most popular items, and always sold out around town.

She nodded. "I found them at the shop by the park," she said. "They were so cute." I didn't register what she was doing as she unhooked them from the tree. She held the pair of doves in her hands. "Of course, you need these," she said, holding them out to me.

She had no idea as she handed them over that she'd just given me back Christmas. That simple, unselfish gesture melted some of the ice around my heart. Without words, I gave her a tearful hug as a thank-you, completely inadequate considering what she'd just handed me.

Every year since then, I open the boxes as they come down from the attic and search for the doves. They are the first items to go on the tree. Sometimes, people don't even notice them, nestled in the branches, but I know they're there. On quiet evenings when it's just me at home with a good book, I'll sit by the tree and admire the twinkling lights and ornaments. When I see the doves perched in the tree, I always think of Mom, and her talent and creativity.

But I also think of Mrs. Edlin. I'd like her to know that I'm paying it forward. I try each year to give spontaneously and unselfishly, often to someone I hardly know. I've heard that you never know how some small thing you do might be a giant thing in someone else's life. I know that very well. Once upon a time, my Christmas miracle was two turtle doves.

—Bonnie Blaylock—

97

Fleece Navidad

Every gift which is given, even though it be small,
is in reality great, if it is given with affection.
~Pindar

My husband and I were hooked on a TV series during the pandemic, so when I saw an ad for clothing emblazoned with the logo from the show, I decided to get something for George. I picked out a pullover fleece in an attractive, dark green. It looked classy in the photo. George is a classy guy, so I was sure he'd love it. I impulsively ordered the item without my customary investigation.

I should have realized it was too easy. Usually I struggled to find his Christmas gift.

Weeks passed with no shipping notification. I began to worry. Would it get here in time?

Finally, I received a puffy, plastic envelope. Behind closed doors, I tore open the package. Some furry thing vaguely resembling a matted, dirty puppy sprang from the pouch and hung from my hands. I held it out in front of me and gasped in horror. I recognized the logo of the TV show.

"Oh, dear Lord, this has to go back," I groaned. "I knew this was too good to be true."

I notified the seller that I was returning the item, printed out the return label, and packaged it up. I handed the bundle to George, who was going to the post office, telling him I was returning something that didn't meet my expectations.

When George came home from running his errands, he tossed the package on the counter and informed me that it was going to cost thirty dollars to send it back.

"Thirty dollars, that's outrageous!" I stood there with my hands on my hips, wondering what to do next.

"What is it anyway?" George edged a little closer.

"It's your Christmas present," I admitted.

"How do you know I won't like it?"

"Trust me," I said with visions of a matted dog in my head.

"Let me see."

I tossed him the package and watched as he tore it open.

I was flustered. "It's supposed to be a fleece, only it doesn't look anything like the picture. If you don't like it, we can donate it to the thrift store."

George examined the garment. "I'm gonna try it on." He disappeared around the corner. In minutes, he reappeared wearing the fuzzy green shirt. "It's comfortable and warm. I'll just wear it around the house."

He walked into the great room and sat in front of the TV. I gazed in wonder at him. The shirt looked like something a late-night comedian would wear in a silly skit.

Days followed when, after dinner, George disappeared into the bedroom and emerged wearing flannel pants, his bedroom slippers, and his furry green shirt.

Finally, one day, I scooped it up and headed to the laundry room. I washed it alone, on delicate, absolutely positive that it would disintegrate. It did not. Then I threw it in the dryer, convinced it would fit my granddaughter's Ken doll when I took it out. That didn't happen either. But when I shook out the shirt, I started laughing. The pullover was even fluffier and reminded me of the shag carpet we used to have in one of our bedrooms.

I laid the fleece on my husband's side of the bed so he could put it away. Arriving home after working out at the gym, George headed for the bedroom and came out wearing his flannel pants and the shaggy pullover. I knew then that it would never be going to the thrift store.

This indestructible, poor imitation of a fleece turned out to be the hit of 2020 for the man who has everything.

—Nancy Emmick Panko—

98

The Twelve Days of Christmas

A friend is someone who knows the song in
your heart and can sing it back to you when
you have forgotten the words.
~Author Unknown

I was watching TV one evening and saw a special segment on helping cancer patients through the holiday season. They were giving tips on how to make an anxious time for them easier and cheerier. One lady said she and her friend always hit all the after-Christmas sales, buying Christmas wrapping and bows at 75–85 percent off so they'd be ready for the next year. When her friend became ill and couldn't join her for the bargain shopping, she bought double the amount and shared her purchases with her friend. It seemed like a small gesture, but it said volumes about their friendship and hope for the future.

The TV segment reminded me of a special Christmas I had shared with a dear friend who was battling cancer. Twelve days before Christmas, I began to sing her "The Twelve Days of Christmas." Each day, I appeared at her door, rang the bell, and sang the verse for that day as I handed her a gift that in some way symbolized that verse. The first day's gift was a basket of pears with an artificial bird tied on the ribbon. The second day's gift was a soap dish with two bars of Dove soap, and so on. I only sang the verse, handed her the gift and then quickly returned to my car and drove away—no chitchat, hugs, or explanation. After the second day, she realized there was more fun to come. She said she tried to guess what the gift would be. The gifts were never expensive, just creative.

The following Christmas, her gift to me was a beautiful box of twelve ornaments, each one representing a verse from "The Twelve Days of Christmas." That Christmas and that song now hold a cherished meaning for both of us.

A couple of years later, another dear friend began her cancer battle. The disease in her body was ferocious and swift, leading to the amputation of her arm shortly before Christmas. I decided, along with some other friends, that we would help her through the holiday with the aid of a song.

The actual twelve days of Christmas begin on December twenty-sixth and end on January sixth. This time, we would hold to tradition and give a friend a new way to look at an old song for those days. I bought a set of ornaments like the ones I had been given, which represented the song, and I made a list of eleven other people I knew would want to be a part of this project. Each of us took a day and an ornament. On our chosen day, we would make our fun run, leaving our friend with a verse in song, a gift and an ornament that illustrated that verse. She could use the twelve ornaments to decorate her tree the following year.

Each evening, our friend met us at the door with her family and camera. On the thirteenth day, we all went together and sang the entire song to her.

These are the gifts I used with my first friend and our whole group used with the next friend:

1. A partridge in a pear tree: pears in a basket, earring tree
2. Two turtle doves: soap dish with Dove soap, Dove chocolate candy
3. Three French hens: baked chicken breasts, fresh/boiled eggs in a basket/KFC chicken bucket
4. Four calling birds: calling card, telephone numbers/address book
5. Five golden rings: five jars of anything with gold rings or lids

6. Six geese a-laying: small pillow, dozen eggs
7. Seven swans a-swimming: sunscreen, sunglasses, beach towel
8. Eight maids a-milking: basket holding cartons of milk, chocolate milk, whipped cream
9. Nine ladies dancing: music CDs
10. Ten lords a-leaping: exercise video, ankle weights, sweatband
11. Eleven pipers piping: decorative piping for a craft item, CD of flute music
12. Twelve drummers drumming: toy drum filled with make-up samples

Edgar Watson Howe wrote, "When a friend is in trouble, don't annoy him by asking if there is anything you can do. Think up something appropriate and do it." I learned that we all have it within us to give, and we should put aside any thoughts that we're interfering and just go for it.

— Andy Skidmore —

99

The Best Christmas Present

Dreams really do come true.
Ours came wrapped in Baby Blue!
~Author Unknown

I folded the tiny shirt and sighed as I carefully placed it in my suitcase. Another move. Though I was used to frequent relocations with my Army husband this one would be tougher with my baby due in only six weeks, on Christmas Day. Would I be able to find an obstetrician I liked in the short amount of time left? Oh, well, it wouldn't help to worry. My husband Randy and I had faith that everything would work out as it should.

Our sweet two-year-old daughter, Annette, wandered in clutching her favorite silky blanket close to her small body. She always wanted to help me with little chores. She would be a good big sister. I closed the suitcase I was packing and gave her a kiss.

Moving day arrived. It went well, with professional movers handling everything. As we settled into our new quarters on the Army post, our neighbors welcomed us with a delicious casserole. Even Sharon, a cousin I barely knew who lived nearby, came to greet us.

Our neighbors in base housing hosted a shower for our soon-to-be bundle of joy, who they nicknamed "the neighborhood baby." Their thoughtfulness reassured us. Everything seemed to be going great—until the week of Christmas. Our military friends had left the base to spend time with their relatives, leaving us with no one to watch Annette if the baby arrived on time. With the move and the new baby, we had not considered that everyone around us would be gone.

Christmas Eve arrived. I wasn't feeling too well, but I didn't want to alarm Randy if the pain I was experiencing was only cramps. Fortunately, Sharon invited us to come over and have dinner with her family. We had a wonderful meal and Annette played with her cousins, six-year-old Debbie and three-year-old James.

After dinner, everyone boarded Jim's motor home and took a trip to see an outdoor reenactment of the Christmas story. I felt lightheaded as the vehicle followed a twisting and bumpy road through the nativity scenes.

When I saw Mary, I thought about her traveling on the back of a donkey while she was nine months pregnant over bumpy, twisting roads past the fields where shepherds were watching their sheep. The experience made Christmas really come alive as I realized I had a common bond with the mother of Jesus. Still, I wasn't sure if I was in labor. These cramps were so different from the back pain and contractions I had experienced with my first delivery.

When we returned home, Annette was sleeping, and Randy soon followed. I wasn't so fortunate. I lay awake all night. Before dawn, I woke Randy and told him we would probably have a Christmas baby.

"Then let's get our little girl up so she can open her presents," he said.

We gently roused her. After opening the packages, Daddy gave her some breakfast while I called the doctor. I was still uncertain if this was a false alarm.

He said, "Come to the hospital just in case."

Unaware of my cramps the night before, Sharon adapted quickly when Randy called to ask if Annette could spend Christmas with her and Jim. By the time we left Sharon's, my pain had intensified. I grabbed my huge belly and doubled over with a contraction.

There was almost no traffic so early on Christmas morning. We whizzed into the hospital parking lot where a nurse was waiting with a wheelchair.

Inside, the receptionist asked me to fill out the insurance forms. I told her my baby was coming. She smiled and handed me a pen anyway.

Between contractions, I cried out, "My... baby... is... coming... now."

I was rushed to the delivery room, and out came my baby on the very next contraction. Cradled in the arms of the nurse was the best Christmas present I had ever received!

I shouldn't have been surprised when Dr. Shephard arrived within moments. He was followed by Randy, who rushed in after parking the car.

Meanwhile, Annette had a nice surprise of her own. Jim and Sharon's little son, James, joined in the miracle of Christmas in his innocent, childish way. He went to the Christmas tree, took one of his gifts, and gave it to Annette so she could open a present with the family. She has never forgotten this unselfish act by a three-year-old when she was away from her family on Christmas morning.

Now I could relate not only to Mary's experience but to the entire Christmas story. Every birth is miraculous, but one on Christmas is extra special. With "shepherds" surrounding me and Magi generosity abounding through the kindness of neighbors, family, and a three-year-old boy, we experienced our own Christmas story reenactment.

— Judith Torgersen Thompson —

Seven Cardinals
for Christmas

I am not alone at all, I thought. I was never alone at all.
And that, of course, is the message of Christmas.
We are never alone.
~Taylor Caldwell

I was about to leave to run an errand — racing against the school bus and my sons arriving home — when the phone rang. The caller delivered words no woman wants to hear. "Something has shown up on your mammogram."

The nurse's words stopped me in my tracks. They scared me to death, and the errand was quickly forgotten. As a single mom of three boys, I worried about them and how I would continue providing their care if the worst-case health scenario came true.

I paced from one end of my home to the other, praying out loud. The school bus rumbling up our hill quickly brought me back to the moment. I dried my tears, gulped a glass of water, and greeted my boys at the front door like I did every afternoon.

But that day was not like every other day. Somehow, though, our after-school routine unfolded without a hitch. Snacks were served. Lunch boxes were emptied. And they went out back to play for a bit before beginning homework.

While they ran around shouting and laughing, I felt my inner world crumbling. I could not bear the thought of not seeing my boys grow up.

The next day, I scheduled a repeat mammogram for the following week. Waiting that week was torturous.

I turned to words of scripture that always gave me comfort and I asked friends to pray. I didn't tell anyone in my family.

Cardinals had often appeared in my life when I needed encouragement or strength. I prayed to see a cardinal but never saw one that week that I waited for the second mammogram.

The day finally came. It was bright and sunny, but freezing cold, only three days before Christmas. I checked in at the hospital and was quickly ushered into the imaging room. As I was waiting for the technician to get everything set up, I noticed her Christmas decorations on the Plexiglas shield between us.

The mammogram proceeded in all its typical uncomfortableness, yet surprisingly I felt wrapped in an undeniable calm. Whatever was to be would be.

After she finished, I commented on how cute the four red partridges and the green pear tree were. She giggled.

"Those aren't partridges in a pear tree. Those are cardinals and a Christmas tree," she said.

She walked out, and I wept as I pulled on my warm sweater. I knew all was well. My heart swelled with relief and gratitude beyond words. I still had to wait for the radiologist to come in and give me the results of his reading. It had been pre-arranged that he would review my film right away so I wouldn't be left hanging over the holidays.

He came in smiling. "All clear," he announced. "Have a very Merry Christmas."

I assured him I would. And I did. But my story doesn't end here.

In a few days, I was at my mom's. She had three beautifully wrapped gifts waiting for me. I began opening them while my boys rushed off to another room to play with their cousins and new toys.

The first package contained a framed print.

The second was a decorative pillow.

And the third was a beautiful Lenox Christmas lamp.

But by the time I had unwrapped the last gift, I was sobbing. My poor mom was bewildered because I hadn't told her anything about my mammogram scare.

At first, all I could utter was, "How did you know?"

All three of her presents for me featured a cardinal.

I quickly filled her in on what I had gone through, and we hugged for a long time.

Seven cardinals appeared for Christmas that year, at a time when a scared, single mom needed them most, from a very loving God who abundantly gives good gifts.

— Sheila Petnuch Fields —

Thick as a Brick

*There is nothing on this earth more
to be prized than true friendship.*
~Thomas Aquinas

The text from Diane arrived amid a flurry of dinner preparations. I considered ignoring it, but what's one more interruption? "My three-year-old granddaughter just asked, 'What the heck is that square thing on the floor?'" she said.

I laughed. I knew exactly what piqued Emily's curiosity, and I texted back, "Tell her if she's lucky, she'll have a treasure just as grand some day!"

Diane and I had met in history class on the first day of high school. The only thing we liked less than history was the teacher, Mr. Butler. But that was okay because we looked across the aisle at each other, and something clicked. I knew it, and she knew it. Moreover, all the gods of friendship knew it, too, and blessed this union from the moment we connected.

Diane and I looked forward to seeing each other every day. We also earned several rebukes a week from Mr. Butler who would admonish "Tait and Company" for our regular hijinks in the back corner of the classroom.

The "square thing" Emily pointed out had debuted fifty years ago. Back then, in Pennsylvania, striking steelworkers like my dad were as common as miniskirts and mood rings. We'd weathered strikes before, but it was always tough when it happened during the holidays.

The local food pantry kept our bellies full, and my grandparents helped with household expenses. But Christmas loomed ahead, and I needed a present for my new best friend. I fretted daily over finding a gift I could give her that would be special but not cost any money.

Desperate for an idea, I followed the scent of the sawdust and found my dad in his basement workshop. This was the guy who transformed two old orange crates into a beautiful Christmas manger for my mom with a swish of his hammer and a few nails. All the neighbors asked where we'd bought it when they saw it on display in our front window. Surely, Dad would have the answer.

"You look like the last rose of summer. Why the long face?" he asked.

"I want to give Diane a present for Christmas, and I don't have any money. Have you got any ideas?"

"Do you want me to make her something?"

"No, thanks. I want to make something myself, but I don't know what."

Stacked in the corner of the workshop were six dirty, old bricks. Dad pointed toward them.

"How about one of those?"

"A brick? What's she supposed to do with that?"

"Nothing much in that condition. But if you paint it and decorate it, it makes a pretty good doorstop."

It never occurred to me that no fourteen-year-old girl in her right mind hankered for a doorstop, let alone one made from a crummy, old brick. Instead, I heard opportunity knocking, and I flung that door wide open.

"How, Dad? Where do I start? What do I do?"

On a shelf above his workbench, two dust-covered cans of paint stood side by side next to a repurposed mayonnaise jar from which protruded a bouquet of brushes. Red and black high-gloss paint plus one dusty, old brick awaited my creative flair.

My dad and a few of my siblings dripped with artistic ability — but me, not so much. I'm the type of person who flees the scene whenever the word "Pictionary" floats through the air.

"Remember, Ann, it's not the color of the paint but the flourish of the artist that makes a masterpiece."

"Right, Dad. Thanks!"

I set about my task without a shred of talent. Undaunted, I doused that brick with shiny red paint and my highest hopes for a stunning outcome.

The next morning, Dad had set out a few artist brushes for me next to the small can of black paint. Some had tapered tips, and others looked angled. All of them intimidated me. Still, I picked up a brush and dabbled a bit here and there. Occasionally, I'd change brushes as if it mattered. Clearly, it didn't, except for the smile it brought to Dad's face, which I could see from the corner of my eye.

It's a good thing that flower power and peace signs were all the rage, for without them that brick would have remained an unadorned, shiny red testament to my lack of talent. Festooned with hearts, daisies and peace signs, my masterpiece was nearly complete. As a final touch, I painted the words "peace," "joy" and "love" in the blank spaces between the "art." Dad and I stood in awe of its rustic beauty!

"She'll love it," he said.

"Really? Are you sure, Dad?"

"What's not to love? It's beautiful and useful all rolled into one."

I never suspected that this was the most ridiculous piece of junk one person could give another. I had made this gift with my own two hands and a whole lot of love, which is well established as the international gift-giving recipe for perfection.

When Diane opened it, I don't think she knew what to make of it, but to her credit she never missed a beat. There were no fake gasps of surprise or excitement.

"This is so cool! I love it!" she said.

"I made it myself. It's a doorstop."

"Of course, it is!" she replied, as if I'd given her the crown jewels.

This gift from my heart is exactly why, all these years later, the brick still stands duty in Diane's house, holding doors open and showing off its peace signs and daisies for all the world to admire. Though she's had a lifetime of opportunity to dump it when I wasn't looking, it, like our relationship, has stood the test of time. It is the brick upon which we built five decades of sharing all that life has placed in our paths.

Fifty years ago, Christmas came early to me when I looked across the aisle on the first day of high school and found myself the friend of a lifetime. After all these years, I can safely say that our friendship is as thick as a brick.

—Annmarie B. Tait—

Meet Our Contributors

Kristi Adams is a *USA Today* bestselling author. She loves sharing tales from the humorous side of military life, travels, and family sagas like escorting Father Christmas on the Washington D.C. metro. Kristi and her husband share their home with a spoiled rotten British Shorthair cat, Tiki. Learn more at www.kristiadamsmedia.com.

Heidi L. Allen is an award-winning television producer, media personality and mentor. Since leaving her high-profile career in television, Heidi has become a popular motivational speaker and recently published her first book, *Stories: Finding your Wings*.

Abishai Ambrose has always been passionate about education. She is dedicated to tutoring and mentoring children to excellence. Abishai loves serving others, spending time with family, and travelling. She also enjoys reading, writing, cooking, and crocheting. Abishai is currently writing her first book.

Monica A. Andermann lives and writes on Long Island where she shares a home with her husband Bill and their faithful tabby, Samson. Her writing has been included in such publications as *Woman's World*, *Guideposts* and *Sasee* as well as many other books in the *Chicken Soup for the Soul* series.

Dave Bachmann is a retired teacher who taught English to special needs students in Arizona for forty years. He now lives and writes in California with his wife Jay, a retired elementary teacher, along with their fourteen-year-old Lab, Scout.

Tamara Bell left her career as a real estate agent in 2018 and is living her lifelong dream of writing and working in an antique shop. She and her husband, Paul, are enjoying restoring a 1930 cottage in

Chautauqua County, NY, and spending time with their family. Seven-year-old granddaughter, Clara, is their greatest joy!

Bonnie Blaylock received her M.A. in creative writing from the University of Tennessee in 1989. She co-owned a veterinary hospital for twenty-plus years and enjoys beekeeping and gardening. In addition to the essays featured on her personal blog, she is currently at work on her third novel.

Loreen Martin Broderick is a Wisconsin native living in Tennessee. She received her M.A. in Counseling and Psychology from TTU. A recipient of the 2003 Beulah Davis Outstanding Writer Award, this is her third story published in the *Chicken Soup for the Soul* series. Her great joy is time spent with her three beloved grandchildren.

After graduating from art school, **Jack Byron** worked as a freelance illustrator. As a gallery artist whose work has been shown throughout the United States, Jack has also worked with Los Angeles-based Savage Interior Design, and has had several of his art essays published, in addition to his stories in the *Chicken Soup for the Soul* series.

Marla Cantrell is an award-winning writer, editor, journalist, and the branch director of a public library in Arkansas. Her short story collection, *Early Morning in the Land of Dreams*, was published in September 2020.

Since 1996 **Jane Cassie's** articles have appeared in more than 8,000 publications. As well as sharing travel stories with armchair adventures, she frequently escapes to her cottage in BC's Cariboo where more stories unfold. Jane is also co-owner/editor of *Travel Writers' Tales*. Learn more at www.travelwriterstales.com.

Kitty Chappell is an international speaker and award-winning nonfiction author of articles, poetry and three books. Her life story book, *Soaring Above the Ashes on the Wings of Forgiveness*, is available in six languages. Kitty welcomes your comments at kittchap@cox.net and kittychappell.com.

Angie Chatman is a freelance writer and storyteller. Her short stories and essays have appeared in *Pangyrus*, *The Rumpus*, *Hippocampus Magazine*, and elsewhere. Angie is one of the three storytellers on the WEBBY award-winning episode "Growing Up Black" seen on *Stories* *from the Stage*. She can also be heard in The Moth Radio Hour's episode "Help Me."

Annette M. Clayton has a master's degree in writing for children and young adults. Her books for kids range from silly to sweet. She is a proud mother of twin girls and an avid hiker. Learn more at www.annettemclayton.com and connect with her on Twitter @AnnetteMClayton.

Anna Cleveland received her Bachelor of Science in English from Appalachian State University. She is a substitute teacher in North Carolina. Anna enjoys reading, writing, and listening to music. She hopes to write books in the future.

Capi Cohen, a Penn State grad and retired homeschooling mom, loves to sew, write, and bake cookies. She reads to her far-flung grandchildren on FaceTime and hopes to use her passport again soon. She is thankful to God for her dear mom, her biggest cheerleader and her first, and bravest, sewing instructor.

Yogyata Singh Davé imagines her life as chapters in a book, each imbued with learning, discovery, and a certain romanticism about the unknown. She enjoys time travel through books, new cultural experiences, and the wonders of vegan cooking. Her work has appeared in *The New York Times*, Indian newspapers and online platforms.

Jenni Clark Dickens is an author who lives in South Carolina with her husband and two children. Originally from Luling, LA, she is a family doctor turned stay-at-home mom. Her desire is to inspire hope and a closer relationship with God through her writing. Connect with her online at JenniClarkDickens.com.

Eileen Joyce Donovan received her M.A. with Distinction in English at Northern Arizona University. Her debut historical novel, *Promises*, was released in 2019, and her next historical fiction novel, *A Lady Newspaperman's Dilemma*, is scheduled for a 2022 release. She enjoys life in Manhattan, surrounded by her books and friends.

Vernita Lea Ediger earned her doctoral degree in environmental anthropology at Stanford University. She works in the field of natural resource conflict resolution, focusing on forestry and water issues. She is currently working on her first novel.

Melissa Face is the author of *I Love You More Than Coffee*, an essay collection for parents who love coffee a lot and their kids… a little more. Her essays and articles have appeared in *Richmond Family Magazine*, *Tidewater Family* magazine, *Scary Mommy*, and twenty-four volumes in the *Chicken Soup for the Soul* series.

Sheila Petnuch Fields, a Hudson Valley-based writer and coach for women, has been published in newspapers and magazines. She is the author of *Awakened YOU! Meditations to EMPOWER Women After Toxic Relationships*, available on Amazon. This is her second story published in the *Chicken Soup for the Soul* series.

Micki Findlay calls herself an "artrepreneur" as she loves exploring all things creative — music, jewelry design, photography, painting and crafting. She lives on Vancouver Island, BC, where she writes for a local magazine. She is also working on her memoir, in hopes it will help women who struggle with low self-worth and depression.

Tara Flowers is a former European fashion marketing director. When not managing her consulting business, Le Papillon Marketing, she is chauffeuring her son and two black Labs all around the suburbs of Philly. A firm believer in the magic of Santa, hope, and faith — she will forever hang her stocking every December 24th.

Sherry Furnish is a graduate of Taylor University and Olivet Nazarene University. After thirty-four years of teaching seventh grade English, she retired in 2020. Happily married, she has three daughters and six grandchildren. Sherry enjoys raising goats and Great Pyrenees.

Carol Gaido-Schmidt is a nurse who enjoys writing short stories and is working on a manuscript for a book. She is a graduate of Penn State University. Her hobbies include writing and cat care.

Buffalo poet and writer, **Sandy McPherson Carrubba Geary** has to travel out of town to visit family. Her travels offer experiences to write about. Her stories have been published in five previous *Chicken Soup for the Soul* books. Her essays, poetry, and short stories have been published in adult and children's magazines.

James A. Gemmell can be found most summers walking one of the Caminos de Santiago in France or Spain. His other hobbies are writing, playing guitar, drawing/painting, golfing and collecting art.

After thirty-five years in Texas, **Annette Glass** retired and moved to Indianapolis. She has one adult son, Oscar, who provides Marine services in the Dallas area. Annette is on the Parish Council of a local Orthodox church and she also serves as their blogger and grant writer. She enjoys doing research for fun.

Beth David Goodwin has celebrated holidays with her husband, Rande, and kids, Sarah and Emily, for twenty years. Beth likes to camp and participate in Ninja Warrior, competing at Nationals in the Masters (old folks) Division. Beth's father, Gunter David, has been previously published in the *Chicken Soup for the Soul* series and she is proud to follow in his footsteps.

Donna Lynne Griggs earned her B.A. in English from UC Berkeley in 2015 and her MFA in Creative Writing and Poetics from the University of Washington, Bothell in 2018. She currently resides in St. Louis, MO with her wife Monica and enjoys reading, camping, and kayaking. She is currently working on a book of inspirational poetry.

Terry Hans, a retired dental hygienist, is compiling a collection of hilarious stories as told to her by patients in the exam room. A previous contributor to the *Chicken Soup for the Soul* series, Terry enjoys spending time with her family, writing, scrapbooking and cheering at grandsons' sporting events. She and her husband are enjoying retirement.

Bradley Harper is a retired U.S. Army pathologist. His debut novel, *A Knife in the Fog*, pitted Arthur Conan Doyle against Jack the Ripper and was a 2019 Finalist for the Edgar Award for Best First Novel. He has been a professional Santa for eight years since retirement as an Army Colonel, serving in a different uniform.

Charles Earl Harrel served as a pastor for thirty years before stepping aside to pursue writing. His stories, devotionals, and articles have appeared in numerous magazines and anthologies. He is also a seven-time contributor to the *Chicken Soup for the Soul* series. Charles enjoys crafts and acrylic painting, and he is currently writing a novel.

Rob Harshman is a retired high school teacher. He travels widely and enjoys gardening and photography. With his wife he lives in Mississauga, ON where he also has two married daughters and four grandchildren. Rob has been a previous contributor to the *Chicken Soup for the Soul* series. He plans to continue writing.

David Hull is a retired teacher who lives in Holley, NY. He enjoys reading, writing, gardening and watching too many *Star Trek* reruns. E-mail him at Davidhull59@aol.com.

Miya Hunter-Willis is a stay-at-home mom to four children whom she affectionately calls the H.A.T.S. She received her master's degree in 2008 in history. Miya enjoys traveling abroad with her husband, tasting new foods, and reading museum exhibition text, much to the chagrin of her family. She can be found laughing… a lot.

Diane Hurles is a born-and-bred Midwesterner who moved to Florida four years ago when she retired. Her career included newspaper writing and editing and public relations. Diane took a memoir writing class several years ago while living in Chicago and has been studying creative nonfiction ever since.

Lori Carpenter Jagow is a ministry consultant, counselor, and speaker in Buffalo, NY. She enjoys traveling with her son's band and photography. She is also an inspirational blogger for Pendleton Center United Methodist Church.

Tanya Janke has worked in three schools, two shopping malls, a theatre, a market research company, and a berry patch. She now spends her days writing. Her first play, an adaptation of *The Little Prince*, was produced in Toronto in 2010.

Christine Jarmola, the author of *Do-Overs* and *Murder Goes to Church* and the soon to be published *Merry Widows* mystery series, spends her days teaching eighth-grade English in Oklahoma and her evenings solving murders for her novels. Her passions are stripping wallpaper, hanging out with her family, and laughing with friends.

When she was nine, **Carrie Karnes-Fannin** read *The Call of the Wild*, leading to an attempt to turn an old Dachshund and confused Beagle into sled dogs. It also inspired her to become a writer. Having given up on mushing, she's now working on a humorous middle-grade series. She lives in Georgia with Langston, a very tame housecat.

With over 500 articles and short stories to her credit, **Kimberly Kimmel** is in love with the written word. She grew up in Los Angeles and majored in music in college. She currently lives in Florida and her passions are dogs, music, reading and writing Western historical romances. She has two children and three grandchildren.

Linda L. Koch is a graduate of the Institute of Children's Literature and has been published in *Good Old Days* and *Willow River Writers Anthology*. Linda has three children and four grandchildren, and enjoys traveling, gardening, and writing. She hopes to publish children's middle-grade novels. E-mail her at Llkoch@gmail.com.

Leslie Lagerstrom works as an advocate for transgender children and their families. Her writing has appeared in *The Huffington Post*, been featured in three anthologies, and has been turned into a stage production. A proud mom of two, she lives in Minnesota where she enjoys hiking with her husband Dave, and her dogs Molly and Olive.

From the time **Traci E. Langston's** mom taught her to read at the age of three, she has had a voracious appetite for books. She has always wanted to be an author. Her biggest fan was always her mother. Finally, at the age of fifty, after the loss of both her parents, she took the plunge and wrote her first children's book about her cat.

Linda L. LaRocque is the author of several award-winning plays. Her numerous short stories have appeared in *Guideposts*, *Signs of the Times*, the *Chicken Soup for the Soul* series and various other anthologies. Her plays are published by Playscripts, Art Age Publishers, Smith and Kraus and Christian Publishers. She resides in Michigan.

Margaret Lea is a writer and private music teacher. She lives in Katy, TX with her amazing husband and three wonderful daughters. She is thrilled to be published in the *Chicken Soup for the Soul* series for a second time.

Pam Lindenau, mother of four, has worked retail her last twenty years but has always wanted to be a writer. Pam enjoys reading, board games, gardening, traveling, and spending time with family. She is in the process of writing her first novel. Read her blog at Pamelalynnblog. wordpress.com.

Barbara LoMonaco is the Senior Editor for the *Chicken Soup for the Soul* series and has had stories published in many titles. She graduated from USC and has a teaching credential. She lives in Southern California where she is surrounded by boys: her husband, her three grown sons and her two grandsons. Thankfully, her three lovely daughters-in-law have diluted the mix somewhat, but the boys are still in the majority.

Ilana M. Long loves to write, travel, act, sing, and hike up mountains. Currently, she lives and teaches in Costa Rica. She is the author of *Ziggy's Big Idea* and several stories in the *Chicken Soup for the Soul* series, and she recently completed a YA sci-fi novel.

Lisa Long knew she wanted to be a writer when she won a city-wide essay contest in second grade. Her interests include reading, cooking, health, and nature. She hopes to continue sharing the stories, thoughts and ideas that provide insight and unite us all. She lives in Chicago, IL.

Carol L. MacKay has often found story inspirations in the nutty behavior of her feline housemates. Many of these tales have been published in children's magazines. Carol lives on Vancouver Island with husband James and cat Victoria, both sources of many laughs over the years. This is her fourth story published in the *Chicken Soup for the Soul* series.

M.C. Manning received her Bachelor of Arts from Athens State University in 2019. She teaches middle-school reading and language arts classes in north Alabama. Though she spends most of her free time with her family, writing is a hobby of hers, along with reading.

Irene Maran is a retired freelance writer living at the Jersey Shore with her four cats and six turtles. She writes for two bi-weekly newspaper columns, runs a prompt writing group, and is a storyteller. A grandmother of five, she enjoys sharing her humorous stories with children and adults.

Donna L. Marsh attended Tennessee Tech University prior to a career in cable TV. She lives in Nashville, where she writes, crafts, volunteers, and enjoys occasional strolls through cemeteries. While she dotes on her fur babies, she most loves spending time with her family, especially her grandchildren.

Emily Marszalek graduated with her B.A. in International Studies from Whitworth University in 2013. She enjoys the simple pleasures in life in the stunning Pacific Northwest with her fiancé Nick and two Goldendoodles, Charlie and Lucy. She is proud to be an American and proud to be a follower of Jesus Christ.

Réjean Mayer is a graduate of communications from the University of Ottawa and a retired manager of communications for the Canadian Federal Public Service. When not being a parent to Courtney or spouse to Chris, Réjean can either be found on stage performing in musicals, or in his kitchen, working on commissioned cakes.

Randi Mazzella is a freelance writer and journalist. She has been published in *The Washington Post*, *Next Avenue*, AARP's *The Girlfriend* and *Reveal* magazine. Randi has been married to her husband for over three decades and is the mother of three amazing grown children. Learn more at www.randimazzella.com.

Richard McIlhenny is a lifelong resident of Philadelphia and a full-time residential Realtor with Remax Services. He is married with two sons: Jesse James and Daniel Boone, who are now nineteen and seventeen. He enjoys golf, fishing, travel, reading and hopes to have time to write the many books he has in him some day.

Baylie Jett Mills is the author and illustrator of *The Adventures of Max* children's book series and has been previously published in the *Chicken Soup for the Soul* series. Baylie is an accomplished pianist and plays the guitar, ukulele, and harmonica. Baylie loves reading, writing, and spending time with her family and four adorable dogs.

Rachel Dunstan Muller is a professional storyteller, podcaster, and the author of four children's novels. She is married to her best friend of thirty-plus years, and they have five children and four grandchildren. Home is on Vancouver Island, on the west coast of Canada. Learn more at racheldunstanmuller.com.

Alice Muschany lives in Flint Hill, MO. She loves retirement — it's true, every day is Saturday! When she's not spending time with her grandchildren, she's busy hiking, taking pictures, reading and writing. E-mail her at aliceandroland@gmail.com.

Margaret Nava writes from her home in New Mexico where she lives and writes about the outdoors and God's creations. In addition to previously being published in the *Chicken Soup for the Soul* series, she has authored six books and written numerous articles for inspirational and Christian living publications.

Nancy Emmick Panko is a retired pediatric RN and frequent contributor to the *Chicken Soup for the Soul* series. An award-winning author of *Guiding Missal*, *Sheltering Angels*, and *Blueberry Moose*, Nancy is also a contributor to many magazines and newsletters. She loves to be in, on, or near the water of Lake Gaston, NC with her family.

Kristiana Pastir graduated from Syracuse University's S.I. Newhouse School of Public Communications with a bachelor's degree in magazine journalism. She freelances for Chicken Soup for the Soul when not chasing after her kids. Kristiana lives with her husband and their children in Connecticut. She enjoys reading, baking, running, CrossFit, and having an uninterrupted conversation.

Rachel R. Perkins is the author of thewelladjustedadult.com, a blog that celebrates the chaos of life while encouraging everyone to find the balance between who we have to be for others, and who we are for ourselves. Rachel is a wife and working mother of four daughters. Find her on Instagram @the_welladjusted_adult.

By far, Christmas is **Kristen Mai Pham's** favorite holiday and she is delighted to be published in the *Chicken Soup for the Soul* series for the twelfth time. When she isn't dreaming of gingerbread cookies, she writes inspirational stories and screenplays. Follow her on Instagram @kristenmaipham or e-mail her at kristenmaipham3@gmail.com.

Christy Piszkiewicz was born on Christmas Eve and always loved reading Christmas stories. As a youngster, she used her creative imagination to entertain her younger brother who was extremely gullible. Finding joy in creating stories, she writes about her serendipitous life. She lives on a "hobby" farm in Ohio.

Connie Kaseweter Pullen lives in rural Sandy, OR, near her five children and several grandchildren. She earned a B.A., with honors, at the University of Portland in 2006, with a double major in Psychology and Sociology. Connie enjoys writing, photography and exploring nature. E-mail her at MyGrandmaPullen@aol.com.

Tim Ramsey has been an educator since 1983. He currently teaches seventh-grade writing. In addition, he teaches reading courses at his local community college. He writes every evening in an attempt to capture a positive moment from the day and to motivate himself and others to remain in the profession.

Peggy Ricks received her Bachelor of Arts degree from Chapman University in Orange, CA in 1972. She has been married for forty-five years, has three married sons and four grandbabies. Currently she has a business making healthy and nutritious dog treats and food for her new furry friends.

Rose Robertson and her husband enjoy a wonderful family composed of three sons, two daughters-in-law, and four grandchildren. Retired, Rose enjoys gardening, bicycling, reading, writing, and needlework. She volunteers as a grief companion to children who have suffered the death of someone significant, and also companions parents who have suffered the death of a child.

Linda W. Rooks is the award-winning author of *Fighting for Your Marriage while Separated*, *Broken Heart on Hold*, and *The Bunny Side of Easter*. Her writings have appeared in numerous publications. She offers a ministry of hope in her blog at lindarooks.com and has appeared on TV and radio across the North American continent.

Patricia Ann Rossi is an outdoor enthusiast. She enjoys running and bicycling. She has a passion for writing and reading. Patricia is a volunteer facilitator for "writing to heal" workshops for cancer survivors. She is an active member in her community. She also serves on her college alumni board.

Tyann Sheldon Rouw lives in Iowa with her husband, three sons, and a yard full of squirrels. She enjoys cooking, reading, baking pies, taking long walks, and writing stories about her family's adventures. Check out her blog at tyannsheldonrouw.weebly.com and follow her on Twitter @TyannRouw.

Debra Rughoo received her Bachelor of Arts in English and Communication Studies. This is her second story published in the *Chicken Soup for the Soul* series. Her writing has also appeared in newspapers and magazines in Canada and the U.S. She is a fan of 80s and 90s music, the Baltimore Orioles, documentaries, and stand-up comedy.

Stephen Rusiniak is from Wayne, NJ and was a police detective specializing in juvenile/family matters. Today he shares his thoughts through his writings, including stories in several titles in the *Chicken Soup for the Soul* series. Contact him via Facebook, Twitter @StephenRusiniak and visit stephenrusiniak.com.

Christy L. Schwan is a native Hoosier, rockhound, wild berry picker, and wildflower seeker. She is pursuing her "encore" career as a poet/author and lives in Wisconsin where she enjoys quiet sports, snowshoeing, kayaking, canoeing, and loon spotting with her husband, children and grandchildren.

Elise Seyfried is the author of four books of humorous essays. Her essays have also appeared in publications including *The Philadelphia Inquirer*, *Purple Clover*, *Modern Loss*, *HuffPost* and *The Independent*. Elise is the mom of five and grandma of two, and is Spiritual Formation Director at a Lutheran church in Oreland, PA.

Andy Skidmore is a Christian woman who has been married to her husband for fifty-four years. She has two sons, one daughter-in-law, three Southern Belle granddaughters and one wonderful husband. Writing, photography and baking take up her spare time. This is her seventh publication in the *Chicken Soup for the Soul* series. E-mail her at andyskid@aol.com.

Tanya Sousa's writing credits include the award-winning picture book, *Life Is a Bowl of Cherry Pits*. Her novel, *The Starling God*, was on the 2015 shortlist for the Green Earth Book Awards. She also writes for magazines and anthologies.

Eleanore R. Steinle writes to encourage and inspire others. She is on the Kids Need More advisory board. Kids Need More helped her family when her daughter, Cassandra, was terminally ill. Eleanore lives in New York with her husband and son. You can contact her through her website at www.EleanoreRSteinle.com and also visit www.KidsNeedMore.org.

Annmarie B. Tait resides in Conshohocken, PA with her husband Joe Beck. She has many stories published in the *Chicken Soup for the Soul* series. Now embarking on retirement, she plans to write many more. Annmarie also enjoys singing and recording Irish and American folk songs with Joe.

Judith Torgersen Thompson received her Bachelor of Design from the University of Florida in 1973. She worked as a computer aided drafting technician until she retired, then wrote two self-published books about her hometown. She and her husband, Randy, have two children and three grandchildren, with another one on the way.

Kathy Boyd Thompson is a published writer of Christian devotions, flash fiction, and short stories. She is a 2016 winner of Guideposts Writers Workshop, a contributing writer to their magazines, and published in Guideposts 2021 publication *In the Arms of Angels*.

Lynn Tremblay lives in Ontario, Canada. She graduated from the University of Toronto in 2010, with an Honours degree in English Literature and a Minor in Professional Writing.

Samantha Ducloux Waltz is an award-winning freelance writer in Portland, OR. Her personal stories appear in numerous anthologies, and she is the author/editor of the anthology *Blended: Writers on the Stepfamily Experience*. Her latest passions are gardening, yoga and her adorable pup. Learn more at www.pathsofthought.com.

Barbara Briggs Ward has been published in two previous *Chicken Soup for the Soul* books. In 2021, her short story, "The Kitchens," earned third place in *The Saturday Evening Post's* annual Great American Fiction Contest. She is the author of a heartwarming Christmas trilogy. Learn more at www.barbarabriggsward.com.

Margery Kisby Warder taught children before becoming a columnist and features writer. As a joyful grandmother seated on her electric recumbent bike, she likes knowing, with just a glance, that her beloved husband is still chasing her. Margery keeps writing and her novels and books are available online.

Dorann Weber is a freelance photographer and a lover of writing, especially for the *Chicken Soup for the Soul* series. She's a contributor for Getty Images and worked as a Photojournalist for many years. In her spare time, she loves, reading, hiking, and spending time with her family in the Pinelands of South New Jersey.

Leslie Wibberley lives in a suburb of Vancouver, Canada with her amazing family and an overly enthusiastic dog. She writes across a wide range of genres, age groups, and narrative styles. Her award-winning work is published in multiple literary journals and anthologies. E-mail her at lawibberley@gmail.com.

Toni Wilbarger has been previously published in the *Chicken*

Soup for the Soul series, *Guideposts, The Upper Room, Church Libraries,* and *Christian Communicator.* Her latest novel, *A Matter of Truth,* was runner up in the 2020 Great Novel Contest sponsored by the Ohio Writers Association. She and her husband live in Curtice, OH.

Dorothy Wills-Raftery is a proud wife, mom, grandmother and award-winning author. Her story "Safely Arrived" was in *Chicken Soup for the Soul: Messages from Heaven and Other Miracles.* She's the creator/writer of FiveSibes blog and longtime K9 epilepsy ambassador. She loves spending time with her family and Siberian Husky, Wolfie.

Amy Catlin Wozniak lives in Northeast Ohio. There she shares her life with her husband, four children, two grandsons, and a Great Pyrenees. She loses all track of time when she's hiking, reading, or writing. Her passion is sharing stories that reflect God's hope. You can find her on Facebook @AmyCatlinWozniakWriter.

Rebecca Wyldewood has degrees in professional writing and history. For over a decade she worked as a magazine features editor for global media companies including Time Inc, Fairfax and NewsCorp. She now lives in a haunted cottage in South Australia where she writes historical novels and teaches seasonal wisdom and folklore.

Deborah Young has enjoyed writing all her life and authored articles on daily life, her spiritual journey, gardening, grief and a book titled *Hanging On: A Painful Pilgrimage.* She plans to continue to write about her life experiences and the lessons and laughter they have provided. Follow her on Facebook at www.facebook.com/Deborah-Young-Author.

Meet Amy Newmark

Amy Newmark is the bestselling author, editor-in-chief, and publisher of the *Chicken Soup for the Soul* book series. Since 2008, she has published 177 new books, most of them national bestsellers in the U.S. and Canada, more than doubling the number of Chicken Soup for the Soul titles in print today. She is also the author of *Simply Happy*, a crash course in Chicken Soup for the Soul advice and wisdom that is filled with easy-to-implement, practical tips for enjoying a better life.

Amy is credited with revitalizing the Chicken Soup for the Soul brand, which has been a publishing industry phenomenon since the first book came out in 1993. By compiling inspirational and aspirational true stories curated from ordinary people who have had extraordinary experiences, Amy has kept the twenty-eight-year-old Chicken Soup for the Soul brand fresh and relevant.

Amy graduated *magna cum laude* from Harvard University where she majored in Portuguese and minored in French. She then embarked on a three-decade career as a Wall Street analyst, a hedge fund manager, and a corporate executive in the technology field. She is a Chartered Financial Analyst.

Her return to literary pursuits was inevitable, as her honors thesis in college involved traveling throughout Brazil's impoverished northeast region, collecting stories from regular people. She is delighted to have come full circle in her writing career — from collecting stories "from the people" in Brazil as a twenty-year-old to, three decades later, collecting stories "from the people" for Chicken Soup for the Soul.

When Amy and her husband Bill, the CEO of Chicken Soup for the Soul, are not working, they are visiting their four grown children and their three grandchildren.

Follow Amy on Twitter @amynewmark. Listen to her free podcast — Chicken Soup for the Soul with Amy Newmark — on Apple, Google, or by using your favorite podcast app on your phone.

Thank You

We owe huge thanks to all our contributors and fans. We received thousands of submissions for this popular topic, and we spent months reading all of them. Our editor Laura Dean was our primary reader, with an assist from Crescent LoMonaco and Jamie Cahill. They all narrowed down the selection for Associate Publisher D'ette Corona and Publisher and Editor-in-Chief Amy Newmark.

Susan Heim did the first round of editing, D'ette chose the perfect quotations to put at the beginning of each story, and Amy edited the stories and shaped the final manuscript.

As we finished our work, D'ette Corona continued to be Amy's right-hand woman in working with all our wonderful writers. Barbara LoMonaco and Elaine Kimbler jumped in to proof, proof, proof. And yes, there will always be typos anyway, so please feel free to let us know about them at webmaster@chickensoupforthesoul.com, and we will correct them in future printings.

The whole publishing team deserves a hand, including our Senior Director of Marketing Maureen Peltier, our Vice President of Production Victor Cataldo, Executive Assistant Mary Fisher, and our graphic designer Daniel Zaccari, who turned our manuscript into this beautiful, inspirational book.

About Toys for Tots

Your purchase of this *Chicken Soup for the Soul* book supports Toys for Tots and helps create Christmas miracles for children who might not receive gifts otherwise! The mission of the U.S. Marine Corps Reserve Toys for Tots Program is to collect new, unwrapped toys during October, November and December each year, and distribute those toys as Christmas gifts to less fortunate children in the community in which the campaign is conducted.

You can contribute to your local Toys for Tots campaign in several ways. You can donate a

toy at one of the area toy drop locations, host a Toys for Tots event at your home, office or other venue and collect toys for Toys for Tots, or volunteer at the local warehouse.

Local campaigns are conducted annually in over 800 communities covering all 50 U.S. states, the District of Columbia and Puerto Rico. Local toy collection campaigns begin in October and last until mid to late December. Toy distribution also takes place mid to late December.

Members of the community drop new, unwrapped toys in collection boxes positioned in local businesses. Coordinators pick up these toys and store them in central warehouses where the toys are sorted by age and gender. At Christmas, Coordinators, with the assistance of local social welfare agencies, church groups, and other local community agencies, distribute the toys to the less fortunate children of the community.

Over the years, Marines have established close working relationships with social welfare agencies, churches and other local community agencies which are well qualified to identify the children in need in the community and play important roles in the distribution of the toys. While Toys for Tots Coordinators organize, coordinate and manage the campaign, the ultimate success depends on the support of the local community and the generosity of the people who donate toys.

You can learn more about Toys for Tots by visiting their website at https://www.toysfortots.org.

Changing lives one story at a time®
www.chickensoup.com